FAITH LESSONS
ON THE
ministry life &
OF THE
Messiah

LEADER'S GUIDE

FAITH LESSONS
ON THE life &
ministry of the
Messiah

LEADER'S GUIDE

Ray Vander Laan

with
Stephen and Amanda Sorenson

ZondervanPublishingHouse
Grand Rapids, Michigan

A Division of HarperCollinsPublishers

Faith Lessons on the Life and Ministry of the Messiah Leader's Guide
Copyright © 1999 by Ray Vander Laan

Requests for information should be addressed to:

ZondervanPublishingHouse
Grand Rapids, Michigan 49530

ISBN 0-310-67858-7

Interior design by Sherri Hoffman

Printed in the United States of America

06 07 08 09 / ❖ ML/ 10 9 8 7 6 5

contents

Introduction 6

How to Use This Guide 9

Session 1
In the Shadow of Herod 12

Session 2
My Rock and My Fortress .50

Session 3
The Time Had Fully Come .92

Session 4
No Greater Love 138

Session 5
The Rabbi 178

Session 6
Language of Culture 220

Session 7
Misguided Faith 266

Session 8
Living Water 304

Additional Resources 337

introduction

Because God speaks to us through the Scriptures, studying them is a rewarding experience. The inspired human authors of the Bible, as well as those to whom the words were originally given, were primarily Jews living in the Near East. God's words and actions spoke to them with such power, clarity, and purpose that they wrote them down and carefully preserved them as an authoritative body of literature.

God's use of human servants in revealing Himself resulted in writings that clearly bear the stamp of time and place. The message of the Scriptures is, of course, eternal and unchanging—but the circumstances and conditions of the people of the Bible are unique to their times. Consequently, we most clearly understand God's truth when we know the cultural context within which He spoke and acted and the perception of the people with whom He communicated. This does not mean that God's revelation is unclear if we don't know the cultural context. Rather, by learning how to think and approach life as Abraham, Moses, Ruth, Esther, and Paul did, modern Christians will deepen their appreciation of God's Word. To fully apply the message of the Bible, we must enter the world of the Hebrews and familiarize ourselves with their culture.

That is the purpose of this study. The events and characters of the Bible are presented in their original settings. Although the videos offer the latest archaeological research, this series is not intended to be a definitive cultural and geographical study of the lands of the Bible. No original scientific discoveries are revealed here. The purpose of this study is to help us better understand God's revealed mission for our lives by enabling us to hear and see His words in their original context.

understanding the world of the Hebrews

More than 3,800 years ago, God spoke to His servant Abraham: "Go, walk through the length and breadth of the land, for I am giving it to you" (Genesis 13:17). From the outset, God's choice of a Hebrew nomad to begin His plan of salvation (that is still unfolding) was linked to the selection of a specific land where His redemptive work would begin. The nature of God's covenant relationship with His people demanded a place where their faith could be exercised and displayed to all nations so that the world would know of *Yahweh,* the true and faithful God. God showed the same care in preparing a land for His chosen people as He did in preparing a people to live in that land. For us to fully understand God's plan and purpose for His people, we must first understand the nature of the place He selected for them.

By New Testament times, the Jewish people had been removed from the Promised Land by the Babylonians due to Israel's failure to live obediently before God (Jeremiah 25:4–11). The exile lasted seventy years, but its impact upon God's people was astounding. New patterns of worship developed, and scribes and experts in God's law shaped the new commitment to be faithful to Him. The prophets predicted the appearance of a Messiah like King David who would revive the kingdom of the Hebrew people.

But the Promised Land was now home to many other groups of people whose religious practices, moral values, and lifestyles conflicted with those of the Jews. Living as God's witnesses took on added difficulty as Greek, Roman, and Samaritan worldviews mingled with that of the Israelites. The Promised Land was divided between kings and governors, usually under the authority of one foreign empire or another. But the mission of God's people did not change. They were still to live *so that the world would know that their God was the true God.* And the land continued to provide them opportunity to encounter the world that desperately needed to know this reality.

The Promised Land was the arena within which God's people were to serve Him faithfully as the world watched. The land God chose for His people was on the crossroads of the world. A major trade route, the Via Maris, ran through it. God intended for the Israelites to take control of the cities along this route and thereby exert influence on the nations around them. Through their righteous living, the Hebrews were to reveal the one true God, *Yahweh,* to the world. They failed to accomplish this mission, however, because of their unfaithfulness.

Western Christianity tends to spiritualize the concept of the Promised Land as it is presented in the Bible. Instead of seeing it as a crossroads from which to influence the world, modern Christians view it as a distant, heavenly city, a glorious "Canaan" toward which we are traveling as we ignore the world around us. We are focused on the destination, not the journey. We have unconsciously separated our walk with God from our responsibility to the world in which He has placed us. In one sense, our earthly experience is simply preparation for an eternity in the "promised land." Preoccupation with this idea, however, distorts the mission God has set for us.

Living by faith is not a vague, otherworldly experience; rather, it is being faithful to God right now, in the place and time in which He has put us. This truth is emphasized by God's choice of Canaan, a crossroads of the ancient world, as the Promised Land for the Israelites. God wants His people to be in the game, not on the bench. Our mission, as Christians today, is the same one He gave to the Israelites. We are to live obediently *within* the world so that through us *the world may know that our God is the one true God.*

The Assumptions of Biblical Writers

Biblical writers assumed that their readers were familiar with Near Eastern geography. The geography of Canaan shaped the culture of the people living there. Their settlements began near sources of water and food. Climate and raw materials shaped their choice of occupation, dress, weapons, diet, and even artistic expression. As their cities grew, they interacted politically. Trade developed, and trade routes were established.

During New Testament times, the Promised Land was called Palestine or Judea. *Judea* (which means "Jewish") technically referred to the land that had been the nation of Judah. Because of the influence that the people of Judea had over the rest of the land, the land itself was called Judea. The Romans divided the land into several provinces, including Judea, Samaria, and Galilee (the three main divisions during Jesus' time); Gaulanitis, the Decapolis, and Perea (east of the Jordan River); and Idumaea (Edom) and Nabatea (in the south). These further divisions of Israel added to the rich historical and cultural background God prepared for the coming of Jesus and the beginning of His church.

Today the names *Israel* and *Palestine* are often used to designate the land God gave to Abraham. Both terms are politically charged. *Palestine* is used by the Arabs living in the central part of the country, while *Israel* is used by the Jews to indicate the State of Israel. In this study, *Israel* is used in the biblical sense. This choice does not indicate a political statement regarding the current struggle in the Middle East but instead is chosen to best reflect the biblical designation for the land.

Unfortunately, many Christians do not have even a basic geographical knowledge of the region. This series is designed to help solve that problem. We will be studying the people and events of the Bible in their geographical and historical contexts. Once we know the *who*, *what*, and *where* of a Bible story, we will be able to understand the *why*. By deepening our understanding of God's Word, we can strengthen our relationship with God.

The biblical writers also used a language that, like all languages, is bound by culture and time. Therefore, understanding the Scriptures involves more than knowing what the words mean. We need to also understand those words from the perspective of the people who used them.

The people whom God chose as His instruments—the people to whom He revealed Himself—were Hebrews living in the Near East. These people described their world and themselves in concrete terms. Their language was one of pictures, metaphors, and examples rather than ideas, definitions, and abstractions. Whereas we might describe God as omniscient or omnipresent (knowing everything and present everywhere), a Hebrew would have preferred to describe God by saying, "The Lord is my shepherd." Thus, the Bible is filled with concrete images from Hebrew culture: God is our Father, and we are His children; God is the potter, and we are the clay; Jesus is the Lamb killed on Passover; heaven is an oasis in the desert, and hell is the city sewage dump; the Last Judgment will be in the Eastern Gate of the heavenly Jerusalem and will include sheep and goats.

These people had an Eastern mind-set rather than a Western mind-set. Eastern thought emphasizes the process of learning as much or more than the end result. Whereas Westerners tend to collect information to find the right answer, Hebrew thought stresses the process of discovery as well as the answer. Thus in the Leader's Guide we have included *suggested responses* to the questions. These are provided primarily to help the leader determine the area(s) on which the participants should focus in discovering the answer(s). These suggested responses are not intended to be the final answers or provide an exhaustive list of possible responses. So, the effective leader will allow the participants to process the information and will stress the learning value of that process.

How to use this guide

This Leader's Guide is divided into five sessions approximately 50–55 minutes in length. Each session corresponds to a videotaped presentation by Ray Vander Laan.

For each session, *the leader* will need:

- Leader's Guide
- Bible
- Video player, monitor, stand, extension cord, etc.
- Videotape

Note: For some sessions, the leader may also want to use an overhead projector, chalkboard, or marker board.

For each session, *the participant* will need:

- Participant's Guide
- Bible
- Pen or pencil

Directions to the leader are enclosed in the shaded boxes and are not meant to be spoken.

Each session is divided into six main parts: **Before You Lead, Introduction, Video Presentation, Group Discovery, Faith Lesson,** and **Closing Prayer.** A brief explanation of each part follows.

I. Before You Lead

Synopsis

This material is presented for the leader's information. It summarizes the material presented in each of the videos.

Key Points of This Lesson

Highlights the key points you'll want to emphasize.

Session Outline

Provides an overview of the content and activities to be covered throughout the session.

Materials

The materials listed above are critical for both the leader and each participant. Additional materials (optional) are listed when appropriate.

2. Introduction

Welcome

Welcomes participants to the session.

What's to Come

A brief summary you may choose to use as you begin the session.

Questions to Think About

Designed to help everyone begin thinking about the theme or topics that will be covered. A corresponding page is included in the Participant's Guide.

3. Video Presentation

This is the time during which you and the participants will watch the video and write down appropriate notes. Key themes have been indicated.

4. Group Discovery

In this section, you'll guide participants in thinking through materials and themes related to the video you've just seen. You may want to read the material word for word, or simply highlight key words and phrases. Feel free to amplify various points with your own material or illustrations.

The Leader's Guide includes a copy of the corresponding pages in the Participant's Guide. Space is also provided in which to write additional planning notes. Having the Participant's Guide pages in front of you allows you to view the pages the participants are seeing as you talk without having to hold two books at the same time. It also lets you know where the participants are in their book when someone asks you a question.

Video Highlights

Use these questions and suggested responses with the entire group. This will guide participants in verbally responding to key points/themes covered in the video.

Small Group Bible Discovery

At this time, if your group has more than seven participants you will break the group into small groups (three to five people) and assign each group a topic. (If you have more groups than topics, assign some topics to more than one group.) Participants will use their Bibles and write down suggested responses to the questions. At the end of this discovery time, participants will reassemble as a large group. As time allows, small group representatives can share key ideas their groups discussed.

Quite often supplementary material—called *Data File, Profile*, etc.—has been inserted near the topics. This material complements the themes but is not required reading to complete the session. Suggest that the participants read and study the supplementary material on their own.

5. faith Lesson

Time for Reflection

At this time, participants will read selected Scripture passages on their own and think about questions that encourage them to apply what they've just discovered to their own lives.

Action Points

At this time, you'll summarize key points (provided for you) with the entire group and encourage participants to act on what they have learned.

6. closing prayer

Close the session with the material or prayer provided.

Before the first session

- Watch the video session.
- Obtain the necessary Participant's Guides for all participants.
- Make sure you have the necessary equipment.

Tips for Leading and promoting group Discussion

1. Allow group members to participate at their own comfort level. Everyone need not answer every question.
2. Ask questions with interest and warmth and then listen carefully to individual responses. Remember: it is important for participants to think through the questions and ideas presented. The *process* is more important than specific *answers*, which is why *suggested responses* are provided.
3. Be flexible. Reword questions if necessary. Choose to spend more time on a topic. Add or delete questions to accommodate the needs of your group members—and your time frame.
4. Suggest that participants, during the coming week, do the Small Group Bible Discovery topics that their individual small groups may not have had the opportunity to do.
5. Allow for (and expect) differences of opinion and experience.
6. Gently guide all participants into discussion. Do not allow any person(s) to monopolize discussion.
7. Should a heated discussion begin on a theological topic, suggest that the participants involved continue their discussion after the session is over.
8. Do not be afraid of silence. Allow people time to think—don't panic. Sometimes ten seconds of silence seems like an eternity. Remember, some of this material requires time to process—so allow people time to digest a question and *then* respond.

In the shadow of Herod

Before You Lead

Synopsis

King Herod the Great ruled Israel from 37 B.C. until his death in 4 B.C. He was king at the time Jesus was born. Herod controlled more territory than almost any king of the Jews who had ruled before him, but he saw threats in every corner and cruelly suppressed all resistance—real or imagined. He especially feared Cleopatra of Egypt, so he built a series of fortress-palaces along an escape route between his palace in Jerusalem and his home country of Edom. From Jerusalem he could travel fewer than ten miles south to the safety of the Herodion, then about thirty miles to the cliff fortress of Masada, and finally the fifty miles to Edom.

This video begins atop the Herodion, the first fortress-palace along Herod's escape route. This spectacular complex, built just over three miles southeast of Bethlehem, is typical of the great building projects for which Herod is known. Built upon a high hill, the walls of the upper palace stood about ninety feet tall, and steep earthen ramparts built against the lower half of the structure gave it the shape of a volcanic cone. In addition, four defensive towers, one on each point of the compass, extended high above the fortress walls. The upper stories of these towers served as homes for the royal family and government officials. The eastern tower, which was the largest, was more than 120 feet high and 55 feet in diameter. It provided luxurious rooms with cool Mediterranean breezes for Herod and his family.

The upper palace dominated the landscape for miles around and even could be seen from Jerusalem—nearly ten miles to the north. As the sun rose and set, the Herodion literally cast its shadow across the surrounding towns. Even today, the view from what remains of the Herodion is spectacular. Just a few miles to the north and west lies Bethlehem, with the Judea Mountains beyond. Looking to the east, one can see the Judea Wilderness, where shepherds sought the green pastures of which David wrote. And beyond, one can even see the waters of the Dead Sea and the distant mountains of Moab.

The Herodion clearly symbolized Herod's visionary genius, power, and splendor. The third largest palace in the ancient world, its buildings covered about forty-five acres surrounded by about two hundred acres of palace grounds. The walls of the upper palace were built as two concentric circles placed about fifteen feet apart. Between those walls, the palace staff bustled through many chambers, apartments, and storage rooms. The protected inner circle of the palace was open to the sky and featured a peristyle garden, a large reception hall, and hot, warm, and cold baths.

To add more glory to his palace complex, Herod added a massive lower palace. It included elaborate halls and guest rooms, a terrace more than one thousand feet long, and a huge swimming pool (140 by 200 feet) surrounded by colonnades and a beautiful garden full of exotic plants. As with Herod's many other magnificent building projects, his efforts were clearly intended to demonstrate his power and make a lasting reputation for himself.

Many significant biblical sites are located close to the Herodion: the hills near Bethlehem where Jacob buried his beloved Rachel, the route Naomi and Ruth traveled when returning from Moab, the fields owned by Boaz in which Ruth gleaned, the valley where Goliath fell dead, and the place where Samuel anointed young David as king of Israel. In fact, the Herodion literally overshadowed the greatest historical event of all time—the humble birth of Jesus the Messiah—in the small town of Bethlehem only several miles away.

Just as the Herodion cast its shadow across the landscape of biblical history, Herod cast his shadow across the history and people of Israel. Although Jesus and Herod were vastly different, God clearly engineered history to bring them together in fulfillment of His purposes. Generations earlier, Isaac, Abraham's son, had prayed on behalf of his barren wife, Rebekah. The Lord answered his prayer, and she conceived twins. "Two nations are in your womb," the Lord said to her, "and two peoples from within you will be separated; one people will be stronger than the other, and the older will serve the younger" (Genesis 25:23). Esau, the older son, founded the nation of Edom. Jacob, the younger son, founded the nation of Israel.

As Ray Vander Laan points out in this video, King Herod (who was an Edomite, a descendant of Esau) seemed to possess all the power, magnificence, and glory. He certainly appeared to rule over a newborn baby in Bethlehem named Jesus. But years earlier, Balaam had prophesied, "A star will come out of Jacob; a scepter will rise out of Israel. . . . Edom will be conquered; . . . but Israel will grow strong" (Numbers 24:17–18). And the prophet Malachi spoke the word of the Lord: ". . . I have loved [Jacob] . . . but Esau I have hated, and I have turned his mountains into a wasteland and left his inheritance to the desert jackals . . ." (Malachi 1:2–3). So, the Jews knew that someday the line of Jacob would assume power.

These prophecies have certainly come true. Today, the awesome projects that King Herod built lie in ruins, and most people remember him only as the king who had innocent babies killed in an attempt to kill the baby Jesus, the promised Messiah. Herod made his mark in the world and then was gone.

In contrast, Jesus didn't leave a single building as a legacy. No one is exactly sure of the locations where He was born or died. Yet His passing changed the world forever. And today He lives! His kingdom has no end, we Christians are His temples, and the eternal truths He revealed remain true today.

No matter how strong and glorious Herod appeared to be, the baby in Bethlehem's manger was stronger. Jesus the Messiah, the Lord of heaven and earth, triumphed over all evil—even death! He will return to conquer all earthly powers.

Key Points of This Lesson

1. *It took great faith for the Jewish people to believe that Jesus, who began His life on earth as a baby in Bethlehem, was truly the Lord of heaven and earth.*

   The contrasts between Jesus and Herod could not have been greater. Herod had all the power, wealth, strength, and glory that his position in the world could offer, yet Jesus, the King of the universe, had nothing of that sort to demonstrate His position. So to believe in Jesus as the Messiah was to believe that regardless of outward appearances, Jesus, the baby in the manger, was indeed Lord of heaven and earth.

2. *King Herod, who personified evil, no doubt seemed to have all the power and control. He ruled with an iron hand, seeking out and destroying every possible enemy—even killing innocent babies. Yet Jesus, the humble King of all creation, was truly in control. He had the power to overcome every evil— including that of Herod.*

   Today, Christians are asked to believe that no matter how powerful Wall Street appears to be, no matter how controlling a government seems, no matter how influential the morals of Hollywood appear to be, no matter how evil pornography seems, no matter how overwhelming hunger, racism, or AIDS appear to be—Jesus Christ is King. Because His power, which has conquered all evil, resides within us, we do not need to fear the evil we face.

   Although it is easier and safer to avoid evil than to confront it, the crucial question that all Christians must answer for themselves is: "Will I dare to live as if God is greater than any evil I face in my life and my culture, as if the power within me is greater than every power of evil that I will encounter?"

Session Outline (53 minutes)

  I. Introduction (5 minutes)
   Welcome
   What's to Come
   Questions to Think About

  II. Show Video "In the Shadow of Herod" (18 minutes)

  III. Group Discovery (20 minutes)
   Video Highlights
   Small Group Bible Discovery

  IV. Faith Lesson (9 minutes)
   Time for Reflection
   Action Points

  V. Closing Prayer (1 minute)

Materials

No additional materials are needed for this session. Simply view the video prior to leading the session so you are familiar with its main points.

in the shadow of Herod

introduction

Welcome

> Assemble the participants together. Welcome them to session one of *Faith Lessons on the Life and Ministry of the Messiah.*

What's to Come

The Herodion, the third largest palace complex of its day, was a monument to Herod's glory, power, and engineering mastery. Its upper palace could be seen for miles, and it literally overshadowed the most significant event in history—Jesus' birth in Bethlehem. But today, only ruins of the great Herodion remain, and that little baby—the Lord of heaven and earth—grew up to make a profound and lasting impact on the entire world. Just as Jesus triumphed over evil, we—His followers—can also be used by God to confront the powers of evil in the world in which we live.

Questions to Think About

> *Participant's Guide page 11.*

> Ask each question and solicit a few responses from group members.

1. Think of some instances in the Bible when that which appeared to be weak and powerless defeated that which appeared to be stronger and more powerful. What thoughts and feelings do these instances bring to mind?

    Suggested Responses: Allow participants to share their examples and feelings. These might include David's defeat of the great warrior Goliath, blind Samson's destruction of the Philistine temple, Esther's exposure of Haman's plot to destroy the Jews, etc. Feelings might include pride, hope, amazement, an awareness of God's faithfulness, etc.

2. What do you think are the most powerful, undefeatable evidences of evil in our world today?

    Suggested Responses: These will vary, but might include the growth of the occult; pornography; rampant pursuit of wealth, fame, relationships; racism; blatant disobedience of God's laws; gangs; organized crime; abuse in the home; etc.

SESSION ONE

In the Shadow of Herod

Questions to Think About

1. Think of some instances in the Bible when that which appeared to be weak and powerless defeated that which appeared to be stronger and more powerful. What thoughts and feelings do these instances bring to mind?

2. What do you think are the most powerful, undefeatable evidences of evil in our world today?

3. Do you agree or disagree with the statement: "It doesn't seem as though God can do much about evil." Explain your view.

PLANNING NOTES:

✏ 3.   Do you agree or disagree with the statement: "It doesn't seem as though God can do much about evil." Explain your view.

Suggested Responses: These will vary. Allow participants to share their perspectives.

Let's keep these ideas in mind as we view the video.

video presentation

18 minutes

Participant's Guide page 12.

On page 12 of your Participant's Guide, you will find a space in which to take notes on key points as we watch this video.

Leader's Video Observations

The Herodion in Its Setting

Israel and Edom, a History of Conflict

Herod the Edomite Versus Jesus the King of Kings

In the shadow of Herod

questions to think about

1. Think of some instances in the Bible when that which appeared to be weak and powerless defeated that which appeared to be stronger and more powerful. What thoughts and feelings do these instances bring to mind?

2. What do you think are the most powerful, undefeatable evidences of evil in our world today?

3. Do you agree or disagree with the statement: "It doesn't seem as though God can do much about evil." Explain your view.

video notes

The Herodion in Its Setting

Israel and Edom, a History of Conflict

Herod the Edomite Versus Jesus the King of Kings

PLANNING NOTES:

group Discovery

2O minutes

If your group has seven or more members, use the **Video Highlights** with the entire group (5 minutes), then break into small groups of three to five to discuss the **Small Group Bible Discovery** (10 minutes). Then reassemble the group to discuss the key points discovered (5 minutes).

If your group has fewer than seven members, begin with the **Video Highlights** (5 minutes), then do one or more of the topics found in the **Small Group Bible Discovery** as a group (10 minutes). Finally, spend five minutes at the end discussing points that had an impact on participants.

Video Highlights (5 minutes)

Here you'll ask one or more of the following questions that directly relate to the video the participants have just seen.

1. Which details about the Herodion made the greatest impression on you?

   Suggested Responses: Allow participants to share their views, which may include the double walls, size of the ramparts, tunnel entrance, or other unique construction features; the sheer size of the entire complex; the magnificent view from atop the ruins; how magnificent the upper and lower palaces must have been; the huge swimming pool and gardens; etc.

2. What is significant about the Herodion's proximity to Bethlehem?

   Suggested Responses: The glorious Herodion towered above everything else, reflecting Herod's genius, power, and glory. Nothing within sight could compare to its majesty. Its towers dwarfed neighboring small towns such as Bethlehem. Yet, in Bethlehem was born a tiny baby—Jesus—who was the King of Kings and would change the world forever.

3. What are some of the contrasts highlighted between King Herod and Jesus?

   Suggested Responses: Jesus was born as a baby in the shadow of the magnificent Herodion; Jesus left a legacy of faith and relationship with God, in contrast to the buildings Herod left; King Herod appeared to have power, but Jesus—the Creator of the universe who appeared to have nothing—really had the power; etc.

4. How do the birth of the twins, Jacob and Esau, and Balaam's prophecy relate to Jesus and Herod?

   Suggested Responses: Jacob was the father of the Jewish people; Esau was the father of the Edomites. As Balaam prophesied, the "star" did come from Jacob when Jesus came to earth. Jesus triumphed over evil, even though it seemed as if evil Herod, an Edomite, was much more powerful.

5. How has this video changed your view of the step of faith that was required for the Jews to believe that Jesus was the Messiah?

   Suggested Responses: will vary. Encourage participants to feel the impact of Herod's presence on the lives of ordinary Jews.

video нighlights

1. Which details about the Herodion made the greatest impression on you?

2. What is significant about the Herodion's proximity to Bethlehem?

3. What are some of the contrasts highlighted between King Herod and Jesus?

4. How do the birth of the twins, Jacob and Esau, and Balaam's prophecy relate to Jesus and Herod?

5. How has this video changed your view of the step of faith that was required for the Jews to believe that Jesus was the Messiah?

PLANNING NOTES:

PROFILE OF A FORTRESS

The Awesome Herodion

- Built about thirty years before Jesus' birth on a hilltop at the edge of the Judea Wilderness to provide an escape for Herod in the event of danger in Jerusalem.
- Rose more than forty-five feet above the hilltop and could be seen from as far as ten miles away in Jerusalem.
- Located near the site of Herod's battlefield victory over the Hasmonaeans, which earned him the Roman nomination to be the earthly king of the Jews.

The Herodion: A Mountaintop Fortress

- Overshadowed Bethlehem, about three miles away, where Jesus, the almighty King, was born.
- Was often passed by shepherds (such as those who came to see the baby Jesus) and farmers who lived in Bethlehem—a small town of at most several hundred people. Bethlehem had fertile farmland and was also close to the wilderness where flocks were kept.

The Upper Palace

The Herodion

- Had double cylindrical walls about fifteen feet apart with an outside diameter of nearly 220 feet. Between the walls were seven stories of apartments, chambers, and storage rooms. Herod covered the lower four stories with packed dirt, creating the unique, volcanic-cone shape.
- Was protected by smaller defensive towers on the south, north, and west that extended outside the cylindrical structure. The enormous eastern tower was 55 feet in diameter, more than 120 feet tall, and provided royal apartments for King Herod and his family.
- Contained a glorious bath complex that included a vaulted caldarium (hot bath), tepidarium (warm bath), and frigidarium (cold bath)—each of which had floors decorated with mosaics. Herod brought water from more than three miles away through aqueducts and stored it in cisterns at the base of the fortress-palace.

(continued on page 24)

PROFILE OF A FORTRESS

The Awesome Herodion

- Built about thirty years before Jesus' birth on a hilltop at the edge of the Judea Wilderness to provide an escape for Herod in the event of danger in Jerusalem.
- Rose more than forty-five feet above the hilltop and could be seen from as far as ten miles away in Jerusalem.
- Located near the site of Herod's battlefield victory over the Hasmonaeans, which earned him the Roman nomination to be the earthly king of the Jews.

The Herodion: A Mountaintop Fortress

- Overshadowed Bethlehem, about three miles away, where Jesus, the almighty King, was born.
- Was often passed by shepherds (such as those who came to see the baby Jesus) and farmers who lived in Bethlehem—a small town of at most several hundred people. Bethlehem had fertile farmland and was also close to the wilderness where flocks were kept.

The Upper Palace

The Herodion

- Had double cylindrical walls about fifteen feet apart with an outside diameter of nearly 220 feet. Between the walls were seven stories of apartments, chambers, and storage rooms. Herod covered the lower four stories with packed dirt, creating the unique, volcanic-cone shape.
- Was protected by smaller defensive towers on the south, north, and west that extended outside the cylindrical structure. The enormous

PLANNING NOTES:

(continued from page 22)

Inside the Herodion

- Could accommodate many guests in its large, roofed reception hall that had colored plaster walls. During the Jewish revolts long after Herod's death, the Zealots made this hall into a synagogue.

- Had an open-air garden with columns on three sides and a niche at each end for statues.

- Was entered by a three-hundred-step stairway on the outside of the mountain followed by a two-hundred-foot tunnel that led into the fortress.

The Lower Palace

- Consisted of a complex of buildings and a pool at the foot of the mountain. The pool—one of the largest in the ancient world—was 10 feet deep, 140 feet long, 200 feet wide, and was surrounded by colonnaded gardens—quite a sight given that the water came via aqueduct from more than three miles away. In the middle of the pool was an island more than forty feet in diameter containing a colonnaded circular building in which Herod and guests could relax in complete privacy.

- Contained a huge building complex between the pool and the upper fortress, with more than 400 feet of elaborate halls and guest rooms. In front was a terrace more than 1,000 feet long.

- Presumably holds the tomb of Herod. However, this largest of the fortress structures has not yet been completely excavated.

The Herodion: Lower Palace

In the Shadow of Herod

eastern tower was 55 feet in diameter, more than 120 feet tall, and provided royal apartments for King Herod and his family.

Inside the Herodion

- Contained a glorious bath complex that included a vaulted caldarium (hot bath), tepidarium (warm bath), and frigidarium (cold bath)—each of which had floors decorated with mosaics. Herod brought water from more than three miles away through aqueducts and stored it in cisterns at the base of the fortress-palace.
- Could accommodate many guests in its large, roofed reception hall that had colored plaster walls. During the Jewish revolts long after Herod's death, the Zealots made this hall into a synagogue.
- Had an open-air garden with columns on three sides and a niche at each end for statues.
- Was entered by a three-hundred-step stairway on the outside of the mountain followed by a two-hundred-foot tunnel that led into the fortress.

The Lower Palace

- Consisted of a complex of buildings and a pool at the foot of the mountain. The pool—one of the largest in the ancient world—was 10 feet deep, 140 feet long, 200 feet wide, and was surrounded by colonnaded gardens—quite a sight given that the water came via aqueduct from more than three miles away. In the middle of the pool was an island more than forty feet in diameter containing a colonnaded circular building in which Herod and guests could relax in complete privacy.
- Contained a huge building complex between the pool and the upper fortress, with more than 400 feet of elaborate halls and guest rooms. In front was a terrace more than 1,000 feet long.

(continued on page 16)

(continued from page 15)

- Presumably holds the tomb of Herod. However, this largest of the fortress structures has not yet been completely excavated.

The Herodion: Lower Palace

Small Group Bible Discovery (15 minutes)

> *Participant's Guide pages 17–26.*
>
> During this time, a group with fewer than seven participants will stay together. A group of seven or more participants will break into small groups and reassemble as a large group during the final five minutes. Assign each group one of the following topics. If you have more than four small groups, assign some topics to more than one group.

Let's break into groups of three to five—people sitting near you—and study some of the Bible passages and truths mentioned in the video.

Turn to pages 17–26 in your Participant's Guide. There you'll find a list of four topics. You'll have ten minutes to read and discuss the topic I'll assign to you. Choose one person in your group to be a spokesperson for your group when we discuss these topics later.

> Assign each group a topic.

I'll signal you when one minute is left.

Topic A: Bethlehem—Small But Significant

Despite its small size, Bethlehem was the location of significant historical events. Discovering its history helps us to appreciate why the town was the perfect place for Jesus' birth.

1. Look at the map of Israel on page 17 of your Participant's Guide. Note Bethlehem's location in relationship to Jerusalem, the Herodion, the Judea Wilderness, the Judea Mountains, Moab, and Edom (Idumaea). Which occupations did Bethlehem's unique location at the border between the mountains and the wilderness enable its people to have?

Topography of Israel: New Testament

small Group Bible Discovery

Topic A: Bethlehem—Small But Significant

Despite its small size, Bethlehem was the location of significant historical events. Discovering its history helps us to appreciate why the town was the perfect place for Jesus' birth.

1. Look at the map of Israel below. Note Bethlehem's location in relationship to Jerusalem, the Herodion, the Judea Wilderness, the Judea Mountains, Moab, and Edom (Idumaea). Which occupations did Bethlehem's unique location at the border between the mountains and the wilderness enable its people to have?

Topography of Israel: New Testament

Suggested Responses: Fertile mountain valleys and hillsides that received adequate rainfall provided valuable croplands for farmers, while the wilderness nearby provided pastures for the shepherds' flocks.

2. Where was Jacob traveling to when Rachel died in childbirth? (See Genesis 35:16–19.)

Suggested Response: Ephrath (Bethlehem).

3. What do King David and Ruth, who are mentioned in the following verses, have in common? (See Ruth 1:22; 1 Samuel 16:1–3; Matthew 1:1, 5.)

Suggested Responses: King David and Ruth (who was originally from Moab) lived in Bethlehem during a portion of their lives. Both of them are also listed in the lineage of Jesus the Messiah.

4. What does Scripture reveal about Moab, the country in which Ruth was reared? (See Genesis 19:36–37; Numbers 24:17; 1 Kings 11:7; 2 Kings 3:26–27.) What does the fact that God blessed the entire world through Ruth reveal about how God uses people in His plan of salvation?

Suggested Responses: The Moabite nation began when Lot's daughters committed incest. The nation eventually would be destroyed by Israel. The Moabites worshiped pagan gods, and its king practiced child sacrifice. Despite her past sinfulness, Ruth had an integral role in God's plan of redemption, which was initiated and fulfilled by the birth of Jesus in Bethlehem.

5. What did Micah predict about seven hundred years before Jesus was born? (See Micah 5:2.)

Suggested Response: The Messiah who would rule over Israel would come out of Bethlehem.

6. Why was it important for Jesus to be born in Bethlehem? (See Matthew 1:1, 17; Luke 1:29–33; 2:4–7.)

Suggested Responses: Jesus—the Son of God, the King of the universe—would be of the line of David and would be given the throne of David. He would rule over the house of David forever. Bethlehem links Jesus to the lineage and family of David.

2. Where was Jacob traveling to when Rachel died in child-birth? (See Genesis 35:16–19.)

3. What do King David and Ruth, who are mentioned in the following verses, have in common? (See Ruth 1:22; 1 Samuel 16:1–3; Matthew 1:1, 5.)

4. What does Scripture reveal about Moab, the country in which Ruth was reared? (See Genesis 19:36–37; Numbers 24:17; 1 Kings 11:7; 2 Kings 3:26–27.) What does the fact that God blessed the entire world through Ruth reveal about how God uses people in His plan of salvation?

5. What did Micah predict about seven hundred years before Jesus was born? (See Micah 5:2.)

6. Why was it important for Jesus to be born in Bethlehem? (See Matthew 1:1, 17; Luke 1:29–33; 2:4–7.)

DID YOU KNOW?

Worlds Apart, But Still Within View

The Wilderness East of Bethlehem

East of the Dead Sea, which is barely ten miles from Bethlehem, are the mountains of Moab where Ruth was reared. Thus, when Ruth moved to Bethlehem with Naomi, she probably moved fewer than twenty miles. She could even see her homeland on a clear day. What a significant, but not extensive, trip that turned out to be!

DID YOU KNOW?

The Wilderness East of Bethlehem

Worlds Apart, But Still Within View
East of the Dead Sea, which is barely ten miles from Bethlehem, are the mountains of Moab where Ruth was reared. Thus, when Ruth moved to Bethlehem with Naomi, she probably moved fewer than twenty miles. She could even see her homeland on a clear day. What a significant, but not extensive, trip that turned out to be!

Topic B: God's Plan for the Birth of the Savior Unfolds

1. Read the following verses and note what you discover about the individuals involved and the way in which God used them to bring about the birth of Jesus.

    a. Genesis 38:6–19, 24–26; Matthew 1:1, 3a

        Suggested Responses: Judah and his daughter-in-law Tamar are listed in the genealogy of Jesus, yet theirs is a colorful tale. When Judah refused to arrange a third marriage so that his widowed daughter-in-law could become pregnant and carry on her husband's name, she posed as a prostitute, and Judah had intercourse with her without discovering her identity. When Tamar became pregnant, Judah wanted her to be burned to death—until she proved that he was the father of her baby!

    b. Joshua 2:1–11, 6:22–25; Matthew 1:1, 5a

        Suggested Responses: Rahab, a prostitute in Jericho, hid the two Israelite spies and believed in Yahweh. So she and her entire family were spared when Jericho was captured. Rahab had a place in Jesus' lineage, too.

    c. Ruth 1:1–6, 15–18; 4:9–17; 1 Kings 11:7; 2 Kings 3:26–27; Matthew 1:1, 5b

        Suggested Responses: Ruth, a daughter of Moab, had been reared to worship pagan gods and her king practiced child sacrifice—something God hated. Yet she committed herself to Yahweh, God of the Israelites (see Ruth 1:16). After her marriage to Boaz, who was a descendant of one of the sons of Tamar (see a. above) and the son of Rahab (see b. above), Ruth gave birth to Obed, the grandfather of King David, in whose lineage Jesus was born.

6. Why was it important for Jesus to be born in Bethlehem? (See Matthew 1:1, 17; Luke 1:29–33; 2:4–7.)

DID YOU KNOW?

Worlds Apart, But Still Within View

East of the Dead Sea, which is barely ten miles from Bethlehem, are the mountains of Moab where Ruth was reared. Thus, when Ruth moved to Bethlehem with Naomi, she probably moved fewer than twenty miles. She could even see her homeland on a clear day. What a significant, but not extensive, trip that turned out to be!

The Wilderness East of Bethlehem

Topic B: God's Plan for the Birth of the Savior Unfolds

1. Read the following verses and note what you discover about the individuals involved and the way in which God used them to bring about the birth of Jesus.

   a. Genesis 38:6–19, 24–26; Matthew 1:1, 3a

   b. Joshua 2:1–11, 6:22–25; Matthew 1:1, 5a

   c. Ruth 1:1–6, 15–18; 4:9–17; 1 Kings 11:7; 2 Kings 3:26–27; Matthew 1:1, 5b

   d. 1 Samuel 16:1–13; Matthew 1:1, 6

PLANNING NOTES:

d. 1 Samuel 16:1–13; Matthew 1:1, 6

Suggested Responses: David was the youngest, weakest, and least important of his brothers. Yet, contrary to the expectations of the culture, God selected David to become king of Israel.

e. 2 Samuel 11:1–5, 14–17, 26–27; 12:13–25; Matthew 1:1, 6b

Suggested Responses: King David lusted after Bathsheba, committed adultery with her (resulting in pregnancy), and then had her husband killed in battle. He married her, but their child died because of David's sin. Then Bathsheba conceived again and gave birth to Solomon, who is in the lineage of Jesus.

2. What do the above passages reveal about God's choice of people who participated in His plan of salvation—to be in Jesus' ancestral line?

Suggested Response: Jesus' ancestral line was comprised of people who, in spite of their sinfulness, had committed themselves to Him.

3. Of all the other people God could have chosen, why do you think He selected these people to have a role in helping to accomplish the birth of Messiah the King?

Suggested Responses: These will vary. Encourage participants to think of several messages that God may have intended to communicate to specific types of people.

KEY DATES

586 B.C.	Babylonian captivity of Judah
538 B.C.	Return to Israel
332 B.C.	Alexander the Great conquers Israel
330–198 B.C.	Rule of Hellenistic Ptolemies over the Jews
198–167 B.C.	Oppression under Hellenistic Seleucids
167 B.C.	Maccabee revolt
167–63 B.C.	Hasmonaean kingdom
37 B.C.	Herod the Great begins his reign
4 B.C.	Herod the Great dies
ca. 6 B.C.	Jesus' birth
ca. A.D. 30	Jesus is crucified
A.D. 70	Roman destruction of Jerusalem during First Jewish Revolt
A.D. 131–135	Bar Kochba Revolt (Second Jewish Revolt)

e. 2 Samuel 11:1–5, 14–17, 26–27; 12:13–25; Matthew
1:1, 6b

2. What do the above passages reveal about God's choice of
people who participated in His plan of salvation—to be in
Jesus' ancestral line?

3. Of all the other people God could have chosen, why do
you think He selected these people to have a role in helping to accomplish the birth of Messiah the King?

KEY DATES

586 B.C.	Babylonian captivity of Judah
538 B.C.	Return to Israel
332 B.C.	Alexander the Great conquers Israel
330–198 B.C.	Rule of Hellenistic Ptolemies over the Jews
198–167 B.C.	Oppression under Hellenistic Seleucids
167 B.C.	Maccabee revolt
167–63 B.C.	Hasmonaean kingdom
37 B.C.	Herod the Great begins his reign
4 B.C.	Herod the Great dies
ca. 6 B.C.	Jesus' birth
ca. A.D. 30	Jesus is crucified
A.D. 70	Roman destruction of Jerusalem during First Jewish Revolt
A.D. 131–135	Bar Kochba Revolt (Second Jewish Revolt)

Topic C: A Contrast Between Two Kings

1. Read Matthew 2:1–8, 16–18.

a. Based on the video and your reading, what do you
think motivated Herod the Great?

b. In what way(s) did King Herod respond to his potential rivals, specifically to Jesus?

PLANNING NOTES:

Topic C: A Contrast Between Two Kings

1. Read Matthew 2:1–8, 16–18.

    a. Based on the video and your reading, what do you think motivated Herod the Great?

        Suggested Responses: Herod the Great thought highly of his abilities and power and spared no effort to impress the world with his greatness. He was also a lying schemer who greatly feared the loss of his power.

    b. In what way(s) did King Herod respond to his potential rivals, specifically to Jesus?

        Suggested Responses: Herod ruthlessly destroyed all potential rivals with incredible cruelty and no remorse. History reveals that killing the male babies of Bethlehem was but one event during his bloody reign.

2. What motivated Jesus—the Messiah, the King of the universe—to do what He did on earth? (See John 4:34; 5:30; 8:54; 10:10, 17.)

    Suggested Responses: Jesus sought first to do the will of His Father in heaven—to please, honor, and glorify Him. Jesus also came to bring people abundant life, which required Him to lose His life and then be resurrected and return to heaven.

3. Describe the contrasts between Jesus and Herod that can be found "beneath the surface" of Matthew 2:1.

    Suggested Responses: Jesus was born in Bethlehem; Herod was born in Edom. Jesus the Messiah was sinless; Herod, the king of the Jews, was a cruel tyrant. Herod's earthly power was awesome, but he had nothing in the kingdom of heaven; Jesus had none of the power that the world could give, but His power in heaven is beyond comprehension. Jesus gave His life and ministry as a sacrifice on behalf of other people; Herod's life revolved around sacrificing others in order to bring glory and honor to himself. Jesus and Herod were opposites—morally, culturally, spiritually, and certainly in terms of their worldly status.

4. Given the differences between King Herod and the infant Messiah, why was the shepherds' visit to Bethlehem such an act of faith? (See Luke 2:8–18.)

    Suggested Responses: It took faith for the shepherds to leave their sheep and seek out the infant king, whom Herod would consider to be his rival. It took faith to worship a baby who seemed so weak and insignificant in comparison to Herod. It took faith to tell others the truth about this infant king—especially since Herod was so quick to destroy any opposition.

5. Describe how the wise men exercised their faith after speaking with Herod and continuing on to Bethlehem (with the great Herodion clearly in view) to find the baby Jesus. (See Matthew 2:1–12.)

    Suggested Responses: After following His star for such a long distance, they must have been amazed to find a mere babe in a manger, especially after having been in King Herod's presence and witnessing the material evidence of his greatness. In some ways it is amazing that they worshiped Jesus as they did. Their refusal

KEY DATES

586 B.C.	Babylonian captivity of Judah
538 B.C.	Return to Israel
332 B.C.	Alexander the Great conquers Israel
330–198 B.C.	Rule of Hellenistic Ptolemies over the Jews
198–167 B.C.	Oppression under Hellenistic Seleucids
167 B.C.	Maccabee revolt
167–63 B.C.	Hasmonaean kingdom
37 B.C.	Herod the Great begins his reign
4 B.C.	Herod the Great dies
ca. 6 B.C.	Jesus' birth
ca. A.D. 30	Jesus is crucified
A.D. 70	Roman destruction of Jerusalem during First Jewish Revolt
A.D. 131–135	Bar Kochba Revolt (Second Jewish Revolt)

Topic C: A Contrast Between Two Kings

1. Read Matthew 2:1–8, 16–18.

   a. Based on the video and your reading, what do you think motivated Herod the Great?

   b. In what way(s) did King Herod respond to his potential rivals, specifically to Jesus?

2. What motivated Jesus—the Messiah, the King of the universe—to do what He did on earth? (See John 4:34; 5:30; 8:54; 10:10, 17.)

3. Describe the contrasts between Jesus and Herod that can be found "beneath the surface" of Matthew 2:1.

4. Given the differences between King Herod and the infant Messiah, why was the shepherds' visit to Bethlehem such an act of faith? (See Luke 2:8–18.)

5. Describe how the wise men exercised their faith after speaking with Herod and continuing on to Bethlehem (with the great Herodion clearly in view) to find the baby Jesus. (See Matthew 2:1–12.)

PLANNING NOTES:

to do Herod's bidding and reveal the location of Jesus is an indication of their faith, for their action could easily have brought harm to them.

✏ 6.   By bringing Jesus and King Herod—two kings who couldn't have been more different—together at the same time in history, what was God revealing about how He works?

Suggested Responses: God uses what seems to be weak to accomplish His purposes. He uses people who appear to be weak to triumph over those who appear to be strong. Although Herod's power seemed overwhelming and undefeatable, God's power was stronger still. What is done for God and His kingdom has lasting value, as opposed to what we do to obtain honor for ourselves. We create a lasting legacy through self-sacrifice and servanthood, not through self-glorification.

PROFILES IN CONTRAST

Jesus	Herod the Great
Placed in a manger	Lived in magnificent palaces
Appeared as a weak and powerless baby	Appeared to have great strength and power
Had no earthly status but really had it all—eternal power, glory, authority, etc.	Had great earthly status, but lacked eternal status
Lived to honor His Father	Lived to glorify himself
Used by God to fulfill the purposes of God	Lived to fulfill his own purposes
Built a kingdom of people (Matthew 16:18; 1 Peter 2:4–8)	Built glorious buildings of marble and other stones
Built for the glory of God so others would know Yahweh is truly God	Built to honor himself and maintain good relations with Rome
Dedicated to serving others	Was self-serving
Had ultimate authority and still does (Ephesians 1:18–22)	Had only limited earthly authority
Died in agony on the cross to remove the sins of humankind	Died in agony, hated by his family, after ordering one of his sons to be executed
The Messiah from Jacob's lineage who overcame all evil but was never accepted as King of the Jews	The Edomite whose reign violated God's rules (Deuteronomy 17:15) and was never accepted by the Jews

6. By bringing Jesus and King Herod—two kings who couldn't have been more different—together at the same time in history, what was God revealing about how He works?

PROFILES IN CONTRAST

Jesus	Herod the Great
Placed in a manger	Lived in magnificent palaces
Appeared as a weak and powerless baby	Appeared to have great strength and power
Had no earthly status but really had it all—eternal power, glory, authority, etc.	Had great earthly status, but lacked eternal status
Lived to honor His Father	Lived to glorify himself
Used by God to fulfill the purposes of God	Lived to fulfill his own purposes
Built a kingdom of people (Matthew 16:18; 1 Peter 2:4–8)	Built glorious buildings of marble and other stones
Built for the glory of God so others would know Yahweh is truly God	Built to honor himself and maintain good relations with Rome
Dedicated to serving others	Was self-serving
Had ultimate authority and still does (Ephesians 1:18–22)	Had only limited earthly authority
Died in agony on the cross to remove the sins of humankind	Died in agony, hated by his family, after ordering one of his sons to be executed
The Messiah from Jacob's lineage who overcame all evil but was never accepted as King of the Jews	The Edomite whose reign violated God's rules (Deuteronomy 17:15) and was never accepted by the Jews

PLANNING NOTES:

Topic D: Israel and Edom, Nations in Conflict

1. What does Genesis 25:21–26 reveal about Jacob and Esau, the grandsons of Abraham?

    Suggested Responses: They would be the fathers of nations in conflict. Esau (the older) ultimately would serve Jacob, and Jacob's people would be stronger than Esau's people.

2. Who were the descendants of Esau? (See Genesis 25:29–30; 36:1–9.)

    Suggested Response: The Edomites. Edom means "red," and the Edomites lived in the mountains to the east and south of the Dead Sea.

3. What did Balaam prophesy would happen to Jacob's people—Israel—and to Esau's people—the Edomites? (See Numbers 24:15–19.)

    Suggested Responses: A "star" would come out of Jacob, and a "scepter" would rise out of Israel. (These were both symbols of royalty.) This person would conquer Edom, and Israel would grow strong.

4. What characterized the history of relationships between Israel and Edom? (See Numbers 20:18–21; 1 Kings 11:14–17; 2 Kings 8:20–22; Ezekiel 25:12–14.)

    Suggested Responses: Both nations hated each other and sought to destroy the other. Because of Edom's attacks on Judah, God promised to take revenge on the Edomites.

5. What did Obadiah and other prophets predict would happen to the descendants of Jacob and Esau? (See Jeremiah 49:8–10; Ezekiel 35:15; Amos 1:11–12; 9:11–12; Obadiah 8–14, 18.)

    Suggested Responses: God would destroy the Edomites because of their violence against Israel and their unwillingness to go to Israel's assistance. No one from Esau's household would survive, and other people (including David's descendants) would inhabit the Edomites' land.

6. History reveals that Herod the Great came from Idumaea, which was Edom. How does what Jesus accomplished on earth during Herod's reign fit with the prophecies about Israel and Edom?

    Suggested Responses: Although Herod appeared to be in control, he was powerless to stop God's plan for Jesus, the King of heaven and earth whom God placed on the throne of David. The ruins of the Herodion illustrate Herod's ultimate defeat by Jesus, who lives today in heaven and through His followers.

> After nine minutes, let participants know that they have one minute remaining. Then reassemble the entire group. After everyone is back together, begin asking one person from each small group to briefly share a key idea with the larger group. In some cases, you may not have time for every group to share their discoveries.

As time allows, let's briefly share the key ideas that your group discussed.

Topic D: Israel and Edom, Nations in Conflict

1. What does Genesis 25:21–26 reveal about Jacob and Esau, the grandsons of Abraham?

2. Who were the descendants of Esau? (See Genesis 25:29–30; 36:1–9.)

3. What did Balaam prophesy would happen to Jacob's people—Israel—and to Esau's people—the Edomites? (See Numbers 24:15–19.)

4. What characterized the history of relationships between Israel and Edom? (See Numbers 20:18–21; 1 Kings 11:14–17; 2 Kings 8:20–22; Ezekiel 25:12–14.)

5. What did Obadiah and other prophets predict would happen to the descendants of Jacob and Esau? (See Jeremiah 49:8–10; Ezekiel 35:15; Amos 1:11–12; 9:11–12; Obadiah 8–14, 18.)

6. History reveals that Herod the Great came from Idumaea, which was Edom. How does what Jesus accomplished on earth during Herod's reign fit with the prophecies about Israel and Edom?

faith lesson

Time for Reflection (6 minutes)

It's time for each of us to think quietly about what we've learned today. On page 27 of the Participant's Guide, you'll find a passage of Scripture. Let's each read this passage silently and take the next few minutes to consider some of the questions that follow the Scripture passage.

Please do not talk during this time. It's a time when we can reflect on the great step of faith that was required for the Jews of Jesus' day to believe that He was the Messiah.

> *The Scripture passage and questions are reproduced in their entirety in the Participant's Guide on pages 27–29.*

And there were shepherds living out in the fields nearby, keeping watch over their flocks at night. An angel of the Lord appeared to them, and the glory of the Lord shone around them, and they were terrified. But the angel said to them, "Do not be afraid. I bring you good news of great joy that will be for all the people. Today in the town of David a Savior has been born to you; he is Christ the Lord. This will be a sign to you: You will find a baby wrapped in cloths and lying in a manger."

Suddenly a great company of the heavenly host appeared with the angel, praising God and saying,

"Glory to God in the highest,
   and on earth peace to men on whom his favor rests."

When the angels had left them and gone into heaven, the shepherds said to one another, "Let's go to Bethlehem and see this thing that has happened, which the Lord has told us about."

So they hurried off and found Mary and Joseph, and the baby, who was lying in the manger. When they had seen him, they spread the word concerning what had been told them about this child, and all who heard it were amazed at what the shepherds said to them. But Mary treasured up all these things and pondered them in her heart. The shepherds returned, glorifying and praising God for all the things they had heard and seen, which were just as they had been told.

LUKE 2:8–20

1. Think about what a step of faith it was for the shepherds to respond as they did to the news of the Messiah's birth.

    a. What earthly king would send such an important announcement to mere shepherds?

    b. What would Herod have done to the shepherds if he had discovered they had actually visited and worshiped another king?

    c. Why would it have been frightening for these events to occur, as they did, in plain view of the Herodion?

ꜰaith ʟesson

Time for Reflection

Read the following passage of Scripture and take the next few minutes to reflect on the great step of faith that was required for the Jews of Jesus' day to believe that He was the Messiah.

> And there were shepherds living out in the fields nearby, keeping watch over their flocks at night. An angel of the Lord appeared to them, and the glory of the Lord shone around them, and they were terrified. But the angel said to them, "Do not be afraid. I bring you good news of great joy that will be for all the people. Today in the town of David a Savior has been born to you; he is Christ the Lord. This will be a sign to you: You will find a baby wrapped in cloths and lying in a manger."
>
> Suddenly a great company of the heavenly host appeared with the angel, praising God and saying,
>
> "Glory to God in the highest,
>   and on earth peace to men on
>   whom his favor rests."
>
> When the angels had left them and gone into heaven, the shepherds said to one another, "Let's go to Bethlehem and see this thing that has happened, which the Lord has told us about."
>
> So they hurried off and found Mary and Joseph, and the baby, who was lying in the manger. When they had seen him, they spread the word concerning what had been told them about this child, and all who heard it were amazed at what the shepherds said to them. But Mary treasured up all these things and pondered them in her heart. The shepherds returned, glorifying and praising God for all the things they had heard and seen, which were just as they had been told.

LUKE 2:8–20

1. Think about what a step of faith it was for the shepherds to respond as they did to the news of the Messiah's birth.

   a. What earthly king would send such an important announcement to mere shepherds?

   b. What would Herod have done to the shepherds if he had discovered they had actually visited and worshiped another king?

   c. Why would it have been frightening for these events to occur, as they did, in plain view of the Herodion?

   d. Why was it a great risk to tell others what had happened—that a new king, the King of heaven and earth, had been born?

PLANNING NOTES:

d. Why was it a great risk to tell others what had happened—that a new king, the King of heaven and earth, had been born?

2. If you had been a bystander when Jesus was born, who would you have believed was more powerful and worthy of your honor and allegiance—Jesus or King Herod? Why?

3. How is the commitment to Jesus you are asked to make similar to the one that people during His lifetime on earth were asked to make?

4. How does your commitment to Jesus as Messiah affect the way you relate to the "Herods" (evils) in your daily life?

Action Points (3 minutes)

> *The following points are reproduced on pages 29–31 of the Participant's Guide.*

Now it's time to wrap up our session.

> Give participants a moment to transition from their thoughtfulness to giving you their full attention.

I'd like to take a moment to summarize the key points we explored. After I have reviewed these points, I will give you a moment to jot down an action step (or steps) that you will commit to this week as a result of what you have learned today.

> Read the following points and pause afterward so that participants can consider and write out their commitment.

1. *It took great faith for the Jewish people to believe that Jesus, who began His life on earth as a baby in Bethlehem, was truly the Lord of heaven and earth.*

    The contrasts between Jesus and Herod could not have been greater. Herod had all the power, wealth, strength, and glory that his position in the world could offer, yet Jesus, the King of the universe, had nothing of that sort to demonstrate His position. So to believe in Jesus as the Messiah was to believe that regardless of outward appearances, Jesus, the baby in the manger, was indeed Lord of heaven and earth.

    Today, Christians are asked to walk by faith, confident in the knowledge that things are not always as they appear to be, that God can use the weak to defeat the powerful. In what ways are you demonstrating faith in your walk with God? In what ways are you paying more attention to outward appearances rather than demonstrating faith in God?

2. *King Herod, who personified evil, no doubt seemed to have all the power and control. He ruled with an iron hand, seeking out and destroying every possible enemy—even killing innocent babies. Yet Jesus, the humble King of all creation, was truly in control. He had the power to overcome every evil—including that of Herod.*

2. If you had been a bystander when Jesus was born, who would you have believed was more powerful and worthy of your honor and allegiance—Jesus or King Herod? Why?

3. How is the commitment to Jesus you are asked to make similar to the one that people during His lifetime on earth were asked to make?

4. How does your commitment to Jesus as Messiah affect the way you relate to the "Herods" (evils) in your daily life?

Action Points

Take a moment to review the key points you explored today, then jot down an action step (or steps) that you will commit to this week as a result of what you have learned.

1. *It took great faith for the Jewish people to believe that Jesus, who began His life on earth as a baby in Bethlehem, was truly the Lord of heaven and earth.*

   The contrasts between Jesus and Herod could not have been greater. Herod had all the power, wealth, strength, and glory

that his position in the world could offer, yet Jesus, the King of the universe, had nothing of that sort to demonstrate His position. So to believe in Jesus as the Messiah was to believe that regardless of outward appearances, Jesus, the baby in the manger, was indeed Lord of heaven and earth.

Today, Christians are asked to walk by faith, confident in the knowledge that things are not always as they appear to be, that God can use the weak to defeat the powerful. In what ways are you demonstrating faith in your walk with God? In what ways are you paying more attention to outward appearances rather than demonstrating faith in God?

2. *King Herod, who personified evil, no doubt seemed to have all the power and control. He ruled with an iron hand, seeking out and destroying every possible enemy—even killing innocent babies. Yet Jesus, the humble King of all creation, was truly in control. He had the power to overcome every evil—including that of Herod.*

   Today, Christians are asked to believe that no matter how powerful Wall Street appears to be, no matter how controlling a government seems, no matter how influential the morals of Hollywood appear to be, no matter how evil pornography seems, no matter how overwhelming hunger, racism, or AIDS appear to be—Jesus Christ is King. Because His power, which has conquered all evil, resides within us, we do not need to fear the evil we face.

   Although it is easier and safer to avoid evil than to confront it, the crucial question that all Christians must answer for themselves is: "Will I dare to live as if God is

PLANNING NOTES:

Today, Christians are asked to believe that no matter how powerful Wall Street appears to be, no matter how controlling a government seems, no matter how influential the morals of Hollywood appear to be, no matter how evil pornography seems, no matter how overwhelming hunger, racism, or AIDS appear to be—Jesus Christ is King. Because His power, which has conquered all evil, resides within us, we do not need to fear the evil we face.

Although it is easier and safer to avoid evil than to confront it, the crucial question that all Christians must answer for themselves is: "Will I dare to live as if God is greater than any evil I face in my life and my culture, as if the power within me is greater than every power of evil that I will encounter?"

What or who are the "Herods" of your life today—the powers of evil that seem so strong and glorious or that seem more attractive and important than following Jesus?

Which opportunities has God given you to confront the power of the sinful world around you, based on the confidence that He—not Satan—is in control? Be specific.

I believe that God is greater than any evil I will face, so I will dare to:

_____

_____

_____

_____

closing prayer

I minute

I hope that this lesson has challenged you, as it has me, to think about ways in which we can, in the power of God, confront evil around us. Let's close in prayer now, asking God to give us the courage to fulfill the calling He has given us and commit all parts of our lives to Him.

Dear God, please draw us closer to You. Help us to remember that You are strong and that in our own strength we are weak. Help us to trust You more, to remember that You indeed are stronger than any evil. As we have seen in this lesson, Herod lived to honor and praise himself, and all that's left are ruins of his buildings and memories of his cruelty. But when we live for You, what we speak and how we act can truly make an eternal difference. Through Your power, we can confront the evils of our culture even though they seem to be so dominant. Help us to live as if You are stronger than those evils—to walk in faith, obeying You. In Your name we pray, amen.

greater than any evil I face in my life and my culture, as if the power within me is greater than every power of evil that I will encounter?"

What or who are the "Herods" of your life today—the powers of evil that seem so strong and glorious or that seem more attractive and important than following Jesus?

Which opportunities has God given you to confront the power of the sinful world around you, based on the confidence that He—not Satan—is in control?

I believe that God is greater than any evil I will face, so I will dare to:

_____

_____

_____

_____

PLANNING NOTES:

DATA FILE

The Works of a Master Builder

Herod the Great's visionary building programs, ingenious development of trade with other countries, and advancement of his nation's interests are remarkable. He used his magnificent building projects as part of his effort to strengthen his relationship with Rome and establish himself as the greatest king the Jews ever had.

Jerusalem

Herod rebuilt the temple out of marble and gold. The building was taller than a fifteen-story building, and its foundation included limestone blocks weighing more than five hundred tons. On the western hill of the city he built a spectacular palace complex that contained reception halls, apartments, fountains, gardens, baths, and a fortress for his personal guards. He also built a Greek theater and hippodrome, paved the streets, and installed sewers.

The Temple Mount: A.D. **70**

1 Temple	6 Double Gates	11 Barclay's Gate
2 Royal Stoa	7 Triple Gates	12 Wilson's Arch
3 Solomon's Colonnade	8 Ritual Baths	13 Warren's Gate
4 Southern Stairs	9 Plaza	14 Place of Trumpeting
5 South Wall	10 Robinson's Arch	15 Tyropoeon Street

Masada

Perched atop a plateau in the Judea Wilderness, this fortress was one of the wonders of the ancient world. A spectacular palace suspended from one end of the plateau, luxurious hot and cold baths, mosaic floors, swimming pools, huge storehouses, barracks for soldiers, and cisterns holding millions of gallons of water helped to make this hot, dry wilderness outpost bearable for its occupants.

Jericho

This palace was built on both sides of a wadi (a dry, deep riverbed), and a bridge spanned the riverbed. One wing contained a huge, marble-floored hall where Herod received guests. Next to it were peristyle gardens, dining halls, and a

(continued on page 48)

DATA FILE

The Works of a Master Builder

Herod the Great's visionary building programs, ingenious development of trade with other countries, and advancement of his nation's interests are remarkable. He used his magnificent building projects as part of his effort to strengthen his relationship with Rome and establish himself as the greatest king the Jews ever had.

The Temple Mount: A.D. 70

1 Temple	6 Double Gates	11 Barclay's Gate
2 Royal Stoa	7 Triple Gates	12 Wilson's Arch
3 Solomon's Colonnade	8 Ritual Baths	13 Warren's Gate
4 Southern Stairs	9 Plaza	14 Place of Trumpeting
5 South Wall	10 Robinson's Arch	15 Tyropoeon Street

Jerusalem

Herod rebuilt the temple out of marble and gold. The building was taller than a fifteen-story building, and its foundation included limestone blocks weighing more than five hundred tons. On the western hill of the city he built a spectacular palace complex that contained reception halls, apartments, fountains, gardens, baths, and a fortress for his personal guards. He also built a Greek theater and hippodrome, paved the streets, and installed sewers.

The Fortress Masada

(continued from page 46)

complete Roman bath. Across the wadi, another large building housed baths, a swimming pool, and gardens.

Caesarea

Needing contact with the Roman world for its military support and trade opportunities, Herod built Caesarea into one of the most amazing seaports of the ancient world. Founded in 22 B.C., the city housed a large theater, amphitheater, hippodrome, a massive temple to Augustus, and—of course—an elaborate seaside palace. Much of the city was built with imported marble, and the city even had an elaborate sewer system that was cleansed by the sea.

The city's real glory, however, lay in its forty-acre, man-made harbor. A lighthouse guided ships into the harbor that brought Roman legions, marble, granite, and the Hellenistic culture into the region. From that harbor, ships also carried spices, olive oil, grain, and—most important—the gospel to the far reaches of the world.

Caesarea

A Theater	D Harbor (Sebastos)	G Amphitheater
B Palace	E Lighthouse	H Hippodrome
C Temple of Augustus	F Aqueduct	

Masada

Perched atop a plateau in the Judea Wilderness, this fortress was one of the wonders of the ancient world. A spectacular palace suspended from one end of the plateau, luxurious hot and cold baths, mosaic floors, swimming pools, huge storehouses, barracks for soldiers, and cisterns holding millions of gallons of water helped to make this hot, dry wilderness outpost bearable for its occupants.

The Fortress Masada

Jericho

This palace was built on both sides of a wadi (a dry, deep riverbed), and a bridge spanned the riverbed. One wing contained a huge, marble-floored hall where Herod received guests. Next to it were peristyle gardens, dining halls, and a complete Roman bath. Across the wadi, another large building housed baths, a swimming pool, and gardens.

Caesarea

Needing contact with the Roman world for its military support and trade opportunities, Herod built Caesarea into one of the most amazing seaports of the ancient world. Founded in 22 B.C., the city housed a large theater, amphitheater, hippodrome, a massive temple to Augustus, and—

(continued on page 34)

(continued from page 33)

of course—an elaborate seaside palace. Much of the city was built with imported marble, and the city even had an elaborate sewer system that was cleansed by the sea.

The city's real glory, however, lay in its forty-acre, man-made harbor. A lighthouse guided ships into the harbor that brought Roman legions, marble, granite, and the Hellenistic culture into the region. From that harbor, ships also carried spices, olive oil, grain, and—most important—the gospel to the far reaches of the world.

Caesarea

A	Theater	D	Harbor (Sebastos)	G	Amphitheater
B	Palace	E	Lighthouse	H	Hippodrome
C	Temple of Augustus	F	Aqueduct		

PLANNING NOTES:

my rock and my fortress

Before you Lead

Synopsis

The ruins of Masada, one of Herod the Great's spectacular fortress-palaces, still stand high above the Dead Sea in the mountainous Judea Wilderness. Today, however, the fortress is not so much recognized as a testimony to Herod's greatness, but as an inspiring symbol of the longstanding Jewish desire for freedom and political independence. This video focuses our attention on the story of Masada, a story that began around the time Jesus, the Messiah, appeared on earth.

The Jews had seethed under Roman rule ever since Herod the Great was made king in 37 B.C. Things grew even worse under the rule of Herod's successors following his death in 4 B.C. Weary of Roman oppression, the Jews became increasingly nationalistic and eager to escape Roman dominion. That is why they were so eager for the coming of the Messiah, whom they assumed would come to deliver them from the Romans, and were so disappointed in Jesus, who came to offer a different kind of freedom.

Finally, in A.D. 66, a social and political explosion sent shock waves throughout Israel. Jews in Caesarea—Herod the Great's marvelous port city from which early Christian missionaries left to take the gospel to the world—objected to a Gentile sacrifice offered near the synagogue entrance. This set off a series of mass killings and riots throughout Israel and the Roman Empire. For a short time, the Zealots gained control, but in response, Roman troops poured into Caesarea . . . Galilee . . . Gamla, crushing the Zealot movement. Fighting continued until the Romans utterly destroyed the great city of Jerusalem, its temple, and its people in A.D. 70.

A few Jewish Zealots (967 people, including women and children, according to the Jewish historian, Josephus) managed to escape to the refuge of Masada, Herod's mountaintop fortress in the Judea Wilderness. Masada is located just west of the Rift Valley and the mountains of Moab, between the Negev wilderness and the Dead Sea. Herod the Great built this refuge in the wilderness in the event he had to flee Jerusalem. Many years earlier, David also had fled to mountain fortresses in this region in order to escape Saul (1 Samuel 23:14). So the Zealots weren't the first to flee to this region.

Inside Masada, the Zealots had everything they needed: fifteen huge storehouses of food, weapons, and supplies; cisterns holding as much as a million gallons of water; swimming pools; living quarters; and a location that was virtually impossible to defeat. According to Josephus, Herod had stockpiled enough materials to supply thousands of men for up to ten years. So the Zealots set up living quarters, studied the Torah, and waited.

When the Zealots' occupation of Masada became known, the Roman army's Tenth Legion marched from Jerusalem and established eight camps around the base of the mountain on which Masada perched. They had few options: a frontal assault up the narrow pathway, giving up and leaving, or doing a siege. Not about to give up, they first built a wall more than two miles long completely around Masada, then they spent seven months building an enormous siege ramp against the western side of the mountain. For these massive projects, they used the sweat of thousands of captured Jews.

Once the ramp was completed, the Romans used their enormous battering ram to smash a hole in Masada's wall. (The wall wasn't thick because Masada's main protection was its high location out of harm's way.) Not to be outdone, the Zealots feverishly built an adjoining wall of timbers and filled the space in between with dirt, which absorbed the pounding of the battering ram. In response, the Romans set the timber wall on fire.

As the fire burned into the evening, the Zealots faced a tragic choice. Their commander, Eleazar, said in effect, "We Zealots have always known that to live in slavery is wrong. We should not be slaves to anyone. God did not create us to be slaves. The most important thing in the life of a person is the right to be free from oppression." He then emphasized how cruelly the Romans would treat anyone captured in Masada.

Having spent nine years fighting the Romans, the freedom fighters agreed with Eleazar. They had seen their nation and culture destroyed, their holy temple desecrated, and their families and friends tortured, enslaved, or killed. As they thought about God and what they believed life was supposed to be, they made their choice. After burning everything of value except their weapons and food (so the Romans couldn't say they had died of starvation or lack of weaponry), the Zealots chose to die by their own hands rather than surrender to the pagan Romans. Only two old women and five children lived to tell the story.

Certainly, as Ray Vander Laan points out, suicide is a terrible thing. Yet the Zealots at Masada believed that it was wrong to owe allegiance to anyone or anything other than God. As a result, they put their belief into action and died in the final battle of the First Jewish Revolt. That is why Masada symbolizes Jewish freedom to the nation of Israel today.

Key Points of This Lesson

1. *God is our fortress. We are to trust in Him, not in our own efforts, for protection and strength.* In Psalm 18:1–3, David used the Hebrew word that is transliterated in English as *masada* to describe God as his rock and fortress—the strong, unshakable source of his protection and strength.

2. *If we are to know God as our rock and fortress, we must open our eyes and hearts to the protection, strength, and freedom that Jesus offers.* Some Jewish people sought a military messiah who would deliver them from Roman oppression. Thus they misunderstood the gospel of the Messiah

who came to sacrifice Himself on their behalf, and they lost their lives without finding real peace.

3. *Our commitment to God needs to be more than just words.* The Zealots who fled to Masada believed it was wrong to owe allegiance to anyone or anything other than God, and they were willing to die for what they believed.

Session Outline (53 minutes)

I. Introduction (4 minutes)
Welcome
What's to Come
Questions to Think About

II. Show Video "My Rock and My Fortress" (21 minutes)

III. Group Discovery (20 minutes)
Video Highlights
Small Group Bible Discovery

IV. Faith Lesson (7 minutes)
Time for Reflection
Action Points

V. Closing Prayer (1 minute)

Materials

No additional materials are needed for this session. Simply view the video prior to leading the session so you are familiar with its main points. It would also be helpful to read the Data File on the Jewish Revolts on pages 86–90.

my Rock and my fortress

introduction

4 minutes

Welcome

> Assemble the participants together. Welcome them to session two of *Faith Lessons on the Life and Ministry of the Messiah.*

What's to Come

During the years following the death of Herod the Great, Jewish nationalism was on the rise. At the time of Jesus' ministry, the people eagerly anticipated the arrival of the Messiah. But they longed for a nationalistic Messiah who would set them free from the bonds of Rome, not one who would provide release from the bonds of sin. So, not too many years after Jesus died and rose from the dead, the Jewish Zealots revolted. For a short time, they held the upper hand, but Rome responded by crushing Israel and utterly destroying Jerusalem and its people.

When Jerusalem and the temple were destroyed, a few Zealots escaped to the captured stronghold of Masada, Herod's mountaintop fortress, where for a time they were safe. In this session, which was filmed at Masada, Ray Vander Laan shares what happened to the Jewish Zealots. He discusses what they stood for and challenges us to view God as our fortress and to be willing to put everything on the line to back up our commitment to Him.

Questions to Think About

> Participant's Guide page 35.

> Ask each question and solicit a few responses from group members.

✏ 1. Which images come to mind when you hear the word *fortress?*

   Suggested Responses: may include a specific historic site that includes the remains of an old fort, a place of safety, a strong building designed to keep out enemies, etc.

✏ 2. When times get tough, when you face trouble or difficult times, what do you view as your personal "fortress"? What provides feelings of safety or security for you?

   Suggested Responses: may include money in the bank, the help of another person, my own ability to handle problem situations, caring family members, the promises of Scripture, etc.

SESSION TWO

My Rock and My Fortress

Questions to Think About

1. Which images come to mind when you hear the word *fortress?*

2. When times get tough, when you face trouble or difficult times, what do you view as your personal "fortress"? What provides feelings of safety or security for you?

3. In what ways might God be considered our "fortress"?

PLANNING NOTES:

✏ 3.   In what ways might God be considered our "fortress"?

Suggested Responses: He is always with us and exhibits His strength on our behalf when we are weak, His character remains the same no matter what, He wants to be our refuge during times of trouble, we can flee to Him anytime, He is strong and unshakable in character, etc.

Let's keep these ideas in mind as we view the video.

video presentation

21 minutes

Participant's Guide page 36.

On page 36 of your Participant's Guide, you will find a space in which to take notes on key points as we watch this video.

Leader's Video Observations

Wilderness Fortresses

David's Masada

Herod's Masada

The Zealots' Masada

The Zealots' Commitment—More Than Words

SESSION TWO

My Rock and My Fortress

Questions to Think About

1. Which images come to mind when you hear the word *fortress?*

2. When times get tough, when you face trouble or difficult times, what do you view as your personal "fortress"? What provides feelings of safety or security for you?

3. In what ways might God be considered our "fortress"?

---

36   Faith Lessons on the Life and Ministry of the Messiah

Video Notes

Wilderness Fortresses

David's Masada

Herod's Masada

The Zealots' Masada

The Zealots' Commitment—More Than Words

PLANNING NOTES:

Group Discovery

20 minutes

> If your group has seven or more members, use the **Video Highlights** with the entire group (5 minutes), then break into small groups of three to five to discuss the **Small Group Bible Discovery** (10 minutes). Then reassemble the group to discuss the key points discovered (5 minutes).
>
> If your group has fewer than seven members, begin with the **Video Highlights** (5 minutes), then do one or more of the topics found in the **Small Group Bible Discovery** as a group (10 minutes). Finally, spend five minutes at the end discussing points that had an impact on participants.

Video Highlights (5 minutes)

> Here you'll ask one or more of the following questions that directly relate to the video the participants have just seen.

1. Now that you have seen a bit of the Judea Wilderness, what do you think it was like for David and his men to hide out in the wilderness? What dangers and hazards, safety and hope did the wilderness offer?

   Suggested Responses: Allow participants to share their ideas, which may include the dangers of flash floods, ambush by enemies, lack of food or water; the safety of many places to hide, the security of fortresses that would be difficult to attack, a tactical advantage for whoever knew the territory well; etc.

2. In what ways would the type of wilderness experience David had encourage you to depend on God as your fortress? In what ways would it tempt you to depend upon yourself?

   Suggested Responses: Encourage participants to consider their response—would they feel abandoned by God? Realize that their survival depended on Him? Become arrogant or self-sufficient?

3. Which physical details about Masada surprised you?

   Suggested Responses: Its remote and high location, the fact that so much water was available—even a swimming pool—the luxury and beauty of the palaces, the fact that the Zealots were able to capture it, etc.

4. What do you think about the Zealots' belief that it is wrong to owe allegiance to anyone or anything but God? What do you think about the way they carried out that belief?

   Suggested Responses: Encourage participants to think about what motivated the Zealots to capture Masada, what they hoped to accomplish by doing so, why they were willing to lay down their lives for what they believed, etc. Encourage participants to consider the personal implications of their closely held beliefs.

video highlights

1. Now that you have seen a bit of the Judea Wilderness, what do you think it was like for David and his men to hide out in the wilderness? What dangers and hazards, safety and hope did the wilderness offer?

2. In what ways would the type of wilderness experience David had encourage you to depend on God as your fortress? In what ways would it tempt you to depend upon yourself?

3. Which physical details about Masada surprised you?

4. What do you think about the Zealots' belief that it is wrong to owe allegiance to anyone or anything but God? What do you think about the way they carried out that belief?

PLANNING NOTES:

Small Group Bible Discovery (15 minutes)

Participant's Guide pages 38–52.

During this time, a group with fewer than seven participants will stay together. A group with seven or more participants will break into small groups and reassemble as a large group during the final five minutes. Assign each group one of the following topics. If you have more than four small groups, assign some topics to more than one group.

Let's break into groups of three to five—people sitting near you—and study some of the Bible passages and truths mentioned in the video.

Turn to pages 38–52 in your Participant's Guide. There you'll find a list of four topics. You'll have ten minutes to read and discuss the topic I'll assign to you. Choose one person in your group to be a spokesperson for your group when we discuss these topics later.

Assign each group a topic.

I'll signal you when one minute is left.

Topic A: A Fortress in the Wilderness

1. According to 1 Samuel 23:14, 24–29, where did David hide when King Saul was seeking to kill him? (On the map on page 39 of your Participant's Guide, locate the area described.)

Suggested Responses: David fled to the Desert of Ziph west of En Gedi and the Desert of Maon west of Masada, then he lived in the fortresses of En Gedi.

Topography of Israel: New Testament

small Group Bible Discovery

Topic A: A Fortress in the Wilderness

1. According to 1 Samuel 23:14, 24–29, where did David hide when King Saul was seeking to kill him? (On the map on page 39, locate the area described.)

2. Although David found safe hiding places in the wilderness, what, according to the following passages, did he consider to be his true protection?

   a. Psalm 18:1–2

   b. Psalm 18:46–50

PLANNING NOTES:

2. Although David found safe hiding places in the wilderness, what, according to the following passages, did he consider to be his true protection?

   a. Psalm 18:1–2

   Suggested Responses: David wrote that the Lord was his rock, his fortress, and his deliverer. These images communicate that God was his security, his strength, his hiding place during troubled times. The Hebrew word used here, metsudah, which refers to any fortress, is equivalent to the English word, masada.

   b. Psalm 18:46–50

   Suggested Responses: David praised God for being his Rock and Savior who avenged him, who saved him, who subdued his enemies, who exalted him, and who rescued him from violent men. These images portray God as being the source of David's security.

Living Water Brings Life

   c. Psalm 63:1

   Suggested Response: Here David used the imagery of the desert wilderness to reveal his deep need for God, comparing his thirst for God to the thirst a person has in the dry wilderness.

   d. Psalm 71:1–3

   Suggested Response: David clearly stated his dependence on God for refuge and deliverance. He recognized that God was his "rock of refuge" and "fortress" who ordered his salvation.

   e. Psalm 144:2

   Suggested Response: David again described God as his fortress, stronghold, deliverer, and shield who would act on his behalf during challenging times.

3. Long after David sought refuge from King Saul, Herod the Great built the fortress of Masada in the same wilderness. In what ways did David and Herod view their protection differently?

   Suggested Responses: Although he was a powerful king, Herod was extremely fearful of anyone who might try to take his power away. He trusted in his own strength exclusively. That's the main reason he built Masada—to be an extravagant place of refuge in the wilderness. David, although he sought safe strongholds, ultimately trusted in God to save him from his enemies.

small Group Bible Discovery

Topic A: A Fortress in the Wilderness

1. According to 1 Samuel 23:14, 24–29, where did David hide when King Saul was seeking to kill him? (On the map on page 39, locate the area described.)

2. Although David found safe hiding places in the wilderness, what, according to the following passages, did he consider to be his true protection?

   a. Psalm 18:1–2

   b. Psalm 18:46–50

   c. Psalm 63:1

Living Water Brings Life

   d. Psalm 71:1–3

   e. Psalm 144:2

3. Long after David sought refuge from King Saul, Herod the Great built the fortress of Masada in the same wilderness. In what ways did David and Herod view their protection differently?

✏ 4.   With the contrasting views of Herod and David fresh in mind, read Matthew 6:25–34 and consider how Jesus would have you view your efforts to protect and provide for your needs.

Suggested Responses: Encourage participants to reconsider their dependence on and trust in God, to look for the Masadas they may be building in the wilderness of their lives, and to renew their commitment to seek God's kingdom and His righteousness above all else.

DATA FILE

The Glories of Masada

Why Masada?

Herod built the fortress-palace of Masada on a huge rock plateau overlooking the Dead Sea in the barren, remote Judea Wilderness. The top of the plateau, more than twenty-one acres in size, is nearly 1,300 feet above the sea. Obviously Masada's height provided its greatest protection. But Herod also surrounded the summit with a wall and thirty defensive towers. The fortress could be reached only via the Snake Path, the main, twisting path on the eastern side of the mountain, and a path on the western side. Strong, heavily guarded gates protected each of these entrances into the fortress.

Although located in a desert wilderness, Masada was close to more hospitable areas. Herod could quickly leave Jerusalem and flee to Masada if the Jewish people revolted or if Herod's Roman master, Antony, gave Herod's domain to Cleopatra, his enemy to the south. Masada was also near the southern areas of Nabatea and Idumaea, the countries of Herod's origin.

(continued on page 66)

Masada

1. The Mountain
2. Northern Palace
3. Western Palace
4. Roman Bathhouse
5. Cistern
6. Storehouse

My Rock and My Fortress

4. With the contrasting views of Herod and David fresh in mind, read Matthew 6:25–34 and consider how Jesus would have you view your efforts to protect and provide for your needs.

DATA FILE

The Glories of Masada

Why Masada?

Herod built the fortress-palace of Masada on a huge rock plateau overlooking the Dead Sea in the barren, remote Judea Wilderness. The top of the plateau, more than twenty-one acres in size, is nearly 1,300 feet above the sea. Obviously Masada's height provided its greatest protection. But Herod also surrounded the summit with a wall and thirty defensive towers. The fortress could be reached only via the Snake Path, the main, twisting path on the eastern side of the mountain, and a path on the western side. Strong, heavily guarded gates protected each of these entrances into the fortress.

(continued on page 42)

Masada

1. The Mountain
2. Northern Palace
3. Western Palace
4. Roman Bathhouse
5. Cistern
6. Storehouse

PLANNING NOTES:

(continued from page 64)

Masada's Palaces

Built into the northern end of the mountain was a remarkable building known as the "hanging palace." The upper level perched on top of the mountain, and the two lower levels were built into the cliff face.

- The upper terrace featured lavish living quarters with mosaic floors, frescoed walls, and a semicircular balcony that offered spectacular views.
- The round, middle terrace had two concentric rows of columns that created a beautiful balcony for relaxation.
- The lower terrace, surrounded by low walls and columns with a roof in between, provided an open court inside a colonnade. A bathroom on its eastern side had mosaic floors. The great retaining walls that supported this level remain a testimony to the genius of Herod's engineers.

The western palace served as Herod's main living quarters in Masada. Occupying more than 37,000 square feet, this building included royal apartments, bathrooms, a cold-water pool, and a large reception hall with magnificently decorated mosaic pavement. Nearby were servants' quarters, workshops, a huge kitchen, and three richly decorated palaces—probably for the families of Herod's wives, who did not get along. (continued on page 68)

Masada: Northern Palace

Column

Mosaic

(continued from page 41)

Although located in a desert wilderness, Masada was close to more hospitable areas. Herod could quickly leave Jerusalem and flee to Masada if the Jewish people revolted or if Herod's Roman master, Antony, gave Herod's domain to Cleopatra, his enemy to the south. Masada was also near the southern areas of Nabatea and Idumaea, the countries of Herod's origin.

Masada's Palaces

Built into the northern end of the mountain was a remarkable building known as the "hanging palace." The upper level perched on top of the mountain, and the two lower levels were built into the cliff face.

- The upper terrace featured lavish living quarters with mosaic floors, frescoed walls, and a semicircular balcony that offered spectacular views.

Masada: Northern Palace

Column

Mosaic

- The round, middle terrace had two concentric rows of columns that created a beautiful balcony for relaxation.
- The lower terrace, surrounded by low walls and columns with a roof in between, provided an open court inside a colonnade. A bathroom on its eastern side had mosaic floors. The great retaining walls that supported this level remain a testimony to the genius of Herod's engineers.

The western palace served as Herod's main living quarters in Masada. Occupying more than 37,000 square feet, this building included royal apartments, bathrooms, a cold-water pool, and a large reception hall with magnificently decorated mosaic pavement. Nearby were servants' quarters, workshops, a huge kitchen, and three richly decorated palaces—probably for the families of Herod's wives, who did not get along.

Water: Masada's Greatest Luxury

Despite its dry, wilderness location, Masada boasted one of the largest bathing complexes of its time. The largest room of the Roman bathhouse contained a hot bath (caldarium), which was much like a sauna. A warm bath (tepidarium) and cold bath (frigidarium) were adjacent. All of them were elegantly decorated with frescoes and mosaic floors. In addition, there were several swimming pools within the fortress.

To gather the water needed to supply such luxuries in the dry wilderness, Herod and his engineers created a brilliant water system that defied nature. Masada was perched on a mountain between two wadis that occasionally flooded when it rained in the mountains to the west. So Herod diverted some of the floodwater into twelve cisterns cut into the base of the mountain that could hold more than 1,500,000 cubic feet of water—enough water to sustain thousands of people for up to ten years! Water was bucketed up about three hundred feet and stored in large cisterns (perhaps old quarries for building stones) that could hold more than one million gallons on top of the plateau. Thus Masada had an enormous supply of fresh water. The elaborate bathing complexes and water supply reveal much about Herod's obsessive fears concerning safety and his craving for opulence and luxury.

(continued on page 44)

(continued from page 66)

Water: Masada's Greatest Luxury

Despite its dry, wilderness location, Masada boasted one of the largest bathing complexes of its time. The largest room of the Roman bathhouse contained a hot bath (caldarium), which was much like a sauna. A warm bath (tepidarium) and cold bath (frigidarium) were adjacent. All of them were elegantly decorated with frescoes and mosaic floors. In addition, there were several swimming pools within the fortress.

To gather the water needed to supply such luxuries in the dry wilderness, Herod and his engineers created a brilliant water system that defied nature. Masada was perched on a mountain between two wadis that occasionally flooded when it rained in the mountains to the west. So Herod diverted some of the floodwater into twelve cisterns cut into the base of the mountain that could hold more than 1,500,000 cubic feet of water—enough water to sustain thousands of people for up to ten years! Water was bucketed up about three hundred feet and stored in large cisterns (perhaps old quarries for building stones) that could hold more than one million gallons on top of the plateau. Thus Masada had an enormous supply of fresh water. The elaborate bathing complexes and water supply reveal much about Herod's obsessive fears concerning safety and his craving for opulence and luxury.

Masada's Storehouses

Fifteen storehouses at Masada contained food, weapons, and other goods needed to provide security and luxury for Herod and his army. Some storerooms were filled with rows upon rows of amphorae (large pottery jars) in which olive oil, flour, wine, and other provisions were stored. Some storerooms were more than sixty feet long and twelve feet wide.

Storehouses of Masada

- The round, middle terrace had two concentric rows of columns that created a beautiful balcony for relaxation.
- The lower terrace, surrounded by low walls and columns with a roof in between, provided an open court inside a colonnade. A bathroom on its eastern side had mosaic floors. The great retaining walls that supported this level remain a testimony to the genius of Herod's engineers.

The western palace served as Herod's main living quarters in Masada. Occupying more than 37,000 square feet, this building included royal apartments, bathrooms, a cold-water pool, and a large reception hall with magnificently decorated mosaic pavement. Nearby were servants' quarters, workshops, a huge kitchen, and three richly decorated palaces— probably for the families of Herod's wives, who did not get along.

Water: Masada's Greatest Luxury

Despite its dry, wilderness location, Masada boasted one of the largest bathing complexes of its time. The largest room of the Roman bathhouse contained a hot bath (caldarium), which was much like a sauna. A warm bath (tepidarium) and cold bath (frigidarium) were adjacent. All of them were elegantly decorated with frescoes and mosaic floors. In addition, there were several swimming pools within the fortress.

To gather the water needed to supply such luxuries in the dry wilderness, Herod and his engineers created a brilliant water system that defied nature. Masada was perched on a mountain between two wadis that occasionally flooded when it rained in the mountains to the west. So Herod diverted some of the floodwater into twelve cisterns cut into the base of the mountain that could hold more than 1,500,000 cubic feet of water—enough water to sustain thousands of people for up to ten years! Water was bucketed up about three hundred feet and stored in large cisterns (perhaps old quarries for building stones) that could hold more than one million gallons on top of the plateau. Thus Masada had an enormous supply of fresh water. The elaborate bathing complexes and water supply reveal much about Herod's obsessive fears concerning safety and his craving for opulence and luxury.

(continued on page 44)

(continued from page 43)

Masada's Storehouses

Fifteen storehouses at Masada contained food, weapons, and other goods needed to provide security and luxury for Herod and his army. Some storerooms were filled with rows upon rows of amphorae (large pottery jars) in which olive oil, flour, wine, and other provisions were stored. Some storerooms were more than sixty feet long and twelve feet wide.

Storehouses of Masada

Topic B: The Quest for Their Own King

1. What did the Jews of Jesus' day eagerly await? Why did they want it so much? (See John 6:14–15.)

2. How did the desire of the Jewish people in general compare to the desire of the Zealots who captured and defended Masada?

Topic B: The Quest for Their Own King

1. What did the Jews of Jesus' day eagerly await? Why did they want it so much? (See John 6:14–15.)

   Suggested Responses: The Jews longed for their promised Messiah, whom they assumed would drive out their Roman rulers and restore their land to them. Believing that Jesus could be the Messiah, they were ready to make Him their political king. The Jews had had more than enough of Rome's brutal political and religious oppression.

2. How did the desire of the Jewish people in general compare to the desire of the Zealots who captured and defended Masada?

   Suggested Responses: Both groups looked to political/military action to achieve freedom from Rome, which they expected their Messiah to provide. Both groups, particularly the Zealots, were willing to take great risks and even give their lives to make that happen.

3. What kind of freedom, peace, and kingdom did Jesus come to offer? (See John 8:31–32; 14:19–27; 16:33; 18:33–37.)

   Suggested Responses: He came to establish a relationship with those who would love and obey Him and promised that He would give them a different kind of peace, a peace that would enable them to take heart in a troubled world. Jesus told Pilate that He was a king, but not an earthly king. He also explained that He came into the world to reveal the truth.

4. What do Matthew 10:2–4 and Acts 1:13 reveal about Simon, one of Jesus' disciples?

   Suggested Response: Simon was widely recognized as a Zealot.

5. Consider the events that took place in Gethsemane when Jesus was arrested. In each of the following passages of Scripture, what evidence do you see of the disciples' expectations for their Messiah? In contrast, what did Jesus have in mind?

The Gospel Account	The Disciples' Perception of God's Kingdom	The Kingdom of God as Jesus Knew It
Matthew 26:50–56	They thought they needed to fight for God's kingdom with the sword, just as if it were an earthly kingdom.	Jesus made it clear that to fight by the sword meant to die by the sword. He revealed that His power was greater than earthly might, should He decide to use it. He was willing to give up Himself in order to fulfill God's plan.
Luke 22:47–52	They thought they needed to fight with their weapons; some of them asked Jesus what to do, while another began to fight.	Jesus said, "No more of this!" then reached out and healed His wounded enemy. He asked His opponents if they really believed He was leading a rebellion.
John 18:10–11	Simon Peter began to fight as if it were a political battle.	Jesus told him to put his sword away. His intent was to obey His Father, even unto death.

(continued from page 43)

Masada's Storehouses

Fifteen storehouses at Masada contained food, weapons, and other goods needed to provide security and luxury for Herod and his army. Some storerooms were filled with rows upon rows of amphorae (large pottery jars) in which olive oil, flour, wine, and other provisions were stored. Some storerooms were more than sixty feet long and twelve feet wide.

Storehouses of Masada

Topic B: The Quest for Their Own King

1. What did the Jews of Jesus' day eagerly await? Why did they want it so much? (See John 6:14–15.)

2. How did the desire of the Jewish people in general compare to the desire of the Zealots who captured and defended Masada?

3. What kind of freedom, peace, and kingdom did Jesus come to offer? (See John 8:31–32; 14:19–27; 16:33; 18:33–37.)

4. What do Matthew 10:2–4 and Acts 1:13 reveal about Simon, one of Jesus' disciples?

5. Consider the events that took place in Gethsemane when Jesus was arrested. In each of the following passages of Scripture, what evidence do you see of the disciples' expectations for their Messiah? In contrast, what did Jesus have in mind?

The Gospel Account	The Disciples' Perception of God's Kingdom	The Kingdom of God as Jesus Knew It
Matthew 26:50–56		
Luke 22:47–52		
John 18:10–11		

✏ 6. What caused Jesus such deep grief as He approached Jerusalem on what we call "Palm Sunday" to the cheers of the people? (See Luke 19:35–44.)

Suggested Responses: Jesus wept tears on behalf of the people and their blindness to the peace He offered. He mourned the coming destruction of Jerusalem (when Rome put down the First Jewish Revolt in A.D. 70). All of this would come because they were so intent on political salvation that they did not recognize Jesus, the Messiah, God's gift of salvation.

✏ 7. After Jesus' resurrection, what did His disciples ask Him? What does their question reveal? (See Acts 1:1–6.)

Suggested Responses: They asked Jesus if He was going to restore the kingdom to Israel. Apparently they still did not fully understand what Jesus came to do and still hoped for political deliverance.

TIMELINE OF EVENTS

198–167 B.C.	Oppression under Hellenistic Seleucids
167 B.C.	Maccabee revolt
167–63 B.C.	Hasmonaean kingdom
37 B.C.	Herod the Great begins his reign
ca. 6 B.C.	Jesus is born
4. B.C.	Herod the Great dies
ca. A.D. 30	Jesus is crucified
A.D. 66–73	First Jewish Revolt
A.D. 70	Jerusalem and the temple are destroyed
A.D. 73	Masada falls

A WORD OF CAUTION

Although many people of Jesus' day believed Him to be the Messiah, some still wanted to make Him into a military-political Messiah who would bring about freedom from Rome. Instead of listening to what and whom Jesus claimed to be, however, some people tried to make Him something else—and missed the peace and salvation He offered.

Today, the same thing is still happening. Many people try to make Jesus into someone other than who He is. (They declare Him to be a good man, for example, but vehemently deny His deity.) The ruins of Masada serve as poignant reminders of the strength and security that God our Fortress provides to His children, and also of what can happen when people misunderstand the gospel of Jesus.

6. What caused Jesus such deep grief as He approached Jerusalem on what we call "Palm Sunday" to the cheers of the people? (See Luke 19:35–44.)

7. After Jesus' resurrection, what did His disciples ask Him? What does their question reveal? (See Acts 1:1–6.)

TIMELINE OF EVENTS

198–167 B.C.	Oppression under Hellenistic Seleucids
167 B.C.	Maccabee revolt
167–63 B.C.	Hasmonaean kingdom
37 B.C.	Herod the Great begins his reign
ca. 6 B.C.	Jesus is born
4. B.C.	Herod the Great dies
ca. A.D. 30	Jesus is crucified
A.D. 66–73	First Jewish Revolt
A.D. 70	Jerusalem and the temple are destroyed
A.D. 73	Masada falls

A WORD OF CAUTION

Although many people of Jesus' day believed Him to be the Messiah, some still wanted to make Him into a military-political Messiah who would bring about freedom from Rome. Instead of listening to what and whom Jesus claimed to be, however, some people tried to make Him something else—and missed the peace and salvation He offered.

Today, the same thing is still happening. Many people try to make Jesus into someone other than who He is. (They declare Him to be a good man, for example, but vehemently deny His deity.) The ruins of Masada serve as poignant reminders of the strength and security that God our Fortress provides to His children, and also of what can happen when people misunderstand the gospel of Jesus.

Topic C: David: Committed to God, Even in the Wilderness

Recalling David's time in the desert wilderness near Masada and En Gedi provides important lessons for us in learning to trust God and depend on Him, particularly during times of trouble. David's faith in God and his willingness to submit to God's will have become a model to believers today.

1. Why did God reject Saul as king and select David? (See 1 Samuel 13:11–14; 15:10–11; 16:6–12.)

PLANNING NOTES:

WORTH OBSERVING

Jesus and the Jewish Revolts

Although Jesus was crucified by the Romans nearly forty years before the First Jewish Revolt, He understood the decision the Jewish people had to make concerning their Messiah. At least one of His disciples, Simon, was a Zealot (Matthew 10:4). His kingdom was not the kingdom of the Zealot or the sword, however (Matthew 26:51–52). Recognizing His people's patriotism, anger against the Romans, and desire for freedom, Jesus didn't trumpet His power. In fact, aware that many false messiahs were proclaiming messages, Jesus frequently commanded the people He taught and/or healed not to tell anyone what He had done for them—possibly because people might misunderstand His role in light of the growing nationalistic climate. (See Matthew 8:1–4; 9:27–30; 12:15–16; Luke 8:51–56; Mark 1:40–44; 3:10–12; 5:38–43; 7:33–36.) Even so, people often saw in Jesus a Davidic king, a military conqueror who would rescue them from the Romans (John 6:14–15; Acts 1:1–6).

Clearly, Jesus predicted the destruction that would result from the revolt (Matthew 24:1–2). His knowledge led Him to weep as He described what would happen (Luke 19:41–44). Some of His fellow Jews were looking for military solutions to their problems rather than spiritual ones, to a political messiah rather than the Lamb of God who came to take away the sins of the world. Jesus warned His followers not to participate in that method of bringing in God's kingdom. Whereas some Jewish people were seeking salvation through political and military might (which led to their future destruction), Jesus lived out and taught completely different truths.

Today, the Jewish people have returned to the land they lost in the First and Second Jewish Revolts, when some Jews sought God in the wrong places and in the wrong ways. Yet, the message of Jesus the Messiah remains unique and relevant, and we must be devoted to it. He alone is God's hope of peace (Luke 2:14).

Topic C: David: Committed to God, Even in the Wilderness

Recalling David's time in the desert wilderness near Masada and En Gedi provides important lessons for us in learning to trust God and depend on Him, particularly during times of trouble. David's faith in God and his willingness to submit to God's will have become a model to believers today.

1. Why did God reject Saul as king and select David? (See 1 Samuel 13:11–14; 15:10–11; 16:6–12.)

   Suggested Responses: God rejected Saul because the king had turned away from Him and disobeyed His commandments. David, on the other hand, had a heart that yearned for God and sought to obey God's commandments.

2. Even before David became a hero, what was his motivation? (See 1 Samuel 17:45–49.)

   Suggested Responses: David sought to represent God before the Philistines and to kill Goliath so that the world would know that there was a God in Israel. He sought to honor God for his victory.

WORTH OBSERVING

Jesus and the Jewish Revolts

Although Jesus was crucified by the Romans nearly forty years before the First Jewish Revolt, He understood the decision the Jewish people had to make concerning their Messiah. At least one of His disciples, Simon, was a Zealot (Matthew 10:4). His kingdom was not the kingdom of the Zealot or the sword, however (Matthew 26:51–52). Recognizing His people's patriotism, anger against the Romans, and desire for freedom, Jesus didn't trumpet His power. In fact, aware that many false messiahs were proclaiming messages, Jesus frequently commanded the people He taught and/or healed not to tell anyone what He had done for them—possibly because people might misunderstand His role in light of the growing nationalistic climate. (See Matthew 8:1–4; 9:27–30; 12:15–16; Luke 8:51–56; Mark 1:40–44; 3:10–12; 5:38–43; 7:33–36.) Even so, people often saw in Jesus a Davidic king, a military conqueror who would rescue them from the Romans (John 6:14–15; Acts 1:1–6).

Clearly, Jesus predicted the destruction that would result from the revolt (Matthew 24:1–2). His knowledge led Him to weep as He described what would happen (Luke 19:41–44). Some of His fellow Jews were looking for military solutions to their problems rather than spiritual ones, to a political messiah rather than the Lamb of God who came to take away the sins of the world. Jesus warned His followers not to participate in that method of bringing in God's kingdom. Whereas some Jewish people were seeking salvation through political and military might (which led to their future destruction), Jesus lived out and taught completely different truths.

Today, the Jewish people have returned to the land they lost in the First and Second Jewish Revolts, when some Jews sought God in the wrong places and in the wrong ways. Yet, the message of Jesus the Messiah remains unique and relevant, and we must be devoted to it. He alone is God's hope of peace (Luke 2:14).

A WORD OF CAUTION

Although many people of Jesus' day believed Him to be the Messiah, some still wanted to make Him into a military-political Messiah who would bring about freedom from Rome. Instead of listening to what and whom Jesus claimed to be, however, some people tried to make Him something else—and missed the peace and salvation He offered.

Today, the same thing is still happening. Many people try to make Jesus into someone other than who He is. (They declare Him to be a good man, for example, but vehemently deny His deity.) The ruins of Masada serve as poignant reminders of the strength and security that God our Fortress provides to His children, and also of what can happen when people misunderstand the gospel of Jesus.

Topic C: David: Committed to God, Even in the Wilderness

Recalling David's time in the desert wilderness near Masada and En Gedi provides important lessons for us in learning to trust God and depend on Him, particularly during times of trouble. David's faith in God and his willingness to submit to God's will have become a model to believers today.

1. Why did God reject Saul as king and select David? (See 1 Samuel 13:11–14; 15:10–11; 16:6–12.)

The Judea Wilderness

3.   Saul hated David and tried to kill him various times (1 Samuel 18:10–11; 19:9–10). Read Psalm 62:4–8, which may have been written during this time. How would you describe David's state of mind while Saul was pursuing him?

Suggested Responses: David seemed to feel betrayed, vulnerable, and troubled. Yet during this difficult time, he trusted God to defend his honor and provide a refuge and strength for him. He could pour his heart out to God and count on Him to meet his needs.

4.   For each of the following passages, describe David's circumstances and the "fortresses," or provision, that God made for him in the wilderness:

Scripture	Circumstance	God's Provision
2 Samuel 22:1–7	Threatened nearly to the point of death	Saved from violent enemies, rescued from the floods of death and destruction
Psalm 18:1–6	Oppressed by enemies nearly to the point of death	Strength, refuge, deliverance, rescued from floods of destruction and snares of death
Psalm 31:1–5, 9–13	Overwhelmed by grief, slander, weakness; entrapped by enemies who desired his life	Deliverance, strength, refuge, guidance, spiritual redemption, mercy
Psalm 71:1–4, 9	Pursued by cruel enemies, weakness	Deliverance, strong protection, faithful refuge
Psalm 91:1–16	Deadly traps, terrors, pestilence, plagues, disasters	Safe, strong dwelling place; faithful protection; freedom from fear; honor; rescue; long life; salvation
Psalm 144:1–4	Conflict, war, death	Training, strength, refuge, deliverance

2. Even before David became a hero, what was his motivation? (See 1 Samuel 17:45–49.)

3. Saul hated David and tried to kill him various times (1 Samuel 18:10–11; 19:9–10). Read Psalm 62:4–8, which may have been written during this time. How would you describe David's state of mind while Saul was pursuing him?

The Judea Wilderness

50   Faith Lessons on the Life and Ministry of the Messiah

4. For each of the following passages, describe David's circumstances and the "fortresses," or provision, that God made for him in the wilderness:

Scripture	Circumstance	God's Provision
2 Samuel 22:1–7		
Psalm 18:1–6		
Psalm 31:1–5, 9–13		
Psalm 71:1–4, 9		
Psalm 91:1–16		
Psalm 144:1–4		

Topic D: The Lord Is Our Rock

Many parts of Israel are quite rocky, especially the wilderness. This geographical condition, combined with the Hebrews' practice of describing spiritual reality by using the concrete images of the world in which they lived, led to the Jews' frequent use of the term "rock" to describe the character of their God. Let's look at some of these images.

Topic D: The Lord Is Our Rock

Many parts of Israel are quite rocky, especially the wilderness. This geographical condition, combined with the Hebrews' practice of describing spiritual reality by using the concrete images of the world in which they lived, led to the Jews' frequent use of the term "rock" to describe the character of their God. Let's look at some of these images.

1. When David was in the wilderness, to what did he attribute his safety? (See 2 Samuel 22:1–3.)

   Suggested Responses: David declared God to be his rock, fortress, refuge, and deliverer.

2. How do we know that David clearly connected the image of a rock with Israel's God? (See 2 Samuel 22:47; 23:3.)

   Suggested Responses: David used the terms synonymously; he identified God as his rock and savior; used two phrases, "God of Israel" and "Rock of Israel," to identify God's words.

3. Read each of the following passages and note what the image of God as a "rock" conveyed.

Psalm 18:31–35	God arms him with strength; makes his way perfect; gives him quick, safe footing on the mountain heights; trains him for battle; sustains him in battle; gives him victory and makes him great.
Psalm 62:1–2	God provides rest for the soul, salvation, and is a fortress; therefore, David cannot be shaken.
Psalm 62:5–8	God and God alone provides rest and hope; God is David's salvation and fortress; therefore, David cannot be shaken; David's honor comes from God; God is his rock and refuge; therefore, the people can pour out their hearts and trust in Him.

4. Which images did Moses use to describe God in Deuteronomy 32:4, 15, 18?

   Suggested Response: "the Rock," "the Rock his Savior," "the Rock, who fathered you."

5. How did God describe Himself to the people of Israel through the words of the prophet Isaiah? (See Isaiah 44:8.)

   Suggested Response: that there is no God, no other "Rock" besides Yahweh.

6. Who does Paul describe as a rock in 1 Corinthians 10:1–4? What does he say that rock did?

   Suggested Response: Paul described the Hebrews as drinking from the spiritual rock that accompanied them on their journey from Egypt to the Promised Land, and he boldly declared that rock to be Christ.

1. When David was in the wilderness, to what did he attribute his safety? (See 2 Samuel 22:1–3.)

2. How do we know that David clearly connected the image of a rock with Israel's God? (See 2 Samuel 22:47; 23:3.)

3. Read each of the following passages and note what the image of God as a "rock" conveyed.

Psalm 18:31–35	
Psalm 62:1–2	
Psalm 62:5–8	

4. Which images did Moses use to describe God in Deuteronomy 32:4, 15, 18?

5. How did God describe Himself to the people of Israel through the words of the prophet Isaiah? (See Isaiah 44:8.)

6. Who does Paul describe as a rock in 1 Corinthians 10:1–4? What does he say that rock did?

DID YOU KNOW?

David wrote these words: "I love you, O LORD, my strength. The LORD is my rock, my fortress and my deliverer" (Psalm 18:1–2). The word transliterated "fortress" here is really a rendering of a Hebrew word that can be translated *masada* in English. The psalmist recognized the solid, unmovable, unshakable characteristics of the Lord. He confidently placed his trust in the Lord, who is truly our fortress, too.

Water from Rock

Water from Rock

DID YOU KNOW?

David wrote these words: "I love you, O LORD, my strength. The LORD is my rock, my fortress and my deliverer" (Psalm 18:1–2). The word transliterated "fortress" here is really a rendering of a Hebrew word that can be translated masada in English. The psalmist recognized the solid, unmovable, unshakable characteristics of the Lord. He confidently placed his trust in the Lord, who is truly our fortress, too.

After nine minutes, let participants know that they have one minute remaining. Then reassemble the entire group. After everyone is back together, begin asking one person from each small group to briefly share a key idea with the larger group. In some cases, you may not have time for every group to share their discoveries.

As time allows, let's briefly share the key ideas that your group discussed.

faith Lesson

7 minutes

Time for Reflection (4 minutes)

It's time for each of us to think quietly about how we can apply what we've learned today. On page 53 of the Participant's Guide, you'll find a passage of Scripture. Let's each read this passage silently and take the next few minutes to consider God as our *masada*, our fortress.

Please do not talk during this time. It's a time when we can reflect on today's lesson and how it applies to our lives.

The Scripture passage and questions are reproduced in their entirety in the Participant's Guide on pages 53-54.

I love you, O LORD, my strength. The LORD is my rock, my fortress and my deliverer; my God is my rock, in whom I take refuge. He is my shield and the horn of my salvation, my stronghold. I call to the LORD, who is worthy of praise, and I am saved from my enemies. . . .

5. How did God describe Himself to the people of Israel through the words of the prophet Isaiah? (See Isaiah 44:8.)

6. Who does Paul describe as a rock in 1 Corinthians 10:1–4? What does he say that rock did?

DID YOU KNOW?

Water from Rock

David wrote these words: "I love you, O LORD, my strength. The LORD is my rock, my fortress and my deliverer" (Psalm 18:1–2). The word transliterated "fortress" here is really a rendering of a Hebrew word that can be translated *masada* in English. The psalmist recognized the solid, unmovable, unshakable characteristics of the Lord. He confidently placed his trust in the Lord, who is truly our fortress, too.

ꜰaith Lesson

Time for Reflection

Read the following passage of Scripture and take the next few minutes to consider God as your *masada*, your fortress.

> I love you, O LORD, my strength. The LORD is my rock, my fortress and my deliverer; my God is my rock, in whom I take refuge. He is my shield and the horn of my salvation, my stronghold. I call to the LORD, who is worthy of praise, and I am saved from my enemies....
>
> He reached down from on high and took hold of me; he drew me out of deep waters. He rescued me from my powerful enemy, from my foes, who were too strong for me. They confronted me in the day of my disaster, but the LORD was my support. He brought me out into a spacious place; he rescued me because he delighted in me....
>
> To the faithful you show yourself faithful, to the blameless you show yourself blameless, to the pure you show yourself pure, but to the crooked you show yourself shrewd. You save the humble but bring low those whose eyes are haughty. You, O LORD, keep my lamp burning; my God turns my darkness into light. With your help I can advance against a troop; with my God I can scale a wall. As for God, his way is perfect; the word of the LORD is flawless. He is a shield for all who take refuge in him. For who is God besides the LORD? And who is the Rock except our God? It is God who arms me with strength and makes my way perfect. He makes my feet like the feet of a deer; he enables me to stand on the heights. He trains my hands for battle; my arms can bend a bow of bronze. You give me your shield of victory, and your right hand sustains me; you stoop down to make me great. You broaden the path beneath me, so that my ankles do not turn.
>
> PSALM 18:1–3, 16–19, 25–36

He reached down from on high and took hold of me; he drew me out of deep waters. He rescued me from my powerful enemy, from my foes, who were too strong for me. They confronted me in the day of my disaster, but the LORD was my support. He brought me out into a spacious place; he rescued me because he delighted in me. . . .

To the faithful you show yourself faithful, to the blameless you show yourself blameless, to the pure you show yourself pure, but to the crooked you show yourself shrewd. You save the humble but bring low those whose eyes are haughty. You, O LORD, keep my lamp burning; my God turns my darkness into light. With your help I can advance against a troop; with my God I can scale a wall. As for God, his way is perfect; the word of the LORD is flawless. He is a shield for all who take refuge in him. For who is God besides the LORD? And who is the Rock except our God? It is God who arms me with strength and makes my way perfect. He makes my feet like the feet of a deer; he enables me to stand on the heights. He trains my hands for battle; my arms can bend a bow of bronze. You give me your shield of victory, and your right hand sustains me; you stoop down to make me great. You broaden the path beneath me, so that my ankles do not turn.

PSALM 18:1–3, 16–19, 25–36

1. David trusted God to be his "fortress." King Herod, on the other hand, trusted in Masada—the fortress-palace he built—and his own abilities. In what ways are you trusting God as David did? In what ways are you, like King Herod, trusting in the work of your own hands?

2. When Masada was captured, the Zealots who desired a political messiah died. How does their tragic ending relate to what often happens today when people place trust in their "masadas" instead of the living Messiah?

3. Think about a specific time when God was a "rock" in your life—or in the life of someone you know. What did you discover about God during that time?

4. In what practical ways do you depend on God to be your "rock" and fortress? Take a few minutes to describe what it means for God to be your "rock."

Action Points (3 minutes)

The following points are reproduced on pages 55–56 of the Participant's Guide.

Now it's time to wrap up our session.

Give participants a moment to transition from their thoughtfulness to giving you their full attention.

I'd like to take a moment to summarize the key points we explored. After I have reviewed these points, I will give you a moment to jot down an action step

faith Lesson

Time for Reflection

Read the following passage of Scripture and take the next few minutes to consider God as your *masada*, your fortress.

I love you, O LORD, my strength. The LORD is my rock, my fortress and my deliverer; my God is my rock, in whom I take refuge. He is my shield and the horn of my salvation, my stronghold. I call to the LORD, who is worthy of praise, and I am saved from my enemies....

He reached down from on high and took hold of me; he drew me out of deep waters. He rescued me from my powerful enemy, from my foes, who were too strong for me. They confronted me in the day of my disaster, but the LORD was my support. He brought me out into a spacious place; he rescued me because he delighted in me....

To the faithful you show yourself faithful, to the blameless you show yourself blameless, to the pure you show yourself pure, but to the crooked you show yourself shrewd. You save the humble but bring low those whose eyes are haughty. You, O LORD, keep my lamp burning; my God turns my darkness into light. With your help I can advance against a troop; with my God I can scale a wall. As for God, his way is perfect; the word of the LORD is flawless. He is a shield for all who take refuge in him. For who is God besides the LORD? And who is the Rock except our God? It is God who arms me with strength and makes my way perfect. He makes my feet like the feet of a deer; he enables me to stand on the heights. He trains my hands for battle; my arms can bend a bow of bronze. You give me your shield of victory, and your right hand sustains me; you stoop down to make me great. You broaden the path beneath me, so that my ankles do not turn.

PSALM 18:1–3, 16–19, 25–36

1. David trusted God to be his "fortress." King Herod, on the other hand, trusted in Masada—the fortress-palace he built—and his own abilities. In what ways are you trusting God as David did? In what ways are you, like King Herod, trusting in the work of your own hands?

2. When Masada was captured, the Zealots who desired a political messiah died. How does their tragic ending relate to what often happens today when people place trust in their "masadas" instead of the living Messiah?

3. Think about a specific time when God was a "rock" in your life—or in the life of someone you know. What did you discover about God during that time?

4. In what practical ways do you depend on God to be your "rock" and fortress? Take a few minutes to describe what it means for God to be your "rock."

PLANNING NOTES:

(or steps) that you will commit to this week as a result of what you have learned today.

> Read the following points and pause afterward so that participants can consider and write out their commitment.

🖉 1.   *God is our fortress. We are to trust in Him, not in our own efforts, for protection and strength.* In Psalm 18:1–3, David used the Hebrew word that is transliterated in English as *masada* to describe God as his rock and fortress—the strong, unshakable source of his protection and strength.

In what way(s) do you live as though God is your fortress—your protection and security? In what way(s) do you tend to trust in your own efforts when facing difficult challenges?

🖉 2.   *If we are to know God as our rock and fortress, we must open our eyes and hearts to the protection, strength, and freedom that Jesus offers.* Some Jewish people sought a military messiah who would deliver them from Roman oppression. Thus they misunderstood the gospel of the Messiah who came to sacrifice Himself on their behalf, and they lost their lives without finding real peace.

In what ways do you find it easy or difficult to believe the Messiah as He truly is? In what ways do you try to conform Him to your own view of what you would like Him to be?

Are you willing to live according to the purposes and standards of God's kingdom, or would you rather pursue a different type of kingdom? Why?

🖉 3.   *Our commitment to God needs to be more than just words.* The Zealots who fled to Masada believed it was wrong to owe allegiance to anyone or anything other than God, and they were willing to die for what they believed.

To what extent are you willing to owe and live out your allegiance to God alone?

How strong a commitment are you willing to make to religious freedom, for example, in order to safeguard it in a culture that may not recognize God and His eternal, spiritual truth?

closing prayer

I minute

Dear God, this session on Masada reminds us of the fact that Jesus came to earth as the Messiah from Your kingdom, not as someone who would overthrow Rome. Today, we are also reminded that You want to be our Rock, our Fortress, our Messiah who offers us true freedom. Please draw us closer to You. Remind us of what You have done for us in the past—and what You are doing today. Give us the strength to stand firmly for You, remembering that You are our shelter during life's storms. Thank You for being our Fortress in whom we can trust. In Jesus' name we pray, amen.

Action Points

Take a few minutes to review the key points you explored today, then write down an action step (or steps) that you will commit to this week as a result of what you have learned.

1. *God is our fortress. We are to trust in Him, not in our own efforts, for protection and strength.* In Psalm 18:1–3, David used the Hebrew word that is transliterated in English as *masada* to describe God as his rock and fortress—the strong, unshakable source of his protection and strength.

   In what way(s) do you live as though God is your fortress—your protection and security? In what way(s) do you tend to trust in your own efforts when facing difficult challenges?

2. *If we are to know God as our rock and fortress, we must open our eyes and hearts to the protection, strength, and freedom that Jesus offers.* Some Jewish people sought a military messiah who would deliver them from Roman oppression. Thus they misunderstood the gospel of the Messiah who came to sacrifice Himself on their behalf, and they lost their lives without finding real peace.

   In what ways do you find it easy or difficult to believe the Messiah as He truly is? In what ways do you try to conform Him to your own view of what you would like Him to be?

   Are you willing to live according to the purposes and standards of God's kingdom, or would you rather pursue a different type of kingdom? Why?

3. *Our commitment to God needs to be more than just words.* The Zealots who fled to Masada believed it was wrong to owe allegiance to anyone or anything other than God, and they were willing to die for what they believed.

   To what extent are you willing to owe and live out your allegiance to God alone?

   How strong a commitment are you willing to make to religious freedom, for example, in order to safeguard it in a culture that may not recognize God and His eternal, spiritual truth?

DATA FILE

The Jewish Revolts

The Seeds of Revolt

After the Romans began their occupation of Judea in 64 B.C., the Jews became divided on how to respond:

Religious leaders, particularly the Pharisees	Most believed the Messiah would come from the Jewish people (God's instruments) and make Israel a great, free nation; condemned Rome's excesses; viewed Romans as oppressors punishing God's people for their unfaithfulness to the Torah
Sadducees and secular leaders	Many decided to cooperate with the Romans, who gave them various privileges (John 11:49–50)
Zealots	Proclaimed revolution to be God's solution to Roman oppression (Acts 5:37)
Essenes	Waited for the Messiah to lead a violent overthrow of the Romans and their Jewish supporters
Herodians	Were satisfied with Herod's dynasty (Matthew 22:16)

The Sparks of a Firestorm

- Jewish factions longed for various freedoms.
- Many so-called messiahs preached their own brands of salvation (Acts 21:38).
- During Feast days, especially Passover, nationalistic tensions escalated, so Rome increased its military presence.
- After Herod Agrippa I, grandson of Herod the Great, died in A.D. 44 (Acts 12:19–23), the Romans appointed a series of increasingly cruel, corrupt governors to rule the Jews, adding to the confusion, hatred, and division.
- The paganism of Rome's culture offended the Jews.
- Assassins began killing Romans—and the Jews who cooperated with them. (Paul was arrested and accused of being a rebel. See Acts 21:27–38.)
- Jewish priests, who became more dependent on Roman security and support, became more corrupt. Jonathan the high priest was assassinated.
- Common people were attracted to the Zealots' radical approach.
- Felix (Acts 24) was replaced by Festus (Acts 25) as governor. Both were brutal but ineffective in quelling the rising revolt. Ananias, the high priest, used this opportunity to murder his opponents, including James (Jesus' brother) and many other Christians.
- Two priests who succeeded Ananias (each of whom was named Jesus) and their followers fought one another in the streets.
- Florus, a new governor, tried to stop the violence by flogging and crucifying hundreds of people.

(continued on page 88)

DATA FILE

The Jewish Revolts

The Seeds of Revolt

After the Romans began their occupation of Judea in 64 B.C., the Jews became divided on how to respond:

Religious leaders, particularly the Pharisees	Most believed the Messiah would come from the Jewish people (God's instruments) and make Israel a great, free nation; condemned Rome's excesses; viewed Romans as oppressors punishing God's people for their unfaithfulness to the Torah
Sadducees and secular leaders	Many decided to cooperate with the Romans, who gave them various privileges (John 11:49–50)
Zealots	Proclaimed revolution to be God's solution to Roman oppression (Acts 5:37)
Essenes	Waited for the Messiah to lead a violent overthrow of the Romans and their Jewish supporters
Herodians	Were satisfied with Herod's dynasty (Matthew 22:16)

The Sparks of a Firestorm

- Jewish factions longed for various freedoms.
- Many so-called messiahs preached their own brands of salvation (Acts 21:38).
- During Feast days, especially Passover, nationalistic tensions escalated, so Rome increased its military presence.
- After Herod Agrippa I, grandson of Herod the Great, died in A.D. 44 (Acts 12:19–23), the Romans appointed a series of increasingly

(continued on page 58)

(continued from page 57)

cruel, corrupt governors to rule the Jews, adding to the confusion, hatred, and division.
- The paganism of Rome's culture offended the Jews.
- Assassins began killing Romans—and the Jews who cooperated with them. (Paul was arrested and accused of being a rebel. See Acts 21:27–38.)
- Jewish priests, who became more dependent on Roman security and support, became more corrupt. Jonathan the high priest was assassinated.
- Common people were attracted to the Zealots' radical approach.
- Felix (Acts 24) was replaced by Festus (Acts 25) as governor. Both were brutal but ineffective in quelling the rising revolt. Ananias, the high priest, used this opportunity to murder his opponents, including James (Jesus' brother) and many other Christians.
- Two priests who succeeded Ananias (each of whom was named Jesus) and their followers fought one another in the streets.
- Florus, a new governor, tried to stop the violence by flogging and crucifying hundreds of people.

The Revolt Begins

In A.D. 66, while Christians and Jews were being thrown to wild animals in Rome, a Gentile in Caesarea offered a "pagan" sacrifice next to the synagogue's entrance on the Sabbath. Jewish citizens protested, so Jerusalem authorities ended all foreign sacrifices in the temple—including those to Caesar.

Governor Florus, who lived in Caesarea, then raided the temple treasury in Jerusalem. When protesters gathered, Florus unleashed his troops on innocent civilians. More than 3,500 people were killed, including women and children. Hundreds of women were raped, whipped, and crucified.

In response, Jewish mobs drove the outnumbered Roman soldiers out of Jerusalem, stormed the Antonia (the Roman fort), and burned records of debts kept there. Zealots surprised the Roman garrison at Masada, occupied it, and then distributed its weapons to the Jews. One Zealot leader in Jerusalem was assassinated by another, who then ordered the slaughter of all Roman prisoners left in Jerusalem.

PLANNING NOTES:

(continued from page 86)

The Revolt Begins

In A.D. 66, while Christians and Jews were being thrown to wild animals in Rome, a Gentile in Caesarea offered a "pagan" sacrifice next to the synagogue's entrance on the Sabbath. Jewish citizens protested, so Jerusalem authorities ended all foreign sacrifices in the temple—including those to Caesar.

Governor Florus, who lived in Caesarea, then raided the temple treasury in Jerusalem. When protesters gathered, Florus unleashed his troops on innocent civilians. More than 3,500 people were killed, including women and children. Hundreds of women were raped, whipped, and crucified.

In response, Jewish mobs drove the outnumbered Roman soldiers out of Jerusalem, stormed the Antonia (the Roman fort), and burned records of debts kept there. Zealots surprised the Roman garrison at Masada, occupied it, and then distributed its weapons to the Jews. One Zealot leader in Jerusalem was assassinated by another, who then ordered the slaughter of all Roman prisoners left in Jerusalem.

The Violence Escalates

When Gentiles in Caesarea learned about the violence against fellow Romans in Jerusalem, they killed about twenty thousand Jews within a day's time. Fifty thousand Jews were killed in Alexandria, and the slaughter of more Jewish people escalated throughout the empire.

Gallus, the governor of Syria, advanced on Jerusalem with the Twelfth Legion, but the Zealots destroyed his troops in the mountain pass of Beth Horon. For a brief time, the Jews kept their national freedom and all the captured weapons from the imperial legion.

Nero ordered his leading general, Vespasian, to end the Jewish problem. Vespasian began his campaign in A.D. 67 in Galilee, using his army of more than fifty thousand troops. Sepphoris, Jotapata, Gamla (where the Zealot movement began), and other towns fell. Many Jewish men were executed, often by crucifixion; Jewish women and children were sold into slavery or saved for the games in the arena.

Flushed with his success in Galilee, Vespasian then conquered the coast, including Joppa and the lands east of Judea. He captured Jericho (east of Jerusalem) and Emmaus (west of Jerusalem). After Nero's suicide in A.D. 68, Vespasian became the Roman emperor and left his son, Titus, to complete the campaign against Jerusalem.

Meanwhile, factions of Zealots, blaming each other for their defeats, fought each other in Jerusalem. Another self-proclaimed messiah fought the Zealots. Confusion and terror reigned. Apparently most Christians had already fled to the mountains, acting on Jesus' words (Matthew 24:15–16). The long separation of Jews and Christians had begun.

In A.D. 70, Titus arrived at Jerusalem with at least eighty thousand troops. He captured half the city, slaughtered its inhabitants, and built a siege wall around the remaining portion of the city. Trapped inside, Jewish factions continued to battle one another. People killed one another over scraps of food. Anyone suspected of contemplating surrender was killed. Dead people filled the streets, and Jews who did surrender were crucified just outside the walls. Josephus, the Jewish writer, reported that six hundred thousand bodies were thrown out of the city as a result of the famine. (continued on page 90)

(continued from page 57)

cruel, corrupt governors to rule the Jews, adding to the confusion, hatred, and division.

- The paganism of Rome's culture offended the Jews.
- Assassins began killing Romans—and the Jews who cooperated with them. (Paul was arrested and accused of being a rebel. See Acts 21:27–38.)
- Jewish priests, who became more dependent on Roman security and support, became more corrupt. Jonathan the high priest was assassinated.
- Common people were attracted to the Zealots' radical approach.
- Felix (Acts 24) was replaced by Festus (Acts 25) as governor. Both were brutal but ineffective in quelling the rising revolt. Ananias, the high priest, used this opportunity to murder his opponents, including James (Jesus' brother) and many other Christians.
- Two priests who succeeded Ananias (each of whom was named Jesus) and their followers fought one another in the streets.
- Florus, a new governor, tried to stop the violence by flogging and crucifying hundreds of people.

The Revolt Begins

In A.D. 66, while Christians and Jews were being thrown to wild animals in Rome, a Gentile in Caesarea offered a "pagan" sacrifice next to the synagogue's entrance on the Sabbath. Jewish citizens protested, so Jerusalem authorities ended all foreign sacrifices in the temple—including those to Caesar.

Governor Florus, who lived in Caesarea, then raided the temple treasury in Jerusalem. When protesters gathered, Florus unleashed his troops on innocent civilians. More than 3,500 people were killed, including women and children. Hundreds of women were raped, whipped, and crucified.

In response, Jewish mobs drove the outnumbered Roman soldiers out of Jerusalem, stormed the Antonia (the Roman fort), and burned records of debts kept there. Zealots surprised the Roman garrison at Masada, occupied it, and then distributed its weapons to the Jews. One Zealot leader in Jerusalem was assassinated by another, who then ordered the slaughter of all Roman prisoners left in Jerusalem.

The Violence Escalates

When Gentiles in Caesarea learned about the violence against fellow Romans in Jerusalem, they killed about twenty thousand Jews within a day's time. Fifty thousand Jews were killed in Alexandria, and the slaughter of more Jewish people escalated throughout the empire.

Gallus, the governor of Syria, advanced on Jerusalem with the Twelfth Legion, but the Zealots destroyed his troops in the mountain pass of Beth Horon. For a brief time, the Jews kept their national freedom and all the captured weapons from the imperial legion.

Nero ordered his leading general, Vespasian, to end the Jewish problem. Vespasian began his campaign in A.D. 67 in Galilee, using his army of more than fifty thousand troops. Sepphoris, Jotapata, Gamla (where the Zealot movement began), and other towns fell. Many Jewish men were executed, often by crucifixion; Jewish women and children were sold into slavery or saved for the games in the arena.

Flushed with his success in Galilee, Vespasian then conquered the coast, including Joppa and the lands east of Judea. He captured Jericho (east of Jerusalem) and Emmaus (west of Jerusalem). After Nero's suicide in A.D. 68, Vespasian became the Roman emperor and left his son, Titus, to complete the campaign against Jerusalem.

Meanwhile, factions of Zealots, blaming each other for their defeats, fought each other in Jerusalem. Another self-proclaimed messiah fought the Zealots. Confusion and terror reigned. Apparently most Christians had already fled to the mountains, acting on Jesus' words (Matthew 24:15–16). The long separation of Jews and Christians had begun.

In A.D. 70, Titus arrived at Jerusalem with at least eighty thousand troops. He captured half the city, slaughtered its inhabitants, and built a siege wall around the remaining portion of the city. Trapped inside, Jewish factions continued to battle one another. People killed one another over scraps of food. Anyone suspected of contemplating surrender was killed. Dead people filled the streets, and Jews who did surrender were crucified just outside the walls. Josephus, the Jewish writer, reported that six hundred thousand bodies were thrown out of the city as a result of the famine.

(continued on page 60)

(continued from page 88)

The Revolt Is Crushed

Mid July: Roman troops recaptured the Antonia fortress.

August 6: Sacrifices ceased in the temple.

End of August (the ninth of Ab): Roman troops burned and destroyed the temple—on the same day of the year that the Babylonians destroyed it more than six hundred years earlier.

August 30: The lower city fell.

September: The upper city fell.

Titus ordered all buildings in Jerusalem to be leveled, except for three towers in Herod's palace. All the citizens of Jerusalem were executed, sold into slavery, or saved for games in the arena. Alleys were choked with corpses. Babies were thrown off walls. People were burned alive. Eleven thousand prisoners died of starvation while awaiting their execution. Josephus records that more than one million Jews died, and nearly one hundred thousand were sold into slavery.

The Fortress Masada

A Final Stand

A few Zealots fled to Herod's fortress of Masada, hoping to outlast the Romans. In A.D. 72, the Roman Tenth Legion laid siege to Masada and, using Jewish slaves, built a wall six feet high and more than two miles long around the base of Masada's mountain plateau.

For seven months, the Romans built a siege ramp against the western side of the mountain and then used a battering ram to smash a hole in the fortress wall. The Zealots fortified the wall with timbers, which the Romans burned. So the Zealots in Masada committed mass suicide. Only two old women and five children survived to share the Zealots' story with the world.

A Tragic Postscript: The Second Jewish Revolt

Eventually the Romans built a temple to Jupiter on the Temple Mount, and Emperor Hadrian (A.D. 117–138) wanted to build a Roman city on Jerusalem's ruins. The few Jews who remained in Jerusalem declared Simon Bar Kochba, a descendant of David, as their Messiah. He began a new resistance, and in A.D. 131 the Jews again revolted.

Although Bar Kochba's revolt was initially successful, the Romans struck back swiftly with overwhelming force. Hadrian himself responded with the Roman commander Julius Severus. The Romans destroyed nearly a thousand villages, killing or enslaving any Jews who had not fled. By A.D. 135, the Second Jewish Revolt had come to an end. Jerusalem became Hadrian's Roman city, the Jewish religion was outlawed, and the Jews became a people without a land.

The revolt drove Christianity to the ends of the earth, and it became a largely Gentile faith. Only today are its Jewish roots being recognized. The descendants of the Pharisees established Rabbinic Judaism, the orthodox faith of Jewish people today. The Zealots, Sadducees, and Essenes are no more.

(continued from page 59)

The Revolt Is Crushed

Mid July: Roman troops recaptured the Antonia fortress.

August 6: Sacrifices ceased in the temple.

End of August (the ninth of Ab): Roman troops burned and destroyed the temple—on the same day of the year that the Babylonians destroyed it more than six hundred years earlier.

August 30: The lower city fell.

September: The upper city fell.

Titus ordered all buildings in Jerusalem to be leveled, except for three towers in Herod's palace. All the citizens of Jerusalem were executed, sold into slavery, or saved for games in the arena. Alleys were choked with corpses. Babies were thrown off walls. People were burned alive. Eleven thousand prisoners died of starvation while awaiting their execution. Josephus records that more than one million Jews died, and nearly one hundred thousand were sold into slavery.

A Final Stand

A few Zealots fled to Herod's fortress of Masada, hoping to outlast the Romans. In A.D. 72, the Roman Tenth Legion laid siege to Masada and, using Jewish slaves, built a wall six feet high and more than two miles long around the base of Masada's mountain plateau.

For seven months, the Romans built a siege ramp against the western side of the mountain and then used a battering ram to smash a hole in the fortress wall. The Zealots fortified the wall with timbers, which the Romans burned. So the Zealots in Masada committed mass suicide. Only two old women and five children survived to share the Zealots' story with the world.

A Tragic Postscript: The Second Jewish Revolt

Eventually the Romans built a temple to Jupiter on the Temple Mount, and Emperor Hadrian (A.D. 117–138) wanted to build a Roman city on Jerusalem's ruins. The few Jews who remained in Jerusalem declared Simon Bar Kochba, a descendant of David, as their messiah. He began a new resistance, and in A.D. 131 the Jews again revolted.

The Fortress Masada

Although Bar Kochba's revolt was initially successful, the Romans struck back swiftly with overwhelming force. Hadrian himself responded with the Roman commander Julius Severus. The Romans destroyed nearly a thousand villages, killing or enslaving any Jews who had not fled. By A.D. 135, the Second Jewish Revolt had come to an end. Jerusalem became Hadrian's Roman city, the Jewish religion was outlawed, and the Jews became a people without a land.

The revolt drove Christianity to the ends of the earth, and it became a largely Gentile faith. Only today are its Jewish roots being recognized. The descendants of the Pharisees established Rabbinic Judaism, the orthodox faith of Jewish people today. The Zealots, Sadducees, and Essenes are no more.

The Time Had Fully Come

Before You Lead

Synopsis

You may not know about the Essenes, a Jewish sect that existed at the time of Jesus, but you probably know about what they hid in caves surrounding their isolated community of Qumran—the Dead Sea Scrolls. These ancient scrolls, first discovered by Bedouins in 1947, have to some extent revolutionized our understanding of the Bible. They have affirmed God's protection of His inspired Word, showing that Old Testament books have changed little through the centuries. The scrolls have also provided insight into the theological beliefs and expectations of the people who lived at the time of Jesus.

Furthermore, the Essenes help us to understand God's work of redemption. Their story helps us to see the ways in which God prepared a movement of people (from Noah to Abraham to Moses to David) who anticipated Jesus' coming, prepared the way for His teachings, and were prepared to follow Him. Archaeological studies of the Essenes' community and their writings shed light on these words of Paul: "But when the time had fully come, God sent his Son . . . to redeem . . ." (Galatians 4:4–5). As you view this video, it will become apparent that God sent the Messiah into a carefully prepared, earthly setting that was significant to His ministry—the first-century Jewish culture—and that God's plan for redemption had been unfolding for many years before Jesus was born.

In 167 B.C., the Jewish Hasmonaeans (also called the Maccabees) overthrew their Greek rulers. For the first time in nearly five hundred years, the Jews were independent. But over time, the Hasmonaeans became as Hellenistic as the Greeks before them. When the Hasmonaeans appointed an openly Hellenistic high priest, two separate groups of devout Jews—the Pharisees and the Essenes—formed in opposition to their authority in the temple.

The Essenes were basically devout Jewish separatists who left the city and temple for periods of time in order to establish alternative—and in their minds, more holy—ways of worshiping and honoring Yahweh. Although some Essenes lived in communities found in Galilee, Judea, and even Jerusalem, the majority studied in the community by the Dead Sea that we know as Qumran.

For about two hundred years, the Essenes carried on an almost ascetic way of life. Believing they had been called to isolate themselves from spiritual darkness (Hellenistic society) and live in right relationship with God, they sought to create a new system of purity. When the Messiah arrived—an event they believed was imminent—the Essenes wanted Him to find people who were prepared to reestablish the true priesthood and true kingship of David and to battle the forces of spiritual darkness.

Despite their physical isolation, the Essenes exerted some influence on the theological climate of their day. Essene scribes wrote extensively on copper, leather, and parchment about their order, the Essene lifestyle, the coming Messiah, and the exciting new age that would soon arrive. They also wrote out all but one of the books contained in the Old Testament.

As Ray Vander Laan brings out, the Essenes developed theological concepts and practices that are quite similar to those of the early Christians. For example, they:

- Practiced a form of ritual cleansing by water that is similar to baptism.
- Used many words and phrases that later appeared in New Testament writings.
- Used a method of Scripture interpretation similar to one the early Christians used.
- Established a communal lifestyle similar to that of the early Christians.
- Believed in justification by faith.
- Called themselves the "New Israel."
- Thought of themselves as preparing the "way of the Lord" by obeying His truths.
- Believed that they were living at the end of an age and that two messiahs—a priest messiah, the Son of the most high God, and a king messiah, who would arrive with power and authority and drive out the sons of darkness—would soon appear.
- Viewed themselves as sons of spiritual light who would not compromise with evil and who would battle the sons of spiritual darkness.

When an earthquake in 31 B.C. destroyed the buildings of Qumran, the community was abandoned until about 4 B.C. when Herod the Great died and his son, Archelaus, became ruler. In A.D. 68, Roman troops destroyed Qumran.

Today, no Essenes remain, but they truly helped to "prepare God's way" as He unfolded His plan of redemption. Their influence helped to prepare the Jews to receive Jesus' message. They helped to shape the theological context so that Jesus' teaching could be understood both by its similarity to existing beliefs and by its uniqueness. Clearly, God had prepared a fertile seedbed in which to cultivate the new faith He would plant on earth. The Essenes stand as yet another reminder that our Christian faith is rooted in a long line of Jewish people and their heritage.

Key Points of This Lesson

1. *God's work in history is rarely sudden and dramatic. Rather, God works through the process of history, through the lives of people, to unfold His plan of redemption.* Just as He used the Romans and the Essenes to prepare a culture and a setting in which the life, death, and resurrection of Jesus could be understood and received, He continues to use people to bring about His redemptive plans. So as we seek to understand the culture of

first-century Israel where Jesus lived, we will gain a better understanding of His message.

2. *The Essenes, who recognized that spiritual light and spiritual darkness cannot coexist, committed themselves to godly values and beliefs and refused to compromise with their culture.* Today, we Christians face the same challenge: to seek to remove the spiritual darkness in our hearts, minds, and lives and to live as children of the light.

3. *Whereas the Essenes separated from their culture in order to study how to follow God, God has called Christians to carry His truths into the secular world.* Without compromising our holy calling, we are to interact with people who live in spiritual darkness and to confront evil in the world around us. We are to exhibit God's light to a watching, hurting world.

Session Outline (52 minutes)

I. Introduction (5 minutes)
Welcome

What's to Come

Questions to Think About

II. Show Video "The Time Had Fully Come" (18 minutes)

III. Group Discovery (20 minutes)
Video Highlights

Small Group Bible Discovery

IV. Faith Lesson (8 minutes)
Time for Reflection

Action Points

V. Closing Prayer (1 minute)

Materials
No additional materials are needed for this session. Simply view the video prior to leading the session so you are familiar with its main points.

The Time Had Fully Come

Introduction

5 minutes

Welcome

Assemble the participants together. Welcome them to session three of *Faith Lessons on the Life and Ministry of the Messiah*.

What's to Come

Many years before the birth of Jesus, the Essenes, a group of devout Jews, separated themselves from the predominantly Hellenistic culture of the Jewish leaders. The Essenes established a wilderness study center near the Dead Sea and were the creators of the famous Dead Sea Scrolls—one of the most important archaeological finds of modern times. They also developed some theological concepts that are remarkably similar to Christian beliefs.

Using the Essenes as examples, Ray Vander Laan reminds us of the careful preparations God made for the earthly life and ministry of His Son. He reveals how God gradually unfolds His plan of redemption through His people—and is still unfolding His plan through you and me. He encourages us to deepen our commitment to godly values and to carry His message to the world around us.

Questions to Think About

Participant's Guide page 62.

Ask each question and solicit a few responses from group members.

1. When you are given a great deal of information that is completely new to you, such as when you are taking a class on an unfamiliar subject, what is the result? Do you usually understand it all right away?

   Suggested Responses: will vary but may include confusion, bewilderment, wishing you hadn't taken the class, may only understand parts of it, etc. Most people will not understand all the information right away.

2. What is required for you to learn new information and be able to use it in practical ways?

   Suggested Responses: will vary but may include repeated exposure to the information, someone explaining it to you, linking the new information to what you already know, etc.

SESSION THREE

the time had fully come

questions to think about

1. When you are given a great deal of information that is completely new to you, such as when you are taking a class on an unfamiliar subject, what is the result? Do you usually understand it all right away?

2. What is required for you to learn new information and be able to use it in practical ways?

3. Describe how God has brought special people or experiences into your life at key times in order to teach you important lessons.

4. Have you ever wished that you and other Christians could retreat from life in the world and just focus on living a holy life? Is it possible for normal, ordinary people to live holy lives in the midst of a spiritually dark culture? Explain your viewpoint.

✏ 3. Describe how God has brought special people or experiences into your life at key times in order to teach you important lessons.

Suggested Responses: Encourage participants to share how other people have come alongside to teach and guide them, or how specific experiences helped them to learn what was needed at a particular time.

✏ 4. Have you ever wished that you and other Christians could retreat from life in the world and just focus on living a holy life? Is it possible for normal, ordinary people to live holy lives in the midst of a spiritually dark culture? Explain your viewpoint.

Suggested Responses: Encourage participants to weigh the requirements, challenges, and merits of holy living in both settings—for themselves, for others, and for God's purposes.

Let's keep these ideas in mind as we view the video.

video presentation

18 minutes

Participant's Guide page 63.

On page 63 of your Participant's Guide, you will find a space in which to take notes on key points as we watch this video.

Leader's Video Observations

The Essenes

Their Community

Their Lifestyle and Practices

Their Beliefs

Their Great Contribution

Understanding God's Work in History

SESSION THREE

The Time Had Fully Come

Questions to Think About

1. When you are given a great deal of information that is completely new to you, such as when you are taking a class on an unfamiliar subject, what is the result? Do you usually understand it all right away?

2. What is required for you to learn new information and be able to use it in practical ways?

3. Describe how God has brought special people or experiences into your life at key times in order to teach you important lessons.

4. Have you ever wished that you and other Christians could retreat from life in the world and just focus on living a holy life? Is it possible for normal, ordinary people to live holy lives in the midst of a spiritually dark culture? Explain your viewpoint.

Session Three: The Time Had Fully Come   63

Video Notes

The Essenes

    Their Community

    Their Lifestyle and Practices

    Their Beliefs

    Their Great Contribution

Understanding God's Work in History

PLANNING NOTES:

group Discovery

20 minutes

If your group has seven or more members, use the **Video Highlights** with the entire group (5 minutes), then break into small groups of three to five to discuss the **Small Group Bible Discovery** (10 minutes). Then reassemble the group to discuss the key points discovered (5 minutes).

If your group has fewer than seven members, begin with the **Video Highlights** (5 minutes), then do one or more of the topics found in the **Small Group Bible Discovery** as a group (10 minutes). Finally, spend five minutes at the end discussing points that had an impact on participants.

Video Highlights (5 minutes)

Here you'll ask one or more of the following questions that directly relate to the video the participants have just seen.

1. What new insights into the Dead Sea Scrolls and the Essene community at Qumran did you gain through this video?

    Suggested Responses: will vary but may include the importance of the scrolls in affirming the validity of the Old Testament Scriptures, amazed by the quantity and extent of the Essenes' writings, surprised the scrolls were hidden for so long, never knew such communities existed within Judaism, etc.

2. Why is it significant that the Essenes developed theological concepts and practices that were similar to those of the early Christians?

    Suggested Responses: This shows that God works through people who have a heart for Him to prepare the way for His unfolding plans. The Christian faith didn't suddenly appear out of nowhere; God used the Essenes to establish a fertile seedbed in which the Christian faith and the teachings of Jesus could flourish.

3. The Essenes of Qumran resisted the Hellenism of their culture by separating themselves and moving to the desert in order to study. What are the benefits and the disadvantages of their approach?

    Suggested Responses: Encourage participants to see how escaping their sinful culture enabled the Essenes to focus more fully on their faith and to live out their commitment to God, but also how their isolation lessened their impact on the culture.

4. Which beliefs and values of Christians today are similar to those of the Essenes? Did these similarities surprise you?

    Suggested Responses: Both believe that spiritual light cannot merge with spiritual darkness and that God's people must do battle against spiritual darkness; both believe that we have a part in God's plan for redemption (preparing the way for God's Messiah, bringing the gospel to the world); both demonstrate their commitment to God by not compromising with the evils of a sinful culture; both practice a ritual meal and baptism; etc.

video нighlights

1. What new insights into the Dead Sea Scrolls and the Essene community at Qumran did you gain through this video?

2. Why is it significant that the Essenes developed theological concepts and practices that were similar to those of the early Christians?

3. The Essenes of Qumran resisted the Hellenism of their culture by separating themselves and moving to the desert in order to study. What are the benefits and the disadvantages of their approach?

4. Which beliefs and values of Christians today are similar to those of the Essenes? Did these similarities surprise you?

5. How do you feel as you realize how deeply the Christian faith is rooted in the Jewish people and culture even before the time of Jesus?

DATA FILE

The Dead Sea Scrolls: An Accidental Discovery
It was a typical day in the Judea Wilderness in 1947. Near an old ruin at the northern end of the Dead Sea that scholars would later recognize as Qumran, a Bedouin shepherd rounded up stray goats at the foot of barren cliffs. He noticed a small opening to a cave, and when he threw a stone into the opening he heard the distinctive sound of pottery breaking. After telling two other family members about his discovery, he returned home with his goats.

The next day, Mohammed edh Dhib squeezed into the cave, which was littered with broken pottery. Two of the ten intact jars contained a large scroll and two smaller ones, which the disappointed Mohammed showed to the other shepherds. Little did they know that they had just discovered incredible treasures—the book of Isaiah, the Manual of Discipline

(continued on page 66)

PLANNING NOTES:

✏ 5.   How do you feel as you realize how deeply the Christian faith is rooted in the Jewish people and culture even before the time of Jesus?

Suggested Responses: may include surprise, grateful that God uses people to establish His purposes, wondering why more people haven't talked about the Jewish heritage of Christianity, etc.

DATA FILE

The Dead Sea Scrolls: An Accidental Discovery

It was a typical day in the Judea Wilderness in 1947. Near an old ruin at the northern end of the Dead Sea that scholars would later recognize as Qumran, a Bedouin shepherd rounded up stray goats at the foot of barren cliffs. He noticed a small opening to a cave, and when he threw a stone into the opening he heard the distinctive sound of pottery breaking. After telling two other family members about his discovery, he returned home with his goats.

The next day, Mohammed edh Dhib squeezed into the cave, which was littered with broken pottery. Two of the ten intact jars contained a large scroll and two smaller ones, which the disappointed Mohammed showed to the other shepherds. Little did they know that they had just discovered incredible treasures—the book of Isaiah, the Manual of Discipline (describing Qumran community rules), and a commentary on the book of Habakkuk!

The Caves of Qumran

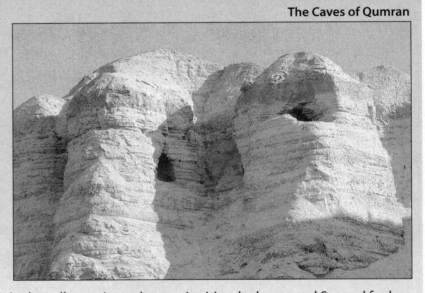

Mohammed hung the scrolls from his tent pole in a bag for several months, then sold them to an antiquities dealer named Kando in Bethlehem. Kando found the cave, located additional scrolls, and then—after showing them to church officials at Jerusalem's Syrian Orthodox Monastery of St. Mark's—sold the three original scrolls to a Jerusalem antiquities dealer named Samuel for less than one hundred dollars.

As word of the discovery spread, Professor E. L. Sukenik of the Hebrew University purchased Kando's additional scrolls. Meanwhile, Samuel had taken the three scrolls to the United States and advertised them in the *Wall Street Journal* on June 1, 1954. Dr. Sukenik's son, Yigael Yadin, happened to see the ad and, through a middleman, purchased the original find for $250,000 and presented the scrolls to the State of Israel. Today, they are in the Israel Museum in Jerusalem.

The Bedouin from Mohammed edh Dhib's tribe soon located more caves near Qumran containing additional scrolls and thousands of scroll fragments. Soon an official archaeological investigation was launched, and the caves and nearby ruins were carefully examined.

(continued on page 104)

4. Which beliefs and values of Christians today are similar to those of the Essenes? Did these similarities surprise you?

5. How do you feel as you realize how deeply the Christian faith is rooted in the Jewish people and culture even before the time of Jesus?

DATA FILE

The Dead Sea Scrolls: An Accidental Discovery

It was a typical day in the Judea Wilderness in 1947. Near an old ruin at the northern end of the Dead Sea that scholars would later recognize as Qumran, a Bedouin shepherd rounded up stray goats at the foot of barren cliffs. He noticed a small opening to a cave, and when he threw a stone into the opening he heard the distinctive sound of pottery breaking. After telling two other family members about his discovery, he returned home with his goats.

The next day, Mohammed edh Dhib squeezed into the cave, which was littered with broken pottery. Two of the ten intact jars contained a large scroll and two smaller ones, which the disappointed Mohammed showed to the other shepherds. Little did they know that they had just discovered incredible treasures—the book of Isaiah, the Manual of Discipline

(continued on page 66)

(continued from page 65)

(describing Qumran community rules), and a commentary on the book of Habakkuk!

Mohammed hung the scrolls from his tent pole in a bag for several months, then sold them to an antiquities dealer named Kando in Bethlehem. Kando found the cave, located additional scrolls, and then—after showing them to church officials at Jerusalem's Syrian Orthodox Monastery of St. Mark's—sold the three original scrolls to a Jerusalem antiquities dealer named Samuel for less than one hundred dollars.

As word of the discovery spread, Professor E. L. Sukenik of the Hebrew University purchased Kando's additional scrolls. Meanwhile, Samuel had taken the three scrolls to the United States and advertised them in the *Wall Street Journal* on June 1, 1954. Dr. Sukenik's son, Yigael Yadin, happened to see the ad and, through a middleman, purchased the original find for $250,000 and presented the scrolls to the State of Israel. Today, they are in the Israel Museum in Jerusalem.

The Bedouin from Mohammed edh Dhib's tribe soon located more caves near Qumran containing additional scrolls and thousands of scroll fragments. Soon an official archaeological investigation was launched, and the caves and nearby ruins were carefully examined.

The Caves of Qumran

(continued from page 102)

Known today as the Dead Sea Scrolls, scrolls (mostly scroll fragments) were found in at least eleven caves near the ruins of Qumran. Among the six hundred scrolls represented, a few of which had been preserved in clay jars (the extremely dry climate aided in preservation), scholars have identified copies of all the books of the Old Testament except Esther; Jewish writings from other sources, such as the apocryphal book of Jubilees; and specific writings from the Qumran community that included Old Testament commentaries, liturgical writing such as hymns, and rules for community conduct.

The most well-known scrolls include the nearly intact Isaiah scroll; the Copper Scroll that describes sixty-four locations where temple treasures were hidden (none of which have been found); the Habakkuk commentary in which the prophecies of God's judgment are applied to the Romans and those who resisted the Essenes' beliefs; and the Manual of Discipline describing the rules of the Essene community.

The scrolls, among the most significant archaeological finds of modern times, have:

- Profoundly affected our understanding of biblical texts.
- Provided striking insight into the theological and cultural setting of Jesus' life, the early church, and the history of Judaism.
- Provided fresh insight into our understanding and application of the Bible's message.
- Affirmed the accuracy of the Scriptures. Until the Dead Sea discoveries, the oldest copies of the Hebrew Bible dated to approximately A.D. 1000. The scrolls take us back beyond 100 B.C. Scholars were amazed to find few differences between old and new texts—most involved spelling changes. Truly, "All Scripture is God-breathed and is useful for teaching, rebuking, correcting and training in righteousness" (2 Timothy 3:16). Although a follower of God trusts the truth of the Bible by faith, the scrolls confirm that our faith in the accuracy of the Bible is fully supported by scholarly evidence.

Author's Note: Scholarly debate continues as to whether the scrolls were written or used at Qumran, whether they were the product of the Essenes, and whether the Essenes actually lived at Qumran. The best evidence to date indicates that the Dead Sea Scrolls were the product of the Essenes and were written or collected at the Qumran settlement. This writer considers this to be the best understanding to date. The actual contents of the scrolls, and the similarity of the writers' beliefs and practices to early Christianity, are subject to much less debate.

Biblical Books Recorded on the Scrolls	Number of Scrolls Found Per Book
The Psalms	36
Deuteronomy	29
Isaiah	21
Exodus	17
Genesis	15
Leviticus	13
Numbers	8

Known today as the Dead Sea Scrolls, scrolls (mostly scroll fragments) were found in at least eleven caves near the ruins of Qumran. Among the six hundred scrolls represented, a few of which had been preserved in clay jars (the extremely dry climate aided in preservation), scholars have identified copies of all the books of the Old Testament except Esther; Jewish writings from other sources, such as the apocryphal book of Jubilees; and specific writings from the Qumran community that included Old Testament commentaries, liturgical writing such as hymns, and rules for community conduct.

The most well-known scrolls include the nearly intact Isaiah scroll; the Copper Scroll that describes sixty-four locations where temple treasures were hidden (none of which have been found); the Habakkuk commentary in which the prophecies of God's judgment are applied to the Romans and those who resisted the Essenes' beliefs; and the Manual of Discipline describing the rules of the Essene community.

The scrolls, among the most significant archaeological finds of modern times, have:

- Profoundly affected our understanding of biblical texts.
- Provided striking insight into the theological and cultural setting of Jesus' life, the early church, and the history of Judaism.
- Provided fresh insight into our understanding and application of the Bible's message.
- Affirmed the accuracy of the Scriptures. Until the Dead Sea discoveries, the oldest copies of the Hebrew Bible dated to approximately A.D. 1000. The scrolls take us back beyond 100 B.C. Scholars were amazed to find few differences between old and new texts—most involved spelling changes. Truly, "All Scripture is God-breathed and is useful for teaching, rebuking, correcting and training in righteousness" (2 Timothy 3:16). Although a follower of God trusts the truth of the Bible by faith, the scrolls confirm that our faith in the accuracy of the Bible is fully supported by scholarly evidence.

Author's Note: Scholarly debate continues as to whether the scrolls were written or used at Qumran, whether they were the product of the Essenes, and whether the Essenes actually lived at Qumran. The best evidence to

(continued on page 68)

(continued from page 67)

date indicates that the Dead Sea Scrolls were the product of the Essenes and were written or collected at the Qumran settlement. This writer considers this to be the best understanding to date. The actual contents of the scrolls, and the similarity of the writers' beliefs and practices to early Christianity, are subject to much less debate.

Biblical Books Recorded on the Scrolls	Number of Scrolls Found Per Book
The Psalms	36
Deuteronomy	29
Isaiah	21
Exodus	17
Genesis	15
Leviticus	13
Numbers	8

Small Group Bible Discovery (15 minutes)

Participant's Guide pages 69-84.

During this time, a group with fewer than seven participants will stay together. A group with seven or more participants will break into small groups and reassemble as a large group during the final five minutes. Assign each group one of the following topics. If you have more than four small groups, assign some topics to more than one group.

Let's break into groups of three to five—people sitting near you—and study some of the Bible passages and truths mentioned in the video.

Turn to pages 69-84 in your Participant's Guide. There you'll find a list of four topics. You'll have ten minutes to read and discuss the topic I'll assign to you. Choose one person in your group to be a spokesperson for your group when we discuss these topics later.

Assign each group a topic.

I'll signal you when one minute is left.

Topic A: Lessons in the Wilderness

The "vast and dreadful" wilderness (Deuteronomy 8:15) had a profound effect on the people of the Bible. There, God disciplined them for their lack of faith, disobedience, and complaining so that they would learn to trust in His faithfulness. There they were transformed from a band of refugees into a powerful nation called to live in obedience to God in His chosen land.

1. Which of Israel's forefathers spent time in the desert in preparation for the missions God gave them? (See Genesis 12:1–9; 13:1; Exodus 3:1; 1 Samuel 23:14.)

   Suggested Responses: Abraham, the father of the nation of Israel; Moses, the lawgiver; and David, the founder of the kingdom of Israel.

2. After God had delivered the Israelites from Egypt and provided their food and water for three months as they traversed the deserts, what did He do? Why do you think He chose that time and place? (See Exodus 19:1–6; 20:1–17.)

   Suggested Responses: While the Israelites were camped in the desert at Mount Sinai, God gave Moses the Ten Commandments, which summarized His covenant with them. They had already experienced months of God's care and provision, which had helped prepare them to carry out the plan God had for them.

3. What do each of the following passages reveal about the Israelites' preparation in the wilderness?

   a. Deuteronomy 8:1–5, 10–18

      Suggested Responses: God had led, humbled, tested, protected, and disciplined them in order to prepare them to keep His commandments. In the

small Group Bible Discovery

Topic A: Lessons in the Wilderness

The "vast and dreadful" wilderness (Deuteronomy 8:15) had a profound effect on the people of the Bible. There, God disciplined them for their lack of faith, disobedience, and complaining so that they would learn to trust in His faithfulness. There they were transformed from a band of refugees into a powerful nation called to live in obedience to God in His chosen land.

1. Which of Israel's forefathers spent time in the desert in preparation for the missions God gave them? (See Genesis 12:1–9; 13:1; Exodus 3:1; 1 Samuel 23:14.)

Topography of Israel: New Testament

2. After God had delivered the Israelites from Egypt and provided their food and water for three months as they traversed the deserts, what did He do? Why do you think He chose that time and place? (See Exodus 19:1–6; 20:1–17.)

3. What do each of the following passages reveal about the Israelites' preparation in the wilderness?

    a. Deuteronomy 8:1–5, 10–18

    b. Psalm 78:9–18

    c. Psalm 95:6–11

    d. Jeremiah 2:1–2

Topography of Israel: New Testament

desert He nurtured and disciplined His people, teaching them to depend solely on Him. He cautioned them to remember, as they grew accustomed to the plenty of the Promised Land, that their blessings came from Him.

b. Psalm 78:9–18

Suggested Responses: Although God had done many miracles, dividing the Red Sea, guiding them with a cloud by day and a fire by night, splitting rocks in the desert in order to provide them with water, etc., the people remained stubborn and rebellious. They continued to sin against God and willfully put Him to the test.

c. Psalm 95:6–11

Suggested Responses: God had led His people through the desert as a shepherd cares for his flock, yet they had hardened their hearts and tested God, provoking His anger.

d. Jeremiah 2:1–2

Suggested Responses: Early in their journey, they had loved and obeyed God as He led them through the desert.

4. When the Israelites turned from God, what did the prophets call on the Israelites to do? (See Jeremiah 2:4–8; 31:31–32; Psalm 81:6–12; Hosea 2:14–15.)

Suggested Response: The prophets reminded them of their time in the wilderness and encouraged them to return to the faith they had first exhibited in the desert.

small Group Bible Discovery

Topic A: Lessons in the Wilderness

The "vast and dreadful" wilderness (Deuteronomy 8:15) had a profound effect on the people of the Bible. There, God disciplined them for their lack of faith, disobedience, and complaining so that they would learn to trust in His faithfulness. There they were transformed from a band of refugees into a powerful nation called to live in obedience to God in His chosen land.

1. Which of Israel's forefathers spent time in the desert in preparation for the missions God gave them? (See Genesis 12:1–9; 13:1; Exodus 3:1; 1 Samuel 23:14.)

Topography of Israel: New Testament

2. After God had delivered the Israelites from Egypt and provided their food and water for three months as they traversed the deserts, what did He do? Why do you think He chose that time and place? (See Exodus 19:1–6; 20:1–17.)

3. What do each of the following passages reveal about the Israelites' preparation in the wilderness?

   a. Deuteronomy 8:1–5, 10–18

   b. Psalm 78:9–18

   c. Psalm 95:6–11

   d. Jeremiah 2:1–2

✏ 5.   What can Christians today learn from the experiences of the Israelites as they journeyed through the wilderness? (See 1 Corinthians 10:1–11.)

Suggested Responses: Although they were led and nourished by God, many of them set their hearts on evil, and they suffered for it. Their experiences serve as an example for us today.

DID YOU KNOW?

The landscape of Israel has played a significant role in biblical history and imagery. Much of Israel's terrain was rugged desert, referred to as "wilderness" in the Scriptures. These wilderness areas were located close to where most Israelites lived. The Negev Wilderness was barely forty miles south of Jerusalem, their holy city. The Judea Wilderness began just east of Jerusalem and was within sight of anyone who lived in the central mountains.

Because the wilderness, particularly the Judea Wilderness, was so close to settled areas, it became a refuge for those seeking solitude or safety from authorities. Here, David hid from Saul (1 Samuel 26), John the Baptist isolated himself from the religious practices of the day (Matthew 3), and Jesus faced the devil (Matthew 4). Here, the Essenes labored over their scrolls, and early Christians built monasteries, some of which still function today.

The Judea Wilderness

The Time Had Fully Come

Session Three: The Time Had Fully Come 71

DID YOU KNOW?

The landscape of Israel has played a significant role in biblical history and imagery. Much of Israel's terrain was rugged desert, referred to as "wilderness" in the Scriptures. These wilderness areas were located close to where most Israelites lived. The Negev Wilderness was barely forty miles south of Jerusalem, their holy city. The Judea Wilderness began just east of Jerusalem and was within sight of anyone who lived in the central mountains.

Because the wilderness, particularly the Judea Wilderness, was so close to settled areas, it became a refuge for those seeking solitude or safety from authorities. Here, David hid from Saul (1 Samuel 26), John the Baptist isolated himself from the religious practices of the day (Matthew 3), and Jesus faced the devil (Matthew 4). Here, the Essenes labored over their scrolls, and early Christians built monasteries, some of which still function today.

The Judea Wilderness

72 Faith Lessons on the Life and Ministry of the Messiah

4. When the Israelites turned from God, what did the prophets call on the Israelites to do? (See Jeremiah 2:4–8; 31:31–32; Psalm 81:6–12; Hosea 2:14–15.)

5. What can Christians today learn from the experiences of the Israelites as they journeyed through the wilderness? (See 1 Corinthians 10:1–11.)

Topic B: The Way of Redemption Led Through the Wilderness

1. What role did the prophets say the wilderness would play in the coming of the Messiah?

2. For what purpose did John the Baptist go into the wilderness? (See Matthew 3:1–3.)

Topic B: The Way of Redemption Led Through the Wilderness

✏ 1. What role did the prophets say the wilderness would play in the coming of the Messiah?

    a. Hosea 2:14–23

       Suggested Response: God's restoration of His people would involve a cleansing in the desert similar to the way He cleansed the Israelites on their way to the Promised Land.

    b. Isaiah 40:1–5

       Suggested Response: The restoration of God's people would include passing through the wilderness, even as it had with Israel the first time.

✏ 2. For what purpose did John the Baptist go into the wilderness? (See Matthew 3:1–3.)

       Suggested Responses: John the Baptist called on the people to repent and helped to cultivate the hearts and minds of the Jewish people for the Messiah who would soon follow. He went into the desert wilderness to "prepare the way for the Lord" in fulfillment of Isaiah 40:3.

✏ 3. Matthew 3:15–4:11 reveals that as soon as Jesus came up out of the Jordan River following His baptism, He was led into the desert—the same wilderness in which the Essene community of Qumran was located—to be tempted by Satan.

    a. Why was the wilderness setting an appropriate place for Jesus' temptation? (See also Isaiah 40:1–3.)

       Suggested Responses: will vary but may include the fact that the desert is where God developed the faith of His people, miraculously providing for their needs and teaching them to depend on Him alone. Just as the hardships of the desert tempted the Israelites to not trust God, Satan appeared

---

DATA FILE

Lessons of the Wilderness

The Hebrews' forty-year wilderness journey made such an impact on them that later biblical writers and prophets referred to those days as reminders of essential truths:

- The psalmist reminded them of God's faithful love that was demonstrated to them in the wilderness (Psalms 105:38–45; 107:4–9).
- Jeremiah (Jeremiah 2:6; 7:22–24) and Micah (Micah 6:3–5) reminded the people of the lessons they learned in the wilderness.
- New Testament writers compared the Israelites' wilderness experience to the lives of believers (Hebrews 3:12–19; 1 Corinthians 10:1–13).
- Jesus, the new "Adam," faced Satan on our behalf in the Judea Wilderness and used lessons from the wilderness to defeat him: "Man does not live on bread alone" (Matthew 4:4; see also Deuteronomy 8:3); and "Do not put the Lord your God to the test" (Matthew 4:7; see also Deuteronomy 6:16).

72   Faith Lessons on the Life and Ministry of the Messiah

4. When the Israelites turned from God, what did the prophets call on the Israelites to do? (See Jeremiah 2:4–8; 31:31–32; Psalm 81:6–12; Hosea 2:14–15.)

5. What can Christians today learn from the experiences of the Israelites as they journeyed through the wilderness? (See 1 Corinthians 10:1–11.)

Topic B: The Way of Redemption Led Through the Wilderness

1. What role did the prophets say the wilderness would play in the coming of the Messiah?

   a. Hosea 2:14–23

   b. Isaiah 40:1–5

2. For what purpose did John the Baptist go into the wilderness? (See Matthew 3:1–3.)

Session Three: The Time Had Fully Come   73

3. Matthew 3:15–4:11 reveals that as soon as Jesus came up out of the Jordan River following His baptism, He was led into the desert—the same wilderness in which the Essene community of Qumran was located—to be tempted by Satan.

   a. Why was the wilderness setting an appropriate place for Jesus' temptation? (See also Isaiah 40:1–3.)

   b. How did Jesus resist Satan's forty-day spiritual attack? (See also Luke 4:1–13.)

DATA FILE

Lessons of the Wilderness

The Hebrews' forty-year wilderness journey made such an impact on them that later biblical writers and prophets referred to those days as reminders of essential truths:

- The psalmist reminded them of God's faithful love that was demonstrated to them in the wilderness (Psalms 105:38–45; 107:4–9).
- Jeremiah (Jeremiah 2:6; 7:22–24) and Micah (Micah 6:3–5) reminded the people of the lessons they learned in the wilderness.
- New Testament writers compared the Israelites' wilderness experience to the lives of believers (Hebrews 3:12–19; 1 Corinthians 10:1–13).
- Jesus, the new "Adam," faced Satan on our behalf in the Judea Wilderness and used lessons from the wilderness to defeat him: "Man does not live on bread alone" (Matthew 4:4; see also Deuteronomy 8:3); and "Do not put the Lord your God to the test" (Matthew 4:7; see also Deuteronomy 6:16).

in the wilderness to tempt Jesus to not trust God. Jesus resisted by completely submitting Himself to obedience and worship of God alone. Furthermore, Isaiah prophesied that the Messiah would come from the wilderness, where a way had been prepared, in order to bring redemption and freedom. God fulfilled prophecy and announced His Son as the true Messiah by placing the beginning of Jesus' ministry in "the wilderness."

b. How did Jesus resist Satan's forty-day spiritual attack? (See also Luke 4:1–13.)

Suggested Responses: Jesus completely submitted Himself to the authority of the Word of God. In response to each temptation, He quoted passages of Scripture that were written during the time the Israelites were in the wilderness.

c. Why did Jesus have to be tempted? What is the importance of Jesus' resistance to Satan compared with Adam's? (See Romans 5:16–19.)

Suggested Responses: Just as the first Adam represented his descendants before God, Jesus represented His "spiritual descendants" before God. He was tempted for those who would follow Him. Just as Adam's sin made us unrighteous, Jesus' victory over temptation enables us to be righteous before God.

d. What do 1 Corinthians 10:13 and Hebrews 2:17–18 reveal about the importance of Jesus' temptation in the wilderness?

Suggested Responses: The temptation, a foundational event during Jesus' earthly life, gives us an encouraging example. Through the power of Jesus, who was tempted just like we are, we can confront the power of the devil directly. We can resist temptation by knowing and trusting God's Word. We can remember that every temptation is, in a sense, the devil's attempt to lure us to follow our own ideas rather than trusting in the words of God. But God is faithful and will give us a way out of our temptation.

Topic C: A Community Set Apart to Fulfill God's Plan

God had worked for centuries to prepare the world for the advent of His Son, the Messiah. God had established His people Israel, the Promised Land, the line of David, the temple system, and even a small, wilderness community of devout Jews—the Essenes—to provide the cultural and theological context for Jesus' life and work.

The Essenes came into being in response to Hellenism, the secular worldview that swept the world around the first century. Hellenism glorified the human being, emphasized physical and sensual practices, and featured erotic themes celebrating the exploits of pagan gods and heroes. Many religious Jews abandoned their biblical worldview in favor of Hellenism. The Essenes, however, made a deliberate choice to remove themselves from Hellenistic culture and create communities in which they could worship and honor Yahweh. Their commitment exerted profound influence on the theological climate of their culture.

Thus, Jesus' message fell on fertile soil—prepared for more than a century by Essenes who waited expectantly for the Messiah to appear. The Essenes' beliefs, which were similar to many teachings and practices of Jesus and the early Christians, enhanced the popular acceptance of Jesus' message. Even today,

c. Why did Jesus have to be tempted? What is the importance of Jesus' resistance to Satan compared with Adam's? (See Romans 5:16–19.)

d. What do 1 Corinthians 10:13 and Hebrews 2:17–18 reveal about the importance of Jesus' temptation in the wilderness?

Topic C: A Community Set Apart to Fulfill God's Plan

God had worked for centuries to prepare the world for the advent of His Son, the Messiah. God had established His people Israel, the Promised Land, the line of David, the temple system, and even a small, wilderness community of devout Jews—the Essenes—to provide the cultural and theological context for Jesus' life and work.

The Essenes came into being in response to Hellenism, the secular worldview that swept the world around the first century. Hellenism glorified the human being, emphasized physical and sensual practices, and featured erotic themes celebrating the exploits of pagan gods and heroes. Many religious Jews abandoned their biblical worldview in favor of Hellenism. The Essenes, however, made a deliberate choice to remove themselves from Hellenistic culture and create communities in which they could worship and honor Yahweh. Their commitment exerted profound influence on the theological climate of their culture.

Thus, Jesus' message fell on fertile soil—prepared for more than a century by Essenes who waited expectantly for the Messiah to appear. The Essenes' beliefs, which were similar to many teachings and practices of Jesus and the early Christians, enhanced the popular the impact of their lifestyle and beliefs provides vivid insights into how God uses people through the events of history to unfold His plan of redemption. Let's take a closer look at how the lifestyle of this community helped to prepare the world to receive the Messiah.

1. The Essenes held all their personal possessions in common. In what ways was this similar to the lifestyle of the early Christians? (See Acts 2:42–45.)

    Suggested Response: The early Christians—in joyful response to what God had done—also shared their possessions with one another, although it was not an official requirement as it was for membership in the Essene community.

2. The Essenes practiced a "ceremonial meal" that symbolized a great messianic banquet they believed would occur when the Messiah arrived. During this meal, they blessed bread and wine. What type of symbolic feast that Jesus established did the early Christians keep? (See Matthew 26:26–29.)

    Suggested Response: The early Christians continued to celebrate the Lord's Supper—a time when they blessed bread and wine in remembrance of Jesus' death on the cross.

3. The Essenes practiced a ceremonial cleansing, using flowing water, that symbolized the spiritual cleansing brought about through repentance and forgiveness. What type of symbolic cleansing did the early Christians practice? (See John 3:22–23; Acts 2:37–41.)

    Suggested Response: Baptism in water to represent repentance and the forgiveness of sins by Jesus.

Qumran

1. Aqueduct and Reservoir
   System
2. Defense Tower
3. Scriptorium
4. Main Assembly Hall and
   Refectory
5. Potters' Workshop
6. Possible Mikveh
7. Cemetery

acceptance of Jesus' message. Even today, the impact of their lifestyle and beliefs provides vivid insights into how God uses people through the events of history to unfold His plan of redemption. Let's take a closer look at how the lifestyle of this community helped to prepare the world to receive the Messiah.

1. The Essenes held all their personal possessions in common. In what ways was this similar to the lifestyle of the early Christians? (See Acts 2:42–45.)

2. The Essenes practiced a "ceremonial meal" that symbolized a great messianic banquet they believed would occur when the Messiah arrived. During this meal, they blessed bread and wine. What type of symbolic feast that Jesus established did the early Christians keep? (See Matthew 26:26–29.)

3. The Essenes practiced a ceremonial cleansing, using flowing water, that symbolized the spiritual cleansing brought about through repentance and forgiveness. What type of symbolic cleansing did the early Christians practice? (See John 3:22–23; Acts 2:37–41.)

4. The Essenes believed there was a great struggle between the sons of light (God's followers) and the sons of darkness (Satan's followers). What do John 3:16–21 and 12:35–36 reveal about the battle between good (light) and evil (darkness) in which the Essenes believed?

Qumran

1. Aqueduct and Reservoir System
2. Defense Tower
3. Scriptorium
4. Main Assembly Hall and Refectory
5. Potters' Workshop
6. Possible Mikveh
7. Cemetery

4. The Essenes believed there was a great struggle between the sons of light (God's followers) and the sons of darkness (Satan's followers). What do John 3:16–21 and 12:35–36 reveal about the battle between good (light) and evil (darkness) in which the Essenes believed?

    Suggested Responses: Jesus identified Himself as the light that God sent into the world, and urged people to put their trust in Him before spiritual darkness overcame them. Jesus also recognized the battle between light and darkness, saying that people who do evil hate the light and that those who live by God's truth enter the light.

5. What does Galatians 4:4–5 reveal about God's redemptive plan, including the part the Essenes played in preparing the Jews?

    Suggested Responses: These verses show that God carefully planned every detail concerning Jesus' coming. Jesus came to first-century Israel when the world was fully prepared to receive Him.

6. In light of Galatians 4:4–5, what does Romans 8:28 reveal about God's timing in the lives of His followers—including you?

    Suggested Response: that God works in all circumstances for His—and our—good.

7. God used the Essenes, who separated themselves from the world in order to know and worship God, to develop the practices and ideas that would help people receive the Messiah. In contrast, what did Jesus command His disciples to do so that they might continue to advance God's plan of redemption? (See Matthew 28:19–20.)

    Suggested Responses: He told them to go and make disciples of all nations. The disciples were to go to where the sinners were, not to invite or wait for sinners to come to them.

Qumran: The Main Assembly Hall

5. What does Galatians 4:4–5 reveal about God's redemptive plan, including the part the Essenes played in preparing the Jews?

6. In light of Galatians 4:4–5, what does Romans 8:28 reveal about God's timing in the lives of His followers—including you?

Qumran: The Main Assembly Hall

7. God used the Essenes, who separated themselves from the world in order to know and worship God, to develop the practices and ideas that would help people receive the Messiah. In contrast, what did Jesus command His disciples to do so that they might continue to advance God's plan of redemption? (See Matthew 28:19–20.)

COMPELLING EVIDENCE

The Remains of Qumran

As is true with many ancient settlements, Qumran was destroyed and rebuilt various times. The earliest settlement on the site dates to the Israelite period shortly before the Babylonian Captivity (ca. 600 B.C.), when it was probably destroyed. Around 140 B.C., Qumran was resettled during the reign of the Hasmonaean king Hyrcanus, but the settlement was abandoned after a damaging earthquake (ca. 31 B.C.). Resettled about the time Jesus was born (ca. 6 B.C.), Qumran became an active community until the Roman army, under Vespasian's command, destroyed it in approximately A.D. 68.

The major structures in Qumran provide significant evidence of the lifestyle and beliefs of the community:

Aqueduct and Reservoir System

Water played an important role in the Essenes' theology. They believed that water used as a symbol of purification must be "living" or moving, not drawn by hand, so they developed a system in which rainwater ran on its own into a ritual bath. At least two cisterns were probably used as ceremonial or ritual baths (*mikvoth)* and had steps that allowed access to the water.

New members were cleansed with water in a type of baptism that apparently symbolized the spiritual cleansing that resulted from repentance and forgiveness after any breaking of God's laws. (See Matthew 3:6, 11.) The Essenes' ritual cleansing likely provided the background for the baptism practiced by John the Baptist and Christian baptism.

The Essenes' commitment to doing what they believed God wanted them to do is exemplary. They created catch basins just west of their community

The Essene Water Tunnel

An Essene Cistern

(continued on page 122)

The Time Had Fully Come

COMPELLING EVIDENCE

The Remains of Qumran

As is true with many ancient settlements, Qumran was destroyed and rebuilt various times. The earliest settlement on the site dates to the Israelite period shortly before the Babylonian Captivity (ca. 600 B.C.), when it was probably destroyed. Around 140 B.C., Qumran was resettled during the reign of the Hasmonaean king Hyrcanus, but the settlement was abandoned after a damaging earthquake (ca. 31 B.C.). Resettled about the time Jesus was born (ca. 6 B.C.), Qumran became an active community until the Roman army, under Vespasian's command, destroyed it in approximately A.D. 68.

The major structures in Qumran provide significant evidence of the lifestyle and beliefs of the community:

Aqueduct and Reservoir System

Water played an important role in the Essenes' theology. They believed that water used as a symbol of purification must be "living" or moving, not drawn by hand, so they developed a system in which rainwater ran on its own into a ritual bath. At least two cisterns were probably used as ceremonial or ritual baths (*mikvoth*) and had steps that allowed access to the water.

The Essene Water Tunnel

New members were cleansed with water in a type of baptism that apparently symbolized the spiritual cleansing that resulted from repentance and forgiveness after any breaking of God's laws. (See Matthew 3:6, 11.) The Essenes' ritual cleansing likely provided the background for the baptism practiced by John the Baptist and Christian baptism.

(continued on page 80)

(continued from page 79)

An Essene Cistern

The Essenes' commitment to doing what they believed God wanted them to do is exemplary. They created catch basins just west of their community where runoff from the Judea Wilderness cascaded over a cliff. They tunneled more than one hundred feet through solid rock to bring the water to the cliff's edge, then directed the water through more than one thousand feet of plaster-coated channels and aqueducts until it reached the community, where it was stored in cisterns.

Defense Tower

Scholars debate the importance of the large tower that once stood in Qumran because it was essentially a religious community of separatists who lived a peaceful, almost monastic existence. The Essenes did, however, believe in the Messiah's imminent arrival and that a great battle would ensue between the sons of light (themselves) and the sons of darkness (followers of evil). The tower most likely provided protection against bandits or other less "military" threats.

Scriptorium

Archaeologists believe the Dead Sea Scrolls were written in this area. Excavation has revealed tables and benches similar to those used by scribes, as well as ink pots and basins in which the Essenes could ritualistically wash their hands before and after writing God's sacred name.

Main Assembly Hall and Refectory

In this room, archaeologists believe the Essenes practiced a ceremonial, communal meal in anticipation of the great banquet of the messianic age. Scholars have discovered many similarities between the

(continued from page 120)

where runoff from the Judea Wilderness cascaded over a cliff. They tunneled more than one hundred feet through solid rock to bring the water to the cliff's edge, then directed the water through more than one thousand feet of plaster-coated channels and aqueducts until it reached the community, where it was stored in cisterns.

Defense Tower

Scholars debate the importance of the large tower that once stood in Qumran because it was essentially a religious community of separatists who lived a peaceful, almost monastic existence. The Essenes did, however, believe in the Messiah's imminent arrival and that a great battle would ensue between the sons of light (themselves) and the sons of darkness (followers of evil). The tower most likely provided protection against bandits or other less "military" threats.

Scriptorium

Archaeologists believe the Dead Sea Scrolls were written in this area. Excavation has revealed tables and benches similar to those used by scribes, as well as ink pots and basins in which the Essenes could ritualistically wash their hands before and after writing God's sacred name.

Main Assembly Hall and Refectory

In this room, archaeologists believe the Essenes practiced a ceremonial, communal meal in anticipation of the great banquet of the messianic age. Scholars have discovered many similarities between the Essenes' ceremonial meal and the Last Supper recorded in the Gospels (Matthew 26:26–29).

In one corner of the room, a small water channel entered where the floor sloped down toward the opposite end of the room. This may have allowed the room to be washed in preparation for the meal. Nearby, archaeologists have unearthed a kitchen with five fireplaces and a smaller room containing the remains of more than one thousand pottery jars, dishes, plates, and cups. Interestingly, community members did not live in this or any other buildings uncovered by archaeologists. They probably lived in nearby caves or tents.

Potters' Workshop

Here, archaeologists have found a basin for preparing clay, a base for a potter's wheel, and two kilns. The clay jars, which helped to preserve the Dead Sea Scrolls for nearly two thousand years, were probably made here.

Cemetery

The main cemetery east of Qumran contains more than one thousand carefully arranged grave sites in orderly rows. Each grave was marked by a small mound of stones, and individuals were buried with their heads facing south. Although ancient writers, including Josephus, indicated that no women lived among the Essenes, several graves contained women's bodies. Scholars have suggested that these were family members of the Qumran community.

(continued from page 79)

An Essene Cistern

The Essenes' commitment to doing what they believed God wanted them to do is exemplary. They created catch basins just west of their community where runoff from the Judea Wilderness cascaded over a cliff. They tunneled more than one hundred feet through solid rock to bring the water to the cliff's edge, then directed the water through more than one thousand feet of plaster-coated channels and aqueducts until it reached the community, where it was stored in cisterns.

Defense Tower

Scholars debate the importance of the large tower that once stood in Qumran because it was essentially a religious community of separatists who lived a peaceful, almost monastic existence. The Essenes did, however, believe in the Messiah's imminent arrival and that a great battle would ensue between the sons of light (themselves) and the sons of darkness (followers of evil). The tower most likely provided protection against bandits or other less "military" threats.

Scriptorium

Archaeologists believe the Dead Sea Scrolls were written in this area. Excavation has revealed tables and benches similar to those used by scribes, as well as ink pots and basins in which the Essenes could ritualistically wash their hands before and after writing God's sacred name.

Main Assembly Hall and Refectory

In this room, archaeologists believe the Essenes practiced a ceremonial, communal meal in anticipation of the great banquet of the messianic age. Scholars have discovered many similarities between the

Essenes' ceremonial meal and the Last Supper recorded in the Gospels (Matthew 26:26–29).

In one corner of the room, a small water channel entered where the floor sloped down toward the opposite end of the room. This may have allowed the room to be washed in preparation for the meal. Nearby, archaeologists have unearthed a kitchen with five fireplaces and a smaller room containing the remains of more than one thousand pottery jars, dishes, plates, and cups. Interestingly, community members did not live in this or any other buildings uncovered by archaeologists. They probably lived in nearby caves or tents.

Potters' Workshop

Here, archaeologists have found a basin for preparing clay, a base for a potter's wheel, and two kilns. The clay jars, which helped to preserve the Dead Sea Scrolls for nearly two thousand years, were probably made here.

Cemetery

The main cemetery east of Qumran contains more than one thousand carefully arranged grave sites in orderly rows. Each grave was marked by a small mound of stones, and individuals were buried with their heads facing south. Although ancient writers, including Josephus, indicated that no women lived among the Essenes, several graves contained women's bodies. Scholars have suggested that these were family members of the Qumran community.

Topic D: The Essenes Prepare the Way for the Messiah

As they devoted themselves to God and the study of the Hebrew Scriptures, the Essenes developed theological concepts and terminology that are similar, or even identical, to those expressed by the New Testament writers. Let's consider the Essenes' understanding of theology and how it contributed to the people's ability to accept Jesus as the Messiah.

1. In the Dead Sea Scrolls, the Essenes used each of the following words or phrases, which are common to the New Testament but not elsewhere, long before Jesus was born. Match the words and phrases below to the following New Testament Scriptures: Matthew 3:3 (Isaiah 40:3); 5:3; 6:22–23; Luke 1:32, 35; John 1:5; 3:19–21; 12:35–36; 2 Corinthians 6:14, 15; Hebrews 7:1–3.

Words or Phrases Used by the Essenes	New Testament Reference
sons of light	John 12:36
light and darkness	Matthew 6:22–23; John 1:5; 3:19–21; 12:35–36; 2 Corinthians 6:14
Belial	2 Corinthians 6:15
poor in spirit	Matthew 5:3
Melchizedek	Hebrews 7:1–3
Son of God (Son of the Most High)	Luke 1:32, 35
way of the Lord	Isaiah 40:3; Matthew 3:3

2. How would the Essenes' use of the above words and phrases (and many others) have prepared Jesus' audience?

Suggested Responses: By using those words and phrases, the Essenes expanded the Jews' vocabulary and theological understanding. This paved the way for Jesus to communicate effectively to His audiences, who understood His meanings more clearly.

3. The Essenes interpreted prophetic Scriptures as being fulfilled by the events of their day, which differed significantly from other religious movements. Why was acceptance, or at least knowledge, of this concept important to God's plan of redemption? (See Matthew 3:1–3; Luke 4:14–21; 18:31–33; Acts 2:14–36.)

Suggested Response: Jesus came in fulfillment of the Scriptures, so the people had to understand that these things could be (and were being!) fulfilled during their lifetime.

Topic D: The Essenes Prepare the Way for the Messiah

As they devoted themselves to God and the study of the Hebrew Scriptures, the Essenes developed theological concepts and terminology that are similar, or even identical, to those expressed by the New Testament writers. Let's consider the Essenes' understanding of theology and how it contributed to the people's ability to accept Jesus as the Messiah.

1. In the Dead Sea Scrolls, the Essenes used each of the following words or phrases, which are common to the New Testament but not elsewhere, long before Jesus was born. Match the words and phrases below to the following New Testament Scriptures: Matthew 3:3 (Isaiah 40:3); 5:3; 6:22–23; Luke 1:32, 35; John 1:5; 3:19–21; 12:35–36; 2 Corinthians 6:14, 15; Hebrews 7:1–3.

Words or Phrases Used by the Essenes	New Testament Reference
sons of light	
light and darkness	
Belial	
poor in spirit	
Melchizedek	
Son of God (Son of the Most High)	
way of the Lord	

2. How would the Essenes' use of the above words and phrases (and many others) have prepared Jesus' audience?

3. The Essenes interpreted prophetic Scriptures as being fulfilled by the events of their day, which differed significantly from other religious movements. Why was acceptance, or at least knowledge, of this concept important to God's plan of redemption? (See Matthew 3:1–3; Luke 4:14–21; 18:31–33; Acts 2:14–36.)

WORTH OBSERVING

God's Perfect Timing

Scripture reveals that God arranged many significant events, movements, and people in order to make the timing of Jesus' birth perfect for the beginning of the church. According to Galatians 4:4–5, "When the time had fully come, God sent his Son, born of a woman ... to redeem." Timing-related factors include:

- The conquests of Alexander the Great, 350 years before Jesus, which made the known world conversant in one language—Greek. This significantly increased the early spread of the Gospel (Acts 9:20–21).
- World dominion by the Roman Empire, which provided world peace and a wide network of roads, built for the Roman legions and trade, that the Christian missionaries would later use. The Romans also executed by crucifixion, and the psalmist had predicted that Jesus would be pierced at His execution (Psalm 22:16–17).

PLANNING NOTES:

> **WORTH OBSERVING**
>
> **God's Perfect Timing**
>
> Scripture reveals that God arranged many significant events, movements, and people in order to make the timing of Jesus' birth perfect for the beginning of the church. According to Galatians 4:4–5, "When the time had fully come, God sent his Son, born of a woman . . . to redeem." Timing-related factors include:
>
> - The conquests of Alexander the Great, 350 years before Jesus, which made the known world conversant in one language—Greek. This significantly increased the early spread of the Gospel (Acts 9:20–21).
> - World dominion by the Roman Empire, which provided world peace and a wide network of roads, built for the Roman legions and trade, that the Christian missionaries would later use. The Romans also executed by crucifixion, and the psalmist had predicted that Jesus would be pierced at His execution (Psalm 22:16–17).

4. The Essenes traced the priesthood of the Messiah to Melchizedek, not Aaron. Why is this belief essential to accepting Jesus as the Messiah? (See Luke 1:31–33; Hebrews 7:1–22.)

    Suggested Responses: Perfection could not be obtained through the law and the Levitical priesthood of Aaron. A new, incorruptible, and indestructible priest—the Son of God—had to come.

5. Even though the Essenes had many beliefs in common with the early Christians, there were key differences between them. Compare the Essenes' belief in two Messiahs (a priest and a king) with Hebrews 7:15–17; 8:1–2; Luke 1:32–33.

    Suggested Response: The New Testament views Jesus as both a king and a priest, not two separate Messiahs.

> After nine minutes, let participants know that they have one minute remaining. Then reassemble the entire group. After everyone is back together, begin asking one person from each small group to briefly share a key idea with the larger group. In some cases, you may not have time for every group to share their discoveries.

As time allows, let's briefly share the key ideas that your group discussed.

3. The Essenes interpreted prophetic Scriptures as being fulfilled by the events of their day, which differed significantly from other religious movements. Why was acceptance, or at least knowledge, of this concept important to God's plan of redemption? (See Matthew 3:1–3; Luke 4:14–21; 18:31–33; Acts 2:14–36.)

WORTH OBSERVING

God's Perfect Timing

Scripture reveals that God arranged many significant events, movements, and people in order to make the timing of Jesus' birth perfect for the beginning of the church. According to Galatians 4:4–5, "When the time had fully come, God sent his Son, born of a woman . . . to redeem." Timing-related factors include:

- The conquests of Alexander the Great, 350 years before Jesus, which made the known world conversant in one language—Greek. This significantly increased the early spread of the Gospel (Acts 9:20–21).
- World dominion by the Roman Empire, which provided world peace and a wide network of roads, built for the Roman legions and trade, that the Christian missionaries would later use. The Romans also executed by crucifixion, and the psalmist had predicted that Jesus would be pierced at His execution (Psalm 22:16–17).

4. The Essenes traced the priesthood of the Messiah to Melchizedek, not Aaron. Why is this belief essential to accepting Jesus as the Messiah? (See Luke 1:31–33; Hebrews 7:1–22.)

5. Even though the Essenes had many beliefs in common with the early Christians, there were key differences between them. Compare the Essenes' belief in two Messiahs (a priest and a king) with Hebrews 7:15–17; 8:1–2; Luke 1:32–33.

PLANNING NOTES:

WAS JOHN THE BAPTIST AN ESSENE?

Did John the Baptist live at Qumran? See the Dead Sea Scrolls? Write any of them? These questions have gripped scholars because the scrolls reveal remarkable similarities between the Essenes and John's teaching and practices. However, John was never identified as an Essene, was not a member of any community, can't be placed definitively at Qumran, and proclaimed his message publicly rather than seeking the shelter of a monastic setting. Note the following comparisons:

John the Baptist	The Essenes
Came from family of priests (Luke 1:5)	Many were priests who disagreed with temple authorities
Lived in the wilderness (Luke 1:80)	Qumran was in the Judea Wilderness
Was called to "prepare the way for the LORD" (Isaiah 40:1–5)	Lived in the wilderness to prepare the way for the Lord
Baptized as a sign of repentance and inner cleansing (Mark 1:4–5)	Practiced ritual cleansing in water as a sign of the soul's cleansing
Proclaimed that the One to come would baptize with the Holy Spirit (Mark 1:7–8)	Believed God would pour out His Spirit like water to cleanse perverse hearts
Was not accepted by most people (Matthew 21:32)	Complained that people ignored their teachings
Didn't participate in the normal lifestyle of his people (Mark 1:6)	Lived an ascetic existence; prepared their own food
His disciples fasted and recited prayers (Mark 2:18; Luke 11:1)	Fasted; had specific prayers
Was in conflict with Jerusalem authorities (Matthew 3:7–10)	Wanted to create a new temple and religious practices

faith lesson

Time for Reflection

Read the following passages of Scripture and take the next few minutes to reflect on how God would have you bring His light into the world without compromising with an ungodly culture.

> This is the message we have heard from him and declare to you: God is light; in him there is no darkness at all. If we claim to have fellowship with him yet walk in the darkness, we lie and do not live by the truth. But if we walk in the light, as he is in the light, we have fellowship with one another, and the blood of Jesus, his Son, purifies us from all sin.
>
> 1 John 1:5–7

> "You are the light of the world. A city on a hill cannot be hidden. Neither do people light a lamp and put it under a bowl. Instead they put it on its stand, and it gives light to everyone in the house. In the same way, let your light shine before men, that they may see your good deeds and praise your Father in heaven."
>
> Matthew 5:14–16

> The night is nearly over; the day is almost here. So let us put aside the deeds of darkness and put on the armor of light. Let us behave decently, as in the daytime, not in orgies and drunkenness, not in sexual immorality and debauchery, not in dissension and jealousy. Rather, clothe yourselves with the Lord Jesus Christ, and do not think about how to gratify the desires of the sinful nature.
>
> Romans 13:12–14

> Do not be yoked together with unbelievers. For what do righteousness and wickedness have in common? Or what fellowship can light have with darkness? What harmony is there between Christ and Belial? What does a believer have in common with an unbeliever? What agreement is there between the temple of God and idols? For we

PLANNING NOTES:

ꜰᴀɪᴛʜ ʟᴇssᴏɴ

Time for Reflection (4 minutes)

It's time for each of us to think quietly about how we can apply what we've learned today. On pages 86–87 of the Participant's Guide, you'll find several passages of Scripture. Let's each read these passages silently and take the next few minutes to consider some of the questions that follow.

Please do not talk during this time. It's a time when we can reflect on how God would have us bring His light into the world without compromising with an ungodly culture.

> *The Scripture passages and questions are reproduced in their entirety in the Participant's Guide on pages 86-87.*

This is the message we have heard from him and declare to you: God is light; in him there is no darkness at all. If we claim to have fellowship with him yet walk in the darkness, we lie and do not live by the truth. But if we walk in the light, as he is in the light, we have fellowship with one another, and the blood of Jesus, his Son, purifies us from all sin.

1 JOHN 1:5–7

"You are the light of the world. A city on a hill cannot be hidden. Neither do people light a lamp and put it under a bowl. Instead they put it on its stand, and it gives light to everyone in the house. In the same way, let your light shine before men, that they may see your good deeds and praise your Father in heaven."

MATTHEW 5:14–16

The night is nearly over; the day is almost here. So let us put aside the deeds of darkness and put on the armor of light. Let us behave decently, as in the daytime, not in orgies and drunkenness, not in sexual immorality and debauchery, not in dissension and jealousy. Rather, clothe yourselves with the Lord Jesus Christ, and do not think about how to gratify the desires of the sinful nature.

ROMANS 13:12–14

Do not be yoked together with unbelievers. For what do righteousness and wickedness have in common? Or what fellowship can light have with darkness? What harmony is there between Christ and Belial? What does a believer have in common with an unbeliever? What agreement is there between the temple of God and idols? For we are the temple of the living God. As God has said: "I will live with them and walk among them, and I will be their God, and they will be my people."

"Therefore come out from them and be
    separate,
                 says the Lord.

faith Lesson

Time for Reflection

Read the following passages of Scripture and take the next few minutes to reflect on how God would have you bring His light into the world without compromising with an ungodly culture.

This is the message we have heard from him and declare to you: God is light; in him there is no darkness at all. If we claim to have fellowship with him yet walk in the darkness, we lie and do not live by the truth. But if we walk in the light, as he is in the light, we have fellowship with one another, and the blood of Jesus, his Son, purifies us from all sin.

1 JOHN 1:5–7

"You are the light of the world. A city on a hill cannot be hidden. Neither do people light a lamp and put it under a bowl. Instead they put it on its stand, and it gives light to everyone in the house. In the same way, let your light shine before men, that they may see your good deeds and praise your Father in heaven."

MATTHEW 5:14–16

The night is nearly over; the day is almost here. So let us put aside the deeds of darkness and put on the armor of light. Let us behave decently, as in the daytime, not in orgies and drunkenness, not in sexual immorality and debauchery, not in dissension and jealousy. Rather, clothe yourselves with the Lord Jesus Christ, and do not think about how to gratify the desires of the sinful nature.

ROMANS 13:12–14

Do not be yoked together with unbelievers. For what do righteousness and wickedness have in common? Or what fellowship can light have with darkness? What harmony is there between Christ and Belial? What does a believer have in common with an unbeliever? What agreement is there between the temple of God and idols? For we

Touch no unclean thing,
    and I will receive you."
"I will be a Father to you,
    and you will be my sons and daughters,
        says the Lord Almighty."

Since we have these promises, dear friends, let us purify ourselves from everything that contaminates body and spirit, perfecting holiness out of reverence for God.

2 CORINTHIANS 6:14–7:1

1.   Reread the first two passages above and meditate on what it means to you to have fellowship with God and to walk in His light rather than to walk in darkness. Consider also what being the light of the world means to you.

2.   Which modern-day values or practices might be similar to the Hellenistic values the Essenes fled? What must you do to flee these values or practices personally, yet remain in the world as a light that shines forth and reveals God to a sinful world?

3.   Select a portion of one of these passages that encourages you to "put aside the deeds of darkness" and live as a light to the world. Place that passage in a place where you can read it frequently and take it to heart.

Action Points (4 minutes)

The following points are reproduced on pages 88-90 of the Participant's Guide:

Now it's time to wrap up our session.

Give participants a moment to transition from their thoughtfulness to giving you their full attention.

I'd like to take a moment to summarize the key points we explored. After I have reviewed these points, I will give you a moment to jot down an action step (or steps) that you will commit to this week as a result of what you have learned today.

Read the following points and pause afterward so that participants can consider and write out their commitment.

1.   *God's work in history is rarely sudden and dramatic. Rather, God works through the process of history, through the lives of people, to unfold His plan of redemption.* Just as He used the Romans and the Essenes to prepare a culture and a setting in which the life, death, and resurrection of Jesus could be understood and received, He continues to use people to bring about His redemptive plans. So as we seek to understand the culture of first-century Israel where Jesus lived, we will gain a better understanding of His message.

What does God's careful preparation for Jesus' coming reveal about His character? About the relationship He desires to have with you?

are the temple of the living God. As God has said: "I will live with them and walk among them, and I will be their God, and they will be my people."

"Therefore come out from them and be
separate,
says the Lord.
Touch no unclean thing,
and I will receive you."
"I will be a Father to you,
and you will be my sons and daughters,
says the Lord Almighty."

Since we have these promises, dear friends, let us purify ourselves from everything that contaminates body and spirit, perfecting holiness out of reverence for God.

2 Corinthians 6:14–7:1

1. Reread the first two passages above and meditate on what it means to you to have fellowship with God and to walk in His light rather than to walk in darkness. Consider also what being the light of the world means to you.

2. Which modern-day values or practices might be similar to the Hellenistic values the Essenes fled? What must you do to flee these values or practices personally, yet remain in the world as a light that shines forth and reveals God to a sinful world?

3. Select a portion of one of these passages that encourages you to "put aside the deeds of darkness" and live as a light

to the world. Place that passage in a place where you can read it frequently and take it to heart.

Action Points

Take a few minutes to review the key points you explored today, then write down an action step (or steps) that you will commit to this week as a result of what you have learned.

1. *God's work in history is rarely sudden and dramatic. Rather, God works through the process of history, through the lives of people, to unfold His plan of redemption.* Just as He used the Romans and the Essenes to prepare a culture and a setting in which the life, death, and resurrection of Jesus could be understood and received, He continues to use people to bring about His redemptive plans. So as we seek to understand the culture of first-century Israel where Jesus lived, we will gain a better understanding of His message.

   What does God's careful preparation for Jesus' coming reveal about His character? About the relationship He desires to have with you?

   Just as God used people, such as the Essenes, in biblical times to help bring about His plan for redemption, God wants to use you as well. In what ways might He be using you in His redemptive plan—among family members, at work, in your neighborhood?

Just as God used people, such as the Essenes, in biblical times to help bring about His plan for redemption, God wants to use you as well. In what ways might He be using you in His redemptive plan—among family members, at work, in your neighborhood?

2. *The Essenes, who recognized that spiritual light and spiritual darkness cannot coexist, committed themselves to godly values and beliefs and refused to compromise with their culture.* Today, we Christians face the same challenge: to seek to remove the spiritual darkness in our hearts, minds, and lives and to live as children of the light.

What personal compromise(s) do you make with ungodly values or beliefs? If you are willing, write out your commitment to remove that spiritual darkness from your life:

Dear Lord, I realize that if I am to shine as a light for You, I must put aside the darkness of _____. Help me to seek Your holiness, to "put on the armor of light" in every area of my life.

3. *Whereas the Essenes separated from their culture in order to study how to follow God, God has called Christians to carry His truths into the secular world.* Without compromising our holy calling, we are to interact with people who live in spiritual darkness and to confront evil in the world around us. We are to exhibit God's light to a watching, hurting world.

Which challenges do you face as you seek to obey and honor God and at the same time live among people who want little or nothing to do with Him?

Begin to pray specifically that God will encourage and strengthen you so that you can walk in His light and carry out His calling.

Instead of abandoning the secular culture, as the Essenes did, God calls you to take His light to people who live in spiritual darkness. Identify one individual with whom you could share God's light. Which step(s) will you take this week to bring God's light into that dark corner?

closing prayer

I minute

I hope that this lesson has challenged you, as it has me, to remember that God is always unfolding His plans for us individually, and the world as a whole. As we close in prayer, let's renew our determination to make choices that will honor Him and enable us to share God's light with people who live in spiritual darkness.

Dear God, Thank You for the way in which You carefully prepared the setting for Jesus' ministry and the ways in which You demonstrate the same care and concern for us. We want to be committed to You, to share Your light with people who live in spiritual darkness. It's tough living in this world without compromising Your beliefs and values. May we learn to be more faithful in bringing spiritual light into our families, workplaces, and communities. In Your name we pray, Jesus, amen.

2. *The Essenes, who recognized that spiritual light and spiritual darkness cannot coexist, committed themselves to godly values and beliefs and refused to compromise with their culture.* Today, we Christians face the same challenge: to seek to remove the spiritual darkness in our hearts, minds, and lives and to live as children of the light.

What personal compromise(s) do you make with ungodly values or beliefs? If you are willing, write out your commitment to remove that spiritual darkness from your life:

Dear Lord, I realize that if I am to shine as a light for You, I must put aside the darkness of _____. Help me to seek Your holiness, to "put on the armor of light" in every area of my life.

3. *Whereas the Essenes separated from their culture in order to study how to follow God, God has called Christians to carry His truths into the secular world.* Without compromising our holy calling, we are to interact with people who live in spiritual darkness and to confront evil in the world around us. We are to exhibit God's light to a watching, hurting world.

Which challenges do you face as you seek to obey and honor God and at the same time live among people who want little or nothing to do with Him?

Begin to pray specifically that God will encourage and strengthen you so that you can walk in His light and carry out His calling.

Instead of abandoning the secular culture, as the Essenes did, God calls you to take His light to people who live in spiritual darkness. Identify one individual with whom you could share God's light. Which step(s) will you take this week to bring God's light into that dark corner?

DATA FILE

A Brief History of the Essenes

In 332 B.C., Alexander the Great's armies swept through Israel, and his successors continued his campaign to bring Greek culture to every part of the known world. The Hellenistic culture deeply offended and disturbed devout Jews, but most of the Jewish people were soon seduced by this secular worldview that glorified the human being through philosophy, athletics, religion, and the arts.

Initially, Alexander's successors—the Ptolemy family from Egypt—allowed significant religious freedom for the Jews. During their rule, the Old Testament was translated into Greek, the translation we know as the *Septuagint.* Later, the Seleucids—Syria's Greek dynasty—brought Israel into their empire. They aggressively promoted Greek culture and defiled the temple in Jerusalem with pigs' blood and dedicated it to their god, Zeus. They banned the Torah, the Sabbath observance, and circumcision. To violate these bans meant death.

DATA FILE

A Brief History of the Essenes

In 332 B.C., Alexander the Great's armies swept through Israel, and his successors continued his campaign to bring Greek culture to every part of the known world. The Hellenistic culture deeply offended and disturbed devout Jews, but most of the Jewish people were soon seduced by this secular worldview that glorified the human being through philosophy, athletics, religion, and the arts.

Initially, Alexander's successors—the Ptolemy family from Egypt—allowed significant religious freedom for the Jews. During their rule, the Old Testament was translated into Greek, the translation we know as the *Septuagint*. Later, the Seleucids—Syria's Greek dynasty—brought Israel into their empire. They aggressively promoted Greek culture and defiled the temple in Jerusalem with pigs' blood and dedicated it to their god, Zeus. They banned the Torah, the Sabbath observance, and circumcision. To violate these bans meant death.

Faithful Jews, led by the Hasmonaean family (also known as the Maccabees) revolted. Through God's blessing, Judah Maccabee and his brothers drove out the pagans and reestablished Jewish independence for the first time in nearly five hundred years. The temple was cleansed and rededicated, and worship of Yahweh resumed. Their great victory became the focus of the Feast of Dedication, known today as Hanukkah (John 10:22).

The Hasmonaean descendants, however, became thoroughly Hellenistic. They openly flaunted pagan practices and fought bitterly with followers of the Torah. When Jonathan the Hasmonaean, who was a Hellenist and not from the line of Zadok (as required by pious Jews), assumed the office of high priest, that was the final straw. The Hasidim, a pious group of Jewish believers that had strongly supported the Maccabean revolt, openly opposed the descendants of Judah.

Out of the Hasidim came two movements that were very important to events of the New Testament: the Pharisees and the Essenes. Scholars believe that when Jonathan was appointed, the Essenes established a religious movement dedicated to the restoration of the true worship of God. Although Essene communities apparently were scattered throughout Galilee, Judea, and in Jerusalem itself, most Essenes (perhaps four thousand) lived in Qumran.

Believing themselves to be the sons of light preparing for a great battle with the sons of darkness, the Essenes felt they needed to be ready to take their place in God's army. Their mission was to prepare the way for the Lord. So they sought to keep their hearts and minds pure and their practices obedient. Stricter than the Pharisees in observing the Sabbath, the Essenes established many practices that set the stage for Jesus' arrival and teaching. They practiced ritual washing to purify themselves of sin, spent much time studying and carefully copying sacred texts, and practiced obedience to God and justice to humankind. Although they were small in number, they exerted significant influence on the religious community of their day.

In A.D. 68, the Romans destroyed Qumran. It is possible that the Essenes placed their sacred scrolls in jars and hid them in nearby caves as the Romans approached. Although this community has disappeared from history, its legacy is only now being realized.

Faithful Jews, led by the Hasmonaean family (also known as the Maccabees) revolted. Through God's blessing, Judah Maccabee and his brothers drove out the pagans and reestablished Jewish independence for the first time in nearly five hundred years. The temple was cleansed and rededicated, and worship of Yahweh resumed. Their great victory became the focus of the Feast of Dedication, known today as Hanukkah (John 10:22).

The Hasmonaean descendants, however, became thoroughly Hellenistic. They openly flaunted pagan practices and fought bitterly with followers of the Torah. When Jonathan the Hasmonaean, who was a Hellenist and not from the line of Zadok (as required by pious Jews), assumed the office of high priest, that was the final straw. The Hasidim, a pious group of Jewish believers that had strongly supported the Maccabean revolt, openly opposed the descendants of Judah.

Out of the Hasidim came two movements that were very important to events of the New Testament: the Pharisees and the Essenes. Scholars believe that when Jonathan was appointed, the Essenes established a religious movement dedicated to the restoration of the true worship of God. Although Essene communities apparently were scattered throughout Galilee, Judea, and in Jerusalem itself, most Essenes (perhaps four thousand) lived in Qumran.

Believing themselves to be the sons of light preparing for a great battle with the sons of darkness, the Essenes felt they needed to be ready to take their place in God's army. Their mission was to prepare the way for the Lord. So they sought to keep their hearts and minds pure and their practices obedient. Stricter than the Pharisees in observing the Sabbath, the Essenes established many practices that set the stage for Jesus' arrival and teaching. They practiced ritual washing to purify themselves of sin, spent much time studying and carefully copying sacred texts, and practiced obedience to God and justice to humankind. Although they were small in number, they exerted significant influence on the religious community of their day.

In A.D. 68, the Romans destroyed Qumran. It is possible that the Essenes placed their sacred scrolls in jars and hid them in nearby caves as the Romans approached. Although this community has disappeared from history, its legacy is only now being realized.

no greater love

before you lead

Synopsis

This video opens on the beautiful site overlooking the Sea of Galilee known as the "Mount of Beatitudes," where Jesus may have delivered His Sermon on the Mount. Ray Vander Laan reads Matthew's account of that message (Matthew 5:3–12), through which Jesus revealed the heart of what His new kingdom was about and provided insight into the lifestyle of the kingdom of heaven. Then he moves on to the ruins of Korazin, just a few miles north of the Mount of Beatitudes. Here, he describes the lifestyle of Jewish families, a metaphor that Jesus used frequently to describe the kingdom of heaven to His audience.

In ancient Israel, when it was time for a man and woman to marry, both fathers would negotiate the bride price to compensate the bride-to-be's family. After exchanging a glass of wine to seal the agreement, the couple was formally engaged. Then the young man would say to his fiancée, in effect, "I'm going home to my father's house and prepare a place for you. When I've done that, I'll return and take you to be my wife."

The son (typically in his mid-twenties) would then build a new house onto his father's existing one. As generations married and built their houses onto the original one, they created a housing complex called an *insula*. Here, family members ate, worked, and lived together. The children knew their grandparents, aunts, uncles, cousins, nieces, and nephews. Everyone benefited as family members shared their lives and values.

As her fiancé and his father prepared her new home, the bride-to-be (typically fourteen or fifteen years old) would remain at her parents' home, preparing her wedding clothes and learning the skills of homemaking. During this time, she was known in the community as "one who had been bought with a price." She might wait six months, nine months, or even longer for her beloved to return. No one knew the exact time when he would come for her.

When the couple's house was completed, the husband-to-be would gather his friends and family and go to his fiancée's house to announce the wedding and take his bride to their new home. People would gather in the open courtyard of the insula, and the "best man" would stand by the door of the wedding chamber and wait while the couple consummated the marriage. Then he would announce that the wedding had taken place, and a joyous seven-day reception would follow.

These insights help us to understand how wonderful heaven and our eternal relationship with God will be. When Jesus spoke of the kingdom of heaven, He compared Himself to a bridegroom who was engaged to be married. "I love you as My bride," He said, in effect, "so I'll pay the bride price. I'll give up My life for you. I'll go to My Father's house where there are many rooms to prepare a place for you. One day I will return and take you to be with Me forever in heaven."

The metaphor Jesus used is one in which people who have accepted Him as Lord and Savior will be together in one family complex. Heaven will be like a joyous wedding reception, celebrating the love between the bride and the Bridegroom. This metaphor also gives new meaning to Jesus' important teaching about love, community, and support. Only by living in that way could the people of Jesus' day (and ours) be the vibrant, caring, influential community Jesus founded in His bride—the church.

As this video comes to an end, Ray takes viewers back to the Sea of Galilee, back to the small "gospel triangle" of Bethsaida, Korazin, and Capernaum where Jesus conducted most of His healing and teaching ministry. After John the Baptist was imprisoned, Jesus left Nazareth and lived in Capernaum, which was a toll stop on the Via Maris, the trade route of the ancient world. By doing so, He fulfilled the words of Isaiah concerning the land of Zebulun and the land of Naphtali: " . . . in the future he will honor Galilee of the Gentiles, by the way of the sea, along the Jordan—The people walking in darkness have seen a great light; on those living in the land of the shadow of death a light has dawned" (Isaiah 9:1–2).

In this region, which God uniquely prepared for His Son, Jesus interacted with many types of people—devout Jews, pagans, Zealots, the power brokers of the Jewish community, and the ordinary farmers and merchants who simply sought to honor and worship God in the ways they knew best. From Galilee, a crossroads of the ancient world, Jesus' message about the kingdom of heaven spread to all the world.

Key Points of This Lesson

1. *In order to communicate His deep love for us, Jesus described His love in terms of a family community—terms that His audience clearly understood. He compared Himself to a bridegroom who chose a bride (the church); who paid a steep price for her (His life on the cross); who has gone to prepare a place for her in his father's house (heaven); and who will come again to take her home.*

   This metaphor was familiar to the people of Jesus' day because a bridegroom customarily left his fiancée to build a home for her, then returned to get her. Likewise, Jesus will one day return to take His followers to His home in heaven, where we will experience joyous community with Him forever.

2. *Through the Beatitudes, Jesus presented to His audience a picture of the lifestyle of the kingdom of heaven. In effect, the Sermon on the Mount outlined the "battle plan" for His kingdom. It gave His followers a new covenant—a new "Torah"—which, if followed, would change the world.*

Session Outline (53 minutes)

I. Introduction (4 minutes)
Welcome
What's to Come
Questions to Think About

II. Show Video "No Greater Love" (22 minutes)

III. Group Discovery (20 minutes)
Video Highlights
Small Group Bible Discovery

IV. Faith Lesson (6 minutes)
Time for Reflection
Action Points

V. Closing Prayer (1 minute)

Materials

View the video prior to leading the session so you are familiar with its main points. It would be helpful to have a marker board, chalkboard, or overhead projector so that you may record the responses to Questions to Think About.

no Greater Love

introduction

4 minutes

Welcome

> Assemble the participants together. Welcome them to session four of *Faith Lessons on the Life and Ministry of the Messiah.*

What's to Come

In this session, we'll come to understand more about the kingdom of heaven. We'll visit the region where Jesus lived and taught as a first-century Jewish rabbi. We'll visit the ruins of ancient Korazin and understand more fully the wedding imagery Jesus used to communicate God's vast love for humankind. We'll also look at the Beatitudes—God's "battle plan" that outlines the strategy for establishing His kingdom.

Questions to Think About

> *Participant's Guide page 92.*

> Ask each question and solicit a few responses from group members. It would be beneficial to write the responses on a marker board, chalkboard, or overhead projector so that the group may view them during this discussion.

✏ 1.   List some experiences that are common to many people in our culture today.

    Suggested Responses: These might be relational experiences such as marriage and family, educational experiences such as going to school or learning how to ride a bicycle, vocational experiences such as going for a job interview or getting a raise, economic experiences such as using a credit card or writing a check, recreational experiences such as skiing or shooting hoops, etc. Encourage the group to think of a dozen or more.

✏ 2.   How would you use some of these common experiences to explain the gospel message to another person?

    Suggested Responses: Allow several participants to share their ideas with the group. For example, a person might say, "When I accept a check from another person, I have to have enough faith in that person's integrity to believe that there's money in the bank to back up the check. I have enough faith in Jesus' integrity that if He says He has gone to heaven to prepare a place for me, I know that place is there."

SESSION FOUR

No Greater Love

Questions to Think About

1. List some experiences that are common to many people in our culture today.

2. How would you use some of these common experiences to explain the gospel message to another person?

As we view the video, let's note how Jesus described His kingdom in terms of common cultural experiences.

video presentation

ユユ minutes

Participant's Guide page 93.

On page 93 of your Participant's Guide, you will find a space in which to take notes on key points as we watch this video.

Leader's Video Observations

The Sermon on the Mount: God's Battle Plan

The Area of Jesus' Ministry: Korazin

Jewish Marriage Customs

Jesus Comes for His Bride

video notes

The Sermon on the Mount: God's Battle Plan

The Area of Jesus' Ministry: Korazin

Jewish Marriage Customs

Jesus Comes for His Bride

PLANNING NOTES:

Group Discovery
20 minutes

If your group has seven or more members, use the **Video Highlights** with the entire group (five minutes), then break into small groups of three to five to discuss the **Small Group Bible Discovery** (10 minutes). Then reassemble the group to discuss the key points discovered (5 minutes).

If your group has fewer than seven members, begin with the **Video Highlights** (5 minutes), then do one or more of the topics found in the **Small Group Bible Discovery** as a group (10 minutes). Finally, spend five minutes at the end discussing points that had an impact on participants.

Video Highlights (5 minutes)

Here you'll ask one or more of the following questions that directly relate to the video the participants have just seen.

1. Look at the map of Galilee on page 95 of your Participant's Guide, and note the cities and towns of the region in which this video was filmed. Note the proximity of Capernaum and Korazin to the Via Maris, Bethsaida's location near Gamla and the Decapolis, and Tiberias across the Sea of Galilee from the Mount of Beatitudes.

2. What impressed you as you viewed the ruins of Korazin?

    Suggested Responses: will vary but may include the prominence of the tabernacle, that a Moses seat has been found only in this location, that family members lived in such close proximity, that an insula could be such a large complex, how small the individual houses actually were, how few material possessions ordinary people had in comparison to Herod's palaces, etc.

Korazin

94   Faith Lessons on the Life and Ministry of the Messiah

video highlights

1. Look at the map of Galilee on page 95 of your Participant's Guide, and note the cities and towns of the region in which this video was filmed. Note the proximity of Capernaum and Korazin to the Via Maris, Bethsaida's location near Gamla and the Decapolis, and Tiberias across the Sea of Galilee from the Mount of Beatitudes.

2. What impressed you as you viewed the ruins of Korazin?

Korazin

Galilee

3. What did you learn about the lifestyle and marriage customs of families in first-century Israel that enhanced your understanding of God's love for you?

   Suggested Responses: will vary but may include that the husband-to-be would prepare a house for his bride, that the husband-to-be paid a price for his bride, that the bride-to-be didn't know exactly when her fiancé would come for her and had to be always ready, that the engagement was taken so seriously that it could only be broken by divorce, etc.

4. Why should the Beatitudes be so important to Christians today?

   Suggested Responses: They reveal the "kingdom lifestyle"; give us a strategy for influencing people for God; are the criteria by which we can evaluate our words, actions, and thoughts; reveal how we, as believers, can confront evil and truly change our world; etc.

Session Four: No Greater Love

95

Galilee

3. What did you learn about the lifestyle and marriage customs of families in first-century Israel that enhanced your understanding of God's love for you?

4. Why should the Beatitudes be so important to Christians today?

DID YOU KNOW?

Jesus Probably Lived with His Extended Family

People in Galilee often lived in family housing complexes sometimes called *insulae* (singular: *insula*). Although not everyone lived this way, many people—particularly extended families—combined living units around an open courtyard. Jesus and His disciples may have lived in such a family compound in Capernaum. (See Matthew 12:46–13:1, 36; Mark 2:1–2; 7:17.) The insula provides the basis for one of the pictures of heaven (God's housing complex) mentioned in John 14:2.

In many places, the New Testament refers to "household," which means "an extended family living together." Jesus, for example, referred to various households (Matthew 10:24–25, 36). After Jesus healed the official's son, "he and all his household believed" (John 4:53). Peter described how an angel had appeared to a Gentile man and said that he (Peter) would bring a message through which the man and all his household would be saved (Acts 11:11–14). Paul and Silas told the jailer how he and all his household could be saved (Acts 16:29–32). (See also Romans 16:10; Ephesians 2:19; 1 Timothy 3:15.)

An *Insula*

DID YOU KNOW?

Jesus Probably Lived with His Extended Family

People in Galilee often lived in family housing complexes sometimes called *insulae* (singular; *insula*). Although not everyone lived this way, many people—particularly extended families—combined living units around an open courtyard. Jesus and His disciples may have lived in such a family compound in Capernaum. (See Matthew 12:46–13:1, 36; Mark 2:1–2; 7:17.) The insula provides the basis for one of the pictures of heaven (God's housing complex) mentioned in John 14:2.

In many places, the New Testament refers to "household," which means "an extended family living together." Jesus, for example, referred to various households (Matthew 10:24–25, 36). After Jesus healed the official's son, "he and all his household believed" (John 4:53). Peter described how an angel had appeared to a Gentile man and said that he (Peter) would bring a message through which the man and all his household would be saved (Acts 11:11–14). Paul and Silas told the jailer how he and all his household could be saved (Acts 16:29–32). (See also Romans 16:10; Ephesians 2:19; 1 Timothy 3:15.)

An *Insula*

Small Group Bible Discovery (15 minutes)

> *Participant's Guide pages 97–112.*
>
> During this time, a group with fewer than seven participants will stay together. A group with seven or more participants will break into small groups and reassemble as a large group during the final five minutes. Assign each group one of the following topics. If you have more than four small groups, assign some topics to more than one group.

Let's break into groups of three to five—people sitting near you—and study some of the Bible passages and truths mentioned in the video.

Turn to pages 97–112 in your Participant's Guide. There you'll find a list of four topics. You'll have ten minutes to read and discuss the topic I'll assign to you. Choose one person in your group to be a spokesperson for your group when we discuss these topics later.

> Assign each group a topic.

I'll signal you when one minute is left.

Topic A: Jesus' Relationship with His Bride—the Church

Jesus often used the metaphor of the marriage relationship to describe His love for His church.

1. In first-century Israel, a bridegroom's family agreed to pay a bride price (usually a large sum) to compensate the bride's family for the loss of their daughter. What price did Jesus pay for you? (See 1 Corinthians 6:19–20; Galatians 3:13–14; 1 Peter 1:18–19.)

   Suggested Response: Jesus bought us at a great price. He died on the cross to redeem us with His precious blood.

2. An engagement in first-century Israel was as serious as marriage. (Breaking an engagement required a divorce.) After the families agreed on the "bride price," the couple drank a glass of wine together to indicate their life commitment to each other. How does your knowledge of this engagement custom enhance your understanding of Luke 22:20?

   Suggested Responses: Jesus was making a life commitment to His followers—a commitment that would require Him to lay down His life. When we participate in the Lord's Supper, we are affirming our life commitment to Him.

3. After his betrothal, the husband-to-be returned to his father's household and, supervised by his father, prepared a place for his bride by adding on to the family insula. Where is Jesus, our Bridegroom, and what is He doing? (See John 14:1–3.)

   Suggested Responses: Jesus is in heaven, preparing a place for each of His followers in His Father's household of many rooms. He will return and take all believers home with Him, where we will live forever in a joyous community.

small Group Bible Discovery

Topic A: Jesus' Relationship with His Bride—the Church

Jesus often used the metaphor of the marriage relationship to describe His love for His church.

1. In first-century Israel, a bridegroom's family agreed to pay a bride price (usually a large sum) to compensate the bride's family for the loss of their daughter. What price did Jesus pay for you? (See 1 Corinthians 6:19–20; Galatians 3:13–14; 1 Peter 1:18–19.)

2. An engagement in first-century Israel was as serious as marriage. (Breaking an engagement required a divorce.) After the families agreed on the "bride price," the couple drank a glass of wine together to indicate their life commitment to each other. How does your knowledge of this engagement custom enhance your understanding of Luke 22:20?

3. After his betrothal, the husband-to-be returned to his father's household and, supervised by his father, prepared a place for his bride by adding on to the family insula.

PLANNING NOTES:

4. In first-century Israel, the bride-to-be remained at her parents' home, preparing for her wedding and learning how to be a wife and mother. One day, often in the evening, the husband-to-be and his friends and family would arrive at her home and announce their arrival with singing, dancing, shouting, and maybe even by blowing a trumpet. After the couple went to their new home and consummated their wedding, a lengthy celebration followed. How and when will Jesus, our spiritual Bridegroom, announce His arrival? (See Matthew 24:36–39; 1 Thessalonians 4:16–17.)

Building a Typical Galilean Home

Suggested Responses: When His Father says the time is right, Jesus will return from heaven with a "loud command, with the voice of the archangel and with the trumpet call of God," and take His followers to His home in heaven forever.

5. The parable of the ten virgins, recorded in Matthew 25:1–13, portrays the return of the bridegroom and the bride's need to be ready. In light of this parable, why must Christians always be ready for Jesus' return?

Suggested Responses: We do not know when Jesus will return for us, so we must always be prepared and live expectantly, just as the brides-to-be in ancient Israel.

6. In light of the imminent return of Jesus, our spiritual Bridegroom, what should be our motive for godly living? (See 1 Corinthians 6:19–20.)

Suggested Responses: Jesus paid the "bride price" for us, so we belong to Him, not to ourselves. Because we are His, we ought to honor Him with our lives.

7. What does Jesus promise, according to Revelation 19:7–9; 21:2–4?

Suggested Response: Jesus (the Lamb) promises to return for us (His beautiful bride, the church) and begin a wedding celebration in honor of God's eternal dwelling with His people in heaven.

Where is Jesus, our Bridegroom, and what is He doing? (See John 14:1–3.)

4. In first-century Israel, the bride-to-be remained at her parents' home, preparing for her wedding and learning how to be a wife and mother. One day, often in the evening, the husband-to-be and his friends and family would arrive at her home and announce their arrival with singing, dancing, shouting, and maybe even by blowing a trumpet. After the couple went to their new home and consummated their

Building a Typical Galilean Home

wedding, a lengthy celebration followed. How and when will Jesus, our spiritual Bridegroom, announce His arrival? (See Matthew 24:36–39; 1 Thessalonians 4:16–17.)

5. The parable of the ten virgins, recorded in Matthew 25:1–13, portrays the return of the bridegroom and the bride's need to be ready. In light of this parable, why must Christians always be ready for Jesus' return?

6. In light of the imminent return of Jesus, our spiritual Bridegroom, what should be our motive for godly living? (See 1 Corinthians 6:19–20.)

7. What does Jesus promise, according to Revelation 19:7–9; 21:2–4?

DATA FILE

Inside a First-Century Jewish House

In Galilee, the ancient village of Qatzrin has been excavated and reconstructed. Although it was populated centuries after Jesus' time, scholars believe that the buildings and artifacts discovered there represent the practices of the first century. Houses in Korazin, Bethsaida, and Capernaum (where Jesus lived, healed, and taught) were also built in this style with these materials. By learning more about the homes and lives of everyday people in biblical times, we can better picture the living conditions with which Jesus was familiar.

A typical Galilean home was built of basalt (dark volcanic rock) and had either one or two stories. A stonemason (sometimes translated as a "carpenter") used a wooden scaffold as he carefully squared the larger rocks and wedged smaller stones in between to provide stability and strength. Sometimes walls were plastered with mud and straw. The doorframe was built of shaped stones and covered by a wooden door. A courtyard, located between various rooms of a family's housing complex, was paved with stones.

Roofs often were made of wooden beams topped with tree branches and covered with clay. When it rained, the clay absorbed water, sealing the roof. (In Korazin, however, roofs were made of stone slabs instead of branches.) Sometimes people did their work and slept on their roofs, which needed to be repaired every year. (See Matthew 24:17; Mark 13:15; Acts 10:9.)

A Galilean Kitchen

A typical Galilean kitchen contained a domed oven for heating and cooking when the weather was cold. Animal dung, the pulp of pressed olives, and small branches were used as fuel. Common kitchen utensils included hand grinders for making flour, cooking pots, reed or palm-leaf baskets for gathering and storing food, a broom, and stone water jars. Small gardens, vineyards with grapes and olive trees, and some small livestock provided most of the people's food. (See Luke 15:8.)

A Galilean family room, the center of family life, was probably used for eating, storing food, and socializing when the weather was inappropriate for being outdoors in the courtyard. Wealthy people reclined as they ate; poorer people sat on the floor or on benches. Food was served on pottery plates or in pottery bowls. Jewish laws regarding "clean" and "unclean" apparently required that different pottery be used for different types of food (so that meat and dairy did not mix, for example). (See Matthew 23:25; 26:23.)

A Galilean Family Room

Provisions such as grain, wine, and oil were stored in large jars in cool places. (See 1 Kings 17:7–14; 2 Kings 4:1–7.) Other foods were hung from the ceiling. Life for first-century Jews depended upon raising food and protecting it from spoilage, rodents, or insects, so the people needed to store it well. Jesus encouraged people to live by faith in God's provision, and He criticized people who were so obsessed with providing for the future that they hoarded goods. (See Matthew 6:25–26, 31–34; Luke 12:16–26.)

(continued on page 158)

DATA FILE

Inside a First-Century Jewish House

In Galilee, the ancient village of Qatzrin has been excavated and reconstructed. Although it was populated centuries after Jesus' time, scholars believe that the buildings and artifacts discovered there represent the practices of the first century. Houses in Korazin, Bethsaida, and Capernaum (where Jesus lived, healed, and taught) were also built in this style with these materials. By learning more about the homes and lives of everyday people in biblical times, we can better picture the living conditions with which Jesus was familiar.

A typical Galilean home was built of basalt (dark volcanic rock) and had either one or two stories. A stonemason (sometimes translated as a "carpenter") used a wooden scaffold as he carefully squared the larger rocks and wedged smaller stones in between to provide stability and strength. Sometimes walls were plastered with mud and straw. The doorframe was built of shaped stones and covered by a wooden door. A courtyard, located between various rooms of a family's housing complex, was paved with stones.

Roofs often were made of wooden beams topped with tree branches and covered with clay. When it rained, the clay absorbed water, sealing the roof. (In Korazin, however, roofs were made of stone slabs instead of branches.) Sometimes people did their work and slept on their roofs, which needed to be repaired every year. (See Matthew 24:17; Mark 13:15; Acts 10:9.)

A Galilean Kitchen

A typical Galilean kitchen contained a domed oven for heating and cooking when the weather was cold. Animal dung,

the pulp of pressed olives, and small branches were used as fuel. Common kitchen utensils included hand grinders for making flour, cooking pots, reed or palm-leaf baskets for gathering and storing food, a broom, and stone water jars. Small gardens, vineyards with grapes and olive trees, and some small livestock provided most of the people's food. (See Luke 15:8.)

A Galilean family room, the center of family life, was probably used for eating, storing food, and socializing when the weather was inappropriate for being outdoors in the courtyard. Wealthy people reclined as they ate; poorer people sat on the floor or on benches. Food was served on pottery plates or in pottery bowls. Jewish laws regarding "clean" and "unclean" apparently required that different pottery be used for different types of food (so that meat and dairy did not mix, for example). (See Matthew 23:25; 26:23.)

A Galilean Family Room

Provisions such as grain, wine, and oil were stored in large jars in cool places. (See 1 Kings 17:7–14; 2 Kings 4:1–7.) Other foods were hung from the ceiling. Life for first-century Jews depended upon raising food and

(continued on page 102)

(continued from page 156)

Sleeping quarters, sometimes located on the second floor and accessed by ladder, had beds made of wooden frames with rope stretched over them. A mat then was laid on each bed. Sometimes more than one family member slept in the same bed (Luke 11:5–7). Poorer people often slept on mats placed on the floor. People could take their mats with them when they traveled. (See Matthew 9:2–6; Mark 2:3–12.)

Lighting was often provided by small, olive-oil lamps that were supplied from a goatskin oil container. Most people, however, went to bed at sunset and got up at dawn. Honest people didn't work after dark, hence the phrase "works of darkness" was developed. (See Luke 22:53; Romans 13:12; Ephesians 5:11–14.)

A storeroom contained the all-important farming tools and supplies that most families needed in order to provide their own food: wooden plow, sickle, brooms, winnowing fork, a sieve for grain, rope made from plant fibers, an animal skin used as a churn for butter or cheese, etc. (The skin was hung and rocked for a long time in order to provide the churning action.) Typically a wooden plow with an iron point was pulled by a donkey or ox over the small fields in which grain was grown.

At harvesttime, farmers cut the grain with the sickle, then placed the grain on a hard stone surface called a "threshing floor" where it was crushed (threshed) by a small sled dragged by animals. Then the straw and grain mixture was thrown into the air on a windy day. The lighter straw and chaff blew away; the grain fell and was collected. Finally, the sieve separated any chaff that remained. (See Matthew 3:11–12; Mark 4:26–29.)

Provisions

The Sleeping Loft

The Lamp

The Storeroom

(continued from page 101)

Provisions

protecting it from spoilage, rodents, or insects, so the people needed to store it well. Jesus encouraged people to live by faith in God's provision, and He criticized people who were so obsessed with providing for the future that they hoarded goods. (See Matthew 6:25–26, 31–34; Luke 12:16–26.)

Sleeping quarters, sometimes located on the second floor and accessed by ladder, had beds made of wooden frames with rope stretched over them. A mat then was laid on each bed. Sometimes more than one family member slept in the same bed (Luke 11:5–7). Poorer people often slept on mats placed on the floor. People could take their mats with them when they traveled. (See Matthew 9:2–6; Mark 2:3–12.)

Lighting was often provided by small olive-oil lamps that were supplied from a goatskin oil container. Most people, however, went to bed at sunset and got up at dawn.

The Sleeping Loft

Honest people didn't work after dark, hence the phrase "works of darkness" was developed. (See Luke 22:53; Romans 13:12; Ephesians 5:11–14.)

A storeroom contained the all-important farming tools and supplies that most families needed in order to provide

The Lamp

their own food: wooden plow, sickle, brooms, winnowing fork, a sieve for grain, rope made from plant fibers, an animal skin used as a churn for butter or cheese, etc. (The skin was hung and rocked for a long time in order to provide the churning action.) Typically a wooden plow with an iron point was pulled by a donkey or ox over the small fields in which grain was grown.

At harvesttime, farmers cut the grain with the sickle, then placed the grain on a hard stone surface called a "threshing floor" where it was crushed (threshed) by a small sled dragged by animals. Then the straw and grain mixture was thrown into the air on a windy day. The lighter straw and chaff blew away; the grain fell and was collected. Finally, the sieve separated any chaff that remained. (See Matthew 3:11–12; Mark 4:26–29.)

The Storeroom

Topic B: The Diverse Communities in Which Jesus Ministered

Many different types of people—religious and nonreligious, Jews and Gentiles, rich and poor, farmers and merchants—populated the area around the Sea of Galilee. Although certain groups tended to predominate in specific areas, people traveled from one area to another in order to hear Jesus and other rabbis teach. Despite His diverse audience, Jesus always tailored His messages appropriately to the beliefs and practices of people in the areas in which He ministered.

As you study this topic, locate each area on the map of Galilee found on page 95 of your Participant's Guide.

Northwestern Shore of the Sea of Galilee

Home of Orthodox Jews, this area had many synagogues. The Pharisees, who were devoted to keeping God's Torah perfectly, predominated. People there knew the Scriptures and longed for the Messiah to come and relieve them of taxes and their scholars' endless debates.

1. Where was the "headquarters" for Jesus' ministry? (See Matthew 4:13–16.)

    Suggested Response: Capernaum.

2. Where did Jesus perform most of His miracles, and what was the result? (See Matthew 11:20–24.)

    Suggested Responses: Most of His miracles were performed in Korazin, Bethsaida, and Capernaum in Galilee, but even with that testimony, the people did not repent.

Northeastern Corner of the Sea of Galilee

Gamla, which was perched on a mountaintop in this region, was the home of Judah of Gamla, a Pharisee who started the Zealot movement. Although the term *zealot* technically applies to people who belonged to the movement that originated in Gamla, the term is often applied to all rebels who resisted Roman authority.

Synagogue of Gamla

Topic B: The Diverse Communities in Which Jesus Ministered

Many different types of people—religious and nonreligious, Jews and Gentiles, rich and poor, farmers and merchants—populated the area around the Sea of Galilee. Although certain groups tended to predominate in specific areas, people traveled from one area to another in order to hear Jesus and other rabbis teach. Despite His diverse audience, Jesus always tailored His messages appropriately to the beliefs and practices of people in the areas in which He ministered.

As you study this topic, locate each area on the map of Galilee found on page 95 of your Participant's Guide.

The Northwestern Shore of the Sea of Galilee

Home of Orthodox Jews, this area had many synagogues. The Pharisees, who were devoted to keeping God's Torah perfectly, predominated. People there knew the Scriptures and longed for the Messiah to come and relieve them of taxes and their scholars' endless debates.

1. Where was the "headquarters" for Jesus' ministry? (See Matthew 4:13–16.)

2. Where did Jesus perform most of His miracles, and what was the result? (See Matthew 11:20–24.)

Synagogue of Gamla

Northeastern Corner of the Sea of Galilee

Gamla, which was perched on a mountaintop in this region, was the home of Judah of Gamla, a Pharisee who started the Zealot movement. Although the term *zealot* technically applies to people who belonged to the movement that originated in Gamla, the term is often applied to all rebels who resisted Roman authority.

3. Where in this region did Jesus teach and heal? Why? (See Matthew 9:35–36.)

3. Where in this region did Jesus teach and heal? Why? (See Matthew 9:35–36.)

    Suggested Response: Jesus went to all the towns and villages in this region, although there is no record that He went specifically to Gamla. He had great compassion on the people whom Matthew described as being "harassed and helpless, like sheep without a shepherd."

4. As Jesus demonstrated His miraculous power in this area populated by Zealots, what unusual request did He make? Why did He do this? (See Matthew 8:1–4; 9:27–30; John 6:14–15.)

    Suggested Responses: He asked people not to tell others what He had done for them because miraculous power would have been very attractive to the Zealots, who wanted to overthrow the Romans. Also, the Zealots would have most likely misinterpreted Jesus' messianic claim as being that of a political-military deliverer. He knew they wanted to make him king by force.

Eastern Shore of the Sea of Galilee: The Decapolis

The Decapolis was an independent region of city-states established by Alexander the Great. For the most part, the people of this area were pagans who worshiped Greek and Roman gods.

5. Read Mark 5:1–20.

    a. Why did many Jews believe that demons lived in the Decapolis, where the "region of the Gerasenes" was located?

        Suggested Responses: Obviously the man who met the boat was demon possessed. The fact that people there raised pigs—animals the Jews considered to be unclean—also contributed to that belief. [Note: The Romans sacrificed pigs to their gods, which the Jewish people considered to be demonic.]

Susita in the Decapolis

4. As Jesus demonstrated His miraculous power in this area populated by Zealots, what unusual request did He make? Why did He do this? (See Matthew 8:1–4; 9:27–30; John 6:14–15.)

Eastern Shore of the Sea of Galilee: The Decapolis

The Decapolis was an independent region of city-states established by Alexander the Great. For the most part, the people of this area were pagans who worshiped Greek and Roman gods.

5. Read Mark 5:1–20.

a. Why did many Jews believe that demons lived in the Decapolis, where the "region of the Gerasenes" was located?

Susita in the Decapolis

b. What did Jesus tell the healed man to do? Why did His instructions differ from those He had given in the region of Gamla? What was the result?

Suggested Responses: After healing the man, Jesus told him to go and tell other people what God had done. The pagans needed to hear what God had done, and they had no political-military expectations of Jesus. The man obeyed, and people in the Decapolis were "amazed."

Southwestern Shore of the Sea of Galilee
Herod Antipas, who executed John the Baptist, built Tiberias, his capital city, on the southwestern shore of the Sea of Galilee. Tradition holds that religious Jews would not live here during Jesus' time because the city was built over a cemetery. So the city's inhabitants were mostly secular Jews who supported Herod's dynasty, in part because of the economic and political power they enjoyed.

6. After Jesus challenged religious leaders to answer whether it was lawful to heal on the Sabbath, He healed a man's shriveled hand. How did the Pharisees respond? (See Mark 3:1–6.)

Suggested Response: The Pharisees plotted with the Herodians about how to kill Jesus.

DATA FILE

The Way of the Sea
During biblical times, Israel was located at the crossroads of the world, where the trade of the civilized world passed through. Since the Arabian desert was in-between the empires of Egypt and Mesopotamia (Persia, Babylon, Assyria), the only trade route passed through Israel, a narrow land bridge between the Mediterranean Sea and the desert to the east. This busy road, the lifeline of the trade route, was known as the Via Maris, the "Way of the Sea."

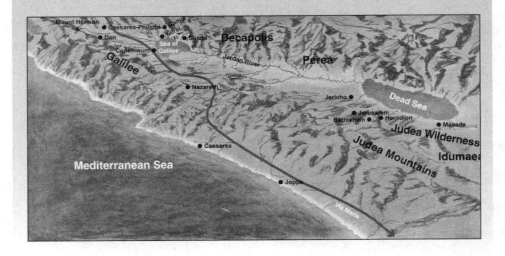

b. What did Jesus tell the healed man to do? Why did His instructions differ from those He had given in the region of Gamla? What was the result?

Southwestern Shore of the Sea of Galilee

Herod Antipas, who executed John the Baptist, built Tiberias, his capital city, on the southwestern shore of the Sea of Galilee. Tradition holds that religious Jews would not live here during Jesus' time because the city was built over a cemetery. So the city's inhabitants were mostly secular Jews who supported Herod's dynasty, in part because of the economic and political power they enjoyed.

6. After Jesus challenged religious leaders to answer whether it was lawful to heal on the Sabbath, He healed a man's shriveled hand. How did the Pharisees respond? (See Mark 3:1–6.)

DATA FILE

The Way of the Sea

During biblical times, Israel was located at the crossroads of the world, where the trade of the civilized world passed through. Since the Arabian desert was in-between the empires of Egypt and Mesopotamia (Persia, Babylon, Assyria), the only trade route passed through Israel, a narrow land bridge between the Mediterranean Sea and the desert to the east. This busy road, the lifeline of the trade route, was known as the Via Maris, the "Way of the Sea."

Topic C: Jesus Presents His Battle Plan

For centuries, the people of Israel had longed for the coming of the Messiah and the establishment of God's kingdom. They had discussed these topics for generations. So when Jesus, the Galilean rabbi, taught that the kingdom of God had arrived, many people listened carefully. Although they longed for the kingdom of God, their idea of what it should be and how they should participate in it differed greatly from what Jesus taught.

So, as He taught in Galilee, Jesus clarified the true meaning of God's kingdom. In fact, we might view the Sermon on the Mount as Jesus' "blueprint" (or battle strategy) for kingdom living. He was willing to become God's sacrifice in order to usher in God's kingdom. What He commanded His followers, His *talmidim*, to do in order to participate

Topic C: Jesus Presents His Battle Plan

For centuries, the people of Israel had longed for the coming of the Messiah and the establishment of God's kingdom. They had discussed these topics for generations. So when Jesus, the Galilean rabbi, taught that the kingdom of God had arrived, many people listened carefully. Although they longed for the kingdom of God, their idea of what it should be and how they should participate in it differed greatly from what Jesus taught.

So, as He taught in Galilee, Jesus clarified the true meaning of God's kingdom. In fact, we might view the Sermon on the Mount as Jesus' "blueprint" (or battle strategy) for kingdom living. He was willing to become God's sacrifice in order to usher in God's kingdom. What He commanded His followers, His *talmidim*, to do in order to participate in His kingdom was no less revolutionary. As we see more clearly how Jesus' presentation of kingdom living came across to the people of His world, we can better understand what it means to obey His call.

1. In Exodus 19:1–3 and 20:1–17, we read how God gave His law to Israel. Compare that event to the Sermon on the Mount, recorded in Matthew 5:1–12.

    Suggested Responses: Moses went up Mount Sinai to receive God's law for the twelve tribes of Israel; Jesus went up a mountainside in Galilee to teach the law of God's kingdom—the new "Torah"—to His twelve disciples.

2. The twelve tribes of Israel received five building blocks: the Old Testament books of Genesis, Exodus, Leviticus, Numbers, and Deuteronomy. Without being too detailed, briefly describe Jesus' five great discourses, which are the building blocks for His followers.

Reference	Brief Description of Discourse
Matthew 5–7	Beatitudes; being salt and light; guilt under the law; do not take oaths, commit adultery, divorce, take revenge, judge others, and worry; how to pray and fast; narrow and wide gates; bear good fruit; build on the right foundation
Matthew 10	Instructions Jesus gave to the Twelve; what commitment to Jesus entails
Matthew 13	Parable of the sower; parable of the weeds; parables of the mustard seed and the yeast; parables of the hidden treasure, the pearl, and the net
Matthew 18	Who is the greatest; parable of the lost sheep; confronting a sinful brother; parable of the unmerciful servant
Matthew 24–25	Signs of the end times; no one knows the exact time Jesus will return; parable of the ten virgins; parable of the eight talents; separating the sheep from the goats; caring for people in need

DATA FILE

The Way of the Sea

During biblical times, Israel was located at the crossroads of the world, where the trade of the civilized world passed through. Since the Arabian desert was in-between the empires of Egypt and Mesopotamia (Persia, Babylon, Assyria), the only trade route passed through Israel, a narrow land bridge between the Mediterranean Sea and the desert to the east. This busy road, the lifeline of the trade route, was known as the Via Maris, the "Way of the Sea."

Topic C: Jesus Presents His Battle Plan

For centuries, the people of Israel had longed for the coming of the Messiah and the establishment of God's kingdom. They had discussed these topics for generations. So when Jesus, the Galilean rabbi, taught that the kingdom of God had arrived, many people listened carefully. Although they longed for the kingdom of God, their idea of what it should be and how they should participate in it differed greatly from what Jesus taught.

So, as He taught in Galilee, Jesus clarified the true meaning of God's kingdom. In fact, we might view the Sermon on the Mount as Jesus' "blueprint" (or battle strategy) for kingdom living. He was willing to become God's sacrifice in order to usher in God's kingdom. What He commanded His followers, His *talmidim*, to do in order to participate

in His kingdom was no less revolutionary. As we see more clearly how Jesus' presentation of kingdom living came across to the people of His world, we can better understand what it means to obey His call.

1. In Exodus 19:1–3 and 20:1–17, we read how God gave His law to Israel. Compare that event to the Sermon on the Mount, recorded in Matthew 5:1–12.

2. The twelve tribes of Israel received five building blocks: the Old Testament books of Genesis, Exodus, Leviticus, Numbers, and Deuteronomy. Without being too detailed, briefly describe Jesus' five great discourses, which are the building blocks for His followers.

Reference	Brief Description of Discourse
Matthew 5–7	
Matthew 10	
Matthew 13	
Matthew 18	
Matthew 24–25	

PLANNING NOTES:

3. Consider how different segments of Jesus' audience would have responded to His unusual battle plan.

a. What do you think the Zealots and the Pharisees may have thought when they heard Jesus speak of what is honored in His kingdom?

Reference	Zealots' Perspective	Pharisees' Perspective
Matthew 5:5	Meek? That will get you nothing! We will have to crush our enemies to inherit the earth.	Meekness is part of what it means to obey the law.
Matthew 5:9	There's no making peace with Rome. We will serve God alone; no one else will master us. We will fight!	We have enough peace to worship our God. When the Messiah comes, He will bring true peace.
Matthew 5:43–47	Love God's enemies? Never! And how dare you compare my actions to those of a tax collector or pagan?	Of course we love God and our neighbors. Perfect obedience to the law includes loving our neighbors, but we don't love our enemies.

b. Read Matthew 6:19–24. How might the Sadducees and Herodians have responded to this message?

Suggested Responses: Jesus' words cut to the heart of their position. They enjoyed the financial benefits and power of serving Rome but wanted to keep the practices of their religion. They wanted to serve both God and money, but Jesus demanded a clear choice.

Topic D: The Burden of Those Who Refused Jesus' Message

Many people near the Sea of Galilee followed Jesus, witnessed His miracles, listened to His words, and became disciples. But others turned away from Him. To those, Jesus gave a strong warning.

1. Read Matthew 11:20–24.

a. What caused Jesus to denounce the cities of Korazin, Bethsaida, and Capernaum?

Suggested Response: Jesus had done most of His miracles there so the people had seen the power of God, yet they did not repent.

b. To which other cities did Jesus compare Korazin and Bethsaida? And Capernaum?

Suggested Response: Jesus compared Korazin and Bethsaida to Tyre and Sidon, and Capernaum to Sodom.

110   Faith Lessons on the Life and Ministry of the Messiah

3. Consider how different segments of Jesus' audience would have responded to His unusual battle plan.

a. What do you think the Zealots and the Pharisees may have thought when they heard Jesus speak of what is honored in His kingdom?

Reference	Zealots' Perspective	Pharisees' Perspective
Matthew 5:5		
Matthew 5:9		
Matthew 5:43–47		

b. Read Matthew 6:19–24. How might the Sadducees and Herodians have responded to this message?

Session Four: No Greater Love   111

Topic D: The Burden of Those Who Refused Jesus' Message

Many people near the Sea of Galilee followed Jesus, witnessed His miracles, listened to His words, and became disciples. But others turned away from Him. To those, Jesus gave a strong warning.

1. Read Matthew 11:20–24.

a. What caused Jesus to denounce the cities of Korazin, Bethsaida, and Capernaum?

b. To which other cities did Jesus compare Korazin and Bethsaida? And Capernaum?

2. What were some of the sins of Tyre and Sidon? (See Amos 1:9–10; 1 Kings 11:33; 16:29–32.)

3. Which sins did the inhabitants of Sodom commit? (See Genesis 19:1–13 and Ezekiel 16:49–50.)

PLANNING NOTES:

📖 **2.** What were some of the sins of Tyre and Sidon? (See Amos 1:9–10; 1 Kings 11:33; 16:29–32.)

Suggested Responses: Amos revealed that Tyre sold Israelite captives to Edom, "disregarding a treaty of brotherhood." Sidon worshiped false gods—Ashtoreth and Baal.

📖 **3.** Which sins did the inhabitants of Sodom commit? (See Genesis 19:1–13 and Ezekiel 16:49–50.)

Suggested Responses: They committed such sins as lust, fornication, homosexuality, ill treatment of foreigners and aliens, anger, arrogance, greed, unconcern for the poor and needy, etc.

📖 **4.** Do people commit the same kinds of sins today? What are some contemporary examples of these sins?

Suggested Responses: Clearly these same sins are common in our world. Some groups of people treat others inhumanely. Many people are unwilling to care for strangers and other needy people. Arrogance is rampant, as people seek to be self-sufficient apart from God. People in some areas are even proud of their acceptance of all kinds of immorality. People worship such false gods as relationships, money, power, fame, material possessions, etc.

📖 **5.** Why was the penalty Jesus pronounced for Korazin, Bethsaida, and Capernaum more severe than that for Tyre, Sidon, and Sodom—who were among the most evil peoples of the Old Testament? (See Matthew 11:21–23.)

Suggested Response: Jesus hadn't taught or healed in Sidon, Tyre, and Sodom, so those people hadn't seen God's power demonstrated through His miracles.

📖 **6.** In light of the above question, can we find people today who have heard all about Jesus but refuse to repent of their sins?

Suggested Response: Many people in developed countries have heard the message of Jesus and turned their backs on it. Many people have grown up attending church or Sunday school, lived in religious homes, and heard quite a bit about Jesus, yet have not chosen to be His disciples. They have, in effect, "seen" most of Jesus' miracles and "heard" much of His teaching, yet have not accepted Him as Lord and Savior.

> After nine minutes, let participants know that they have one minute remaining. Then reassemble the entire group. After everyone is back together, begin asking one person from each small group to briefly share a key idea with the larger group. In some cases, you may not have time for every group to share their discoveries.

As time allows, let's briefly share the key ideas that your group discussed.

Topic D: The Burden of Those Who Refused Jesus' Message

Many people near the Sea of Galilee followed Jesus, witnessed His miracles, listened to His words, and became disciples. But others turned away from Him. To those, Jesus gave a strong warning.

1. Read Matthew 11:20–24.

   a. What caused Jesus to denounce the cities of Korazin, Bethsaida, and Capernaum?

   b. To which other cities did Jesus compare Korazin and Bethsaida? And Capernaum?

2. What were some of the sins of Tyre and Sidon? (See Amos 1:9–10; 1 Kings 11:33; 16:29–32.)

3. Which sins did the inhabitants of Sodom commit? (See Genesis 19:1–13 and Ezekiel 16:49–50.)

4. Do people commit the same kinds of sins today? What are some contemporary examples of these sins?

5. Why was the penalty Jesus pronounced for Korazin, Bethsaida, and Capernaum more severe than that for Tyre, Sidon, and Sodom—who were among the most evil peoples of the Old Testament? (See Matthew 11:21–23.)

6. In light of the above question, can we find people today who have heard all about Jesus but refuse to repent of their sins?

PLANNING NOTES:

ᖴᴀɪᴛʜ ʟᴇꜱꜱᴏɴ

6 minutes   **Time for Reflection (4 minutes)**

It's time for each of us to think quietly about how we can apply what we've learned today. On pages 113–14 of the Participant's Guide, you'll find several Scripture passages. Let's read these silently and take the next few minutes to consider some of the questions that follow.

Please do not talk during this time. It's a time to reflect on how Jesus has chosen to demonstrate His love for us, His bride.

> *The Scripture passages and questions are reproduced in their entirety in the Participant's Guide on pages 113–14.*

. . . You are not your own; you were bought at a price. . . .

1 Corinthians 6:19–20

"Do not let your hearts be troubled. Trust in God; trust also in me. In my Father's house are many rooms; if it were not so, I would have told you. I am going there to prepare a place for you. And if I go and prepare a place for you, I will come back and take you to be with me that you also may be where I am. You know the way to the place where I am going."

John 14:1–4

"Be dressed ready for service and keep your lamps burning, like men waiting for their master to return from a wedding banquet, so that when he comes and knocks they can immediately open the door for him. It will be good for those servants whose master finds them watching when he comes. I tell you the truth, he will dress himself to serve, will have them recline at the table and will come and wait on them. It will be good for those servants whose master finds them ready, even if he comes in the second or third watch of the night. But understand this: If the owner of the house had known at what hour the thief was coming, he would not have let his house be broken into. You also must be ready, because the Son of Man will come at an hour when you do not expect him."

Luke 12:35–40

"No one knows about that day or hour, not even the angels in heaven, nor the Son, but only the Father. . . .

Therefore keep watch, because you do not know on what day your Lord will come."

Matthew 24:36, 42

✏ 1.   What does it mean to you that Jesus presents Himself as your spiritual "husband"—one who has bought you with a price and is even now eagerly preparing an eternal home for you?

faith lesson

Time for Reflection

Read the following Scripture passages and take the next few minutes to reflect on the ways in which Jesus has chosen to demonstrate His love for you, His bride.

> . . . You are not your own; you were bought at a price. . . .
>
> 1 CORINTHIANS 6:19–20

> "Do not let your hearts be troubled. Trust in God; trust also in me. In my Father's house are many rooms; if it were not so, I would have told you. I am going there to prepare a place for you. And if I go and prepare a place for you, I will come back and take you to be with me that you also may be where I am. You know the way to the place where I am going."
>
> JOHN 14:1–4

> "Be dressed ready for service and keep your lamps burning, like men waiting for their master to return from a wedding banquet, so that when he comes and knocks they can immediately open the door for him. It will be good for those servants whose master finds them watching when he comes. I tell you the truth, he will dress himself to serve, will have them recline at the table and will come and wait on them. It will be good for those servants whose master finds them ready, even if he comes in the second or third watch of the night. But understand this: If the owner of the house had known at what hour the thief was coming, he would not have let his house be broken into. You also must be ready, because the Son of Man will come at an hour when you do not expect him."
>
> LUKE 12:35–40

> "No one knows about that day or hour, not even the angels in heaven, nor the Son, but only the Father. . . . Therefore keep watch, because you do not know on what day your Lord will come."
>
> MATTHEW 24:36, 42

1. What does it mean to you that Jesus presents Himself as your spiritual "husband"—one who has bought you with a price and is even now eagerly preparing an eternal home for you?

2. What have you discovered during this session about the depth of Jesus' love for you? In what ways has His love for you as His "bride" been meaningful to you?

3. What is required for you to live every moment as one who is faithfully "engaged" to Jesus and who waits expectantly for Him—your Bridegroom—to return for you?

✏ 2. What have you discovered during this session about the depth of Jesus' love for you? In what ways has His love for you as His "bride" been meaningful to you?

✏ 3. What is required for you to live every moment as one who is faithfully "engaged" to Jesus and who waits expectantly for Him—your Bridegroom—to return for you?

Action Points (2 minutes)

> *The following points are reproduced on pages 115–16 of the Participant's Guide:*

Now it's time to wrap up our session.

> Give participants a moment to transition from their thoughtfulness to giving you their full attention.

I'd like to take a moment to summarize the key points we explored. After I have reviewed these points, I will give you a moment to jot down an action step (or steps) that you will commit to this week as a result of what you have learned today.

> Read the following points and pause afterward so that participants can consider and write out their commitment.

✏ 1. *In order to communicate His deep love for us, Jesus described His love in terms of a family community—terms that His audience clearly understood. He compared Himself to a bridegroom who chose a bride (the church); who paid a steep price for her (His life on the cross); who has gone to prepare a place for her in His Father's house (heaven); and who will come again to take her home.*

This metaphor was familiar to the people of Jesus' day because a bridegroom customarily left his fiancée to build a home for her, then returned to get her. Likewise, Jesus will one day return to take His followers to His home in heaven, where we will experience joyous community with Him forever.

In what way(s) are you, if you are a beloved follower of Jesus the Messiah, preparing for His return?

Which specific things will you do this week to better prepare yourself to be Jesus' bride?

✏ 2. *Through the Beatitudes, Jesus presented to His audience a picture of the lifestyle of the kingdom of heaven. In effect, the Sermon on the Mount outlined the "battle plan" for His kingdom. It gave His followers a new covenant—a new Torah, which, if followed, would change the world.*

Which of the Beatitudes especially helps you understand how a person in Jesus' kingdom should live? Why is it meaningful to you?

Action Points

Take a few moments to review the key points you explored today, then write down an action step (or steps) that you will commit to this week as a result of what you have learned.

1. *In order to communicate His deep love for us, Jesus described His love in terms of a family community—terms that His audience clearly understood. He compared Himself to a bridegroom who chose a bride (the church); who paid a steep price for her (His life on the cross); who has gone to prepare a place for her in His Father's house (heaven); and who will come again to take her home.*

   This metaphor was familiar to the people of Jesus' day because a bridegroom customarily left his fiancée to build a home for her, then returned to get her. Likewise, Jesus will one day return to take His followers to His home in heaven, where we will experience joyous community with Him forever.

   In what way(s) are you, if you are a beloved follower of Jesus the Messiah, preparing for His return?

   Which specific things will you do this week to better prepare yourself to be Jesus' bride?

2. *Through the Beatitudes, Jesus presented to His audience a picture of the lifestyle of the kingdom of heaven. In effect, the Sermon on the Mount outlined the "battle plan" for His kingdom. It gave His followers a new covenant—a new Torah, which, if followed, would change the world.*

   Which of the Beatitudes especially helps you understand how a person in Jesus' kingdom should live? Why is it meaningful to you?

   Select a verse from the Beatitudes to be your "motto verse" during the next several weeks. Read it several times a day.

   How will you seek to live differently in order to carry out that part of the battle plan?

PLANNING NOTES:

Select a verse from the Beatitudes to be your "motto verse" during the next several weeks. Read it several times a day.

How will you seek to live differently in order to carry out that part of the battle plan?

closing prayer

I minute

Let's close in prayer now, thanking God for His love and committing ourselves to live in ways that will honor Him as we await His return.

Dear God, thank You that You sent Your Son, Jesus, to pay the steep bride price necessary to redeem us from sin. You love us so much that You compare Yourself to a loving husband. Please help us to live as if we are engaged to You—to faithfully honor You in what we think, say, and do. Please give us the strength and diligence to expectantly await Jesus' return, just as the brides-to-be of Jesus' day waited for their husbands-to-be. Thank You that You—the living God—listen to and act on our prayers. Amen.

2. *Through the Beatitudes, Jesus presented to His audience a picture of the lifestyle of the kingdom of heaven. In effect, the Sermon on the Mount outlined the "battle plan" for His kingdom. It gave His followers a new covenant—a new Torah, which, if followed, would change the world.*

Which of the Beatitudes especially helps you understand how a person in Jesus' kingdom should live? Why is it meaningful to you?

Select a verse from the Beatitudes to be your "motto verse" during the next several weeks. Read it several times a day.

How will you seek to live differently in order to carry out that part of the battle plan?

PLANNING NOTES:

The Rabbi

Before You Lead

Synopsis

Gamla was an isolated city situated in the mountains northeast of the Sea of Galilee. It was founded in about 150 B.C. by Jews returning to their homeland from Babylon after the Maccabees freed the land from the Seleucid Greeks. The rugged mountain on which the city was built was so steep, even on its more gentle southern slope, that the houses were built on top of one another—the roof of one house was the "front yard" of the house above it. The northern side of the mountain was a sheer cliff.

Like many people who lived north of the Sea of Galilee, the people of Gamla loved God. They built a synagogue as early as 100 B.C, which is one of the earliest ever found. The synagogue functioned as a community center as well as a place to pray, study the Torah, and understand God's will for their lives.

But the people of Gamla were different from many other Jews. They were Zealots—passionate and fiercely independent Jews who were committed to God alone. They viewed violent rebellion against Rome's oppression as a God-ordained responsibility and eagerly awaited a messiah who would exercise political and military might. Jesus, however, offered quite a different freedom. The Zealots rejected the freedom Jesus offered, and He wept for them as He rode into Jerusalem and saw the people wave palm branches in defiance of Rome. He knew how they would suffer because they sought peace in an earthly kingdom rather than the peace of the heavenly kingdom.

That suffering came in the form of the First Jewish Revolt, which began in A.D. 66, years after Jesus' death and resurrection. Because the revolt was led in part by Zealots from Gamla, thirty thousand Roman soldiers surrounded the city to put down the uprising. After the Romans breached the city wall, Gamla's inhabitants and others who had taken refuge there panicked. More than five thousand men, women, and children perished as they jumped or pushed one another over the cliff on the mountain's north side. Then the Romans destroyed Gamla, which remains unsettled to this day.

The synagogue in Gamla provides an opportunity for us to better understand how Jesus participated in His culture, how He ministered as a Jewish rabbi within the Jewish community. Surrounded by the tumultuous political backdrop of pro-Roman Herodians, religious Pharisees, pagans, and fiercely independent Zealots, Jesus used the teaching style of a rabbi to communicate His message to the people of His day. He visited and taught in all the synagogues of Galilee, probably even in Gamla.

Evidence indicates that Jesus also wore the Jewish prayer shawl with its tassels (*tsitsityot*) that reminded Jews of the five books of Moses (their covenant with God) and of the four letters of God's sacred and holy name. According to Jewish tradition, one who touched the *tsitsityot* of the Messiah would be forgiven of sins and healed of diseases. So some Pharisees made their tassels extra long as a way of saying, "Hey, maybe I'm the Messiah. Notice how holy and righteous I am." Jesus criticized them for being hypocrites—actors who pretended to be something they were not—and for believing their human rules to be equal to God's. But as the real Messiah, Jesus did have God's power. That is why it is significant that a woman who had a bleeding disease expressed her faith in Him by reaching out to touch the tassels of His garment. God honored her faith in the Messiah by healing her.

Jesus knew that militaristic rebellion could never bring true freedom to the Jews. So by His lifestyle—by loving and ministering to people whose inner hurts and brokenness led them to commit sinful acts—He encouraged them to use a different method of influencing their culture. His message of restoration, forgiveness, and love still attracts many people, but it repels others.

What will we do? Are we willing to become like Jesus? Will we love our enemies and care about other people more than ourselves? Will we accept His claim to be God's Messiah and also obediently pursue His way of living?

Key Points of This Lesson

1. *Jesus came to earth to minister amidst a cauldron of conflicting ideas and tumultuous politics. Surrounded by a diverse array of belief systems, He assumed the role of a Jewish rabbi and taught a simple message that directed people toward fellowship with God. He also modeled the lifestyle of the kingdom of God and linked people's acceptance of His claim to be the Messiah to their willingness to follow the lifestyle He demonstrated.*

2. *The way Jesus chose to point people toward God was to love them—even those whose inner hurt and brokenness led them to do things that were considered to be unacceptable or immoral.*

   As His followers, we, too, are to point people toward God. Although using the tools of our culture to teach people about God is certainly important, our ultimate focus has to be on the hurts, needs, and cares of people and to minister to them as Jesus did.

Session Outline (53 minutes)

I. Introduction (5 minutes)
Welcome
What's to Come
Questions to Think About

II. Show Video "The Rabbi" (19 minutes)

III. Group Discovery (20 minutes)
Video Highlights
Small Group Bible Discovery

IV. Faith Lesson (8 minutes)

Time for Reflection

Action Points

V. Closing Prayer (1 minute)

Materials

No additional materials are needed for this session. Simply view the video prior to leading the session so you are familiar with its main points.

the rabbi

introduction

5 minutes

Welcome

Assemble the participants together. Welcome them to session five of *Faith Lessons on the Life and Ministry of the Messiah.*

What's to Come

This session takes us to Gamla, home of the Zealot movement. In the setting of Gamla's synagogue, one of the earliest ever built, we will gain a better understanding of Jesus' ministry as a first-century rabbi. We will also learn more about the diverse and tumultuous culture of His time—the God-fearing Zealots, the Rome-honoring Herodians, the pagans, the law-abiding Pharisees, and the powerful Sadducees. We will see how Jesus carried the message of God's kingdom and expressed His love for the hurting, needy people of His world.

Questions to Think About

Participant's Guide page 117.

Ask each question and solicit a few responses from group members.

1. What risks does a deeply committed person take?

   Suggested Responses: Encourage participants to consider the risks of commitment, which may include making choices that may have unpleasant consequences, sacrificing his or her needs for the benefit of others, offending others, being misunderstood, suffering for one's beliefs, etc.

2. When a committed person crosses the line and becomes "fanatical" about something, what additional risks does he or she face?

   Suggested Responses: Encourage participants to explore the differences between commitment and fanaticism. A fanatic may be more inclined to lose perspective, make poor decisions, alienate potential allies, create ultimatums, sacrifice unnecessarily, etc.

3. What do you think attracts people to Jesus? What causes people to reject Jesus?

SESSION FIVE

The Rabbi

Questions to Think About

1. What risks does a deeply committed person take?

2. When a committed person crosses the line and becomes "fanatical" about something, what additional risks does he or she face?

3. What do you think attracts people to Jesus? What causes people to reject Jesus?

PLANNING NOTES:

Suggested Responses: Encourage participants to consider who Jesus is and how different groups of people perceive Him. Sometimes the same things cause some people to accept Him and some to reject Him. Specific examples may include His love, mercy, and compassion; His understanding of us and our life on earth because He lived here also; the simplicity of His message; His claim to be the Son of God; His simple but specific requirement for salvation; etc.

Let's keep these thoughts in mind as we view the video.

video presentation
19 minutes

Participant's Guide page 118.

On page 118 of your Participant's Guide, you will find a space in which to take notes on key points as we watch this video.

Leader's Video Observations

Gamla—Home of the Zealot Movement

The Synagogue—Center of Jewish Community and Religious Life

Jesus the Rabbi

The Rabbi

questions to think about

1. What risks does a deeply committed person take?

2. When a committed person crosses the line and becomes "fanatical" about something, what additional risks does he or she face?

3. What do you think attracts people to Jesus? What causes people to reject Jesus?

---

video notes

Gamla—Home of the Zealot Movement

The Synagogue—Center of Jewish Community and Religious Life

Jesus the Rabbi

PLANNING NOTES:

Group Discovery

20 minutes

If your group has seven or more members, use the **Video Highlights** with the entire group (5 minutes), then break into small groups of three to five to discuss the **Small Group Bible Discovery** (10 minutes). Then reassemble the group to discuss the key points discovered (5 minutes).

If your group has fewer than seven members, begin with the **Video Highlights** (5 minutes), then do one or more of the topics found in the **Small Group Bible Discovery** as a group (10 minutes). Finally, spend five minutes at the end discussing points that had an impact on participants.

Video Highlights (5 minutes)

Here you'll ask one or more of the following questions that directly relate to the video the participants have just seen.

Look at the map on page 119 of your Participant's Guide and locate Gamla. Note its proximity to the Sea of Galilee and the towns of Bethsaida, Capernaum, and Korazin, where Jesus conducted much of His ministry.

1. What about Gamla surprised you?

Suggested Responses: will vary and may include its isolation, that people built a city in such a steep place, the great tragedy that took place in such a peaceful setting, the small breach in the wall that opened the way to Gamla's defeat, that Jesus may have taught there, etc.

Galilee

video highlights

Look at the map below and locate Gamla. Note its proximity to the Sea of Galilee and the towns of Bethsaida, Capernaum, and Korazin, where Jesus conducted much of His ministry.

1. What about Gamla surprised you?

2. Who were the Zealots, and what happened to them?

Galilee

Synagogue of Gamla

📖 2.   Who were the Zealots, and what happened to them?

Suggested Responses: They were a movement of devout Jews who believed that a political-military messiah would come to liberate them from Roman oppression. They were passionate about serving God and God only. They were willing to die to obtain their freedom. They were completely destroyed by the Romans during the First Jewish Revolt.

📖 3.   What new information did you learn about the Jewish synagogue?

Suggested Responses: may include how long ago synagogues were built; that they were initially used as community centers; that male community members, not trained pastors, read the Torah and gave short "sermons" about walking with God; that synagogues were open to women; that worship in the early Christian church was so similar to that in the synagogues; etc.

📖 4.   In what ways was Jesus' role as a rabbi important to God's plan of redemption?

Suggested Responses: will vary and may include that a rabbi typically taught about the kingdom of God; that because Jesus was a rabbi, disciples would gather around Him to learn from Him; that rabbis typically traveled to different towns and synagogues to teach; etc. Because He was a rabbi, Jesus spread His message during His lifetime, and His disciples carried it on following His death and resurrection.

Session Five: The Rabbi 119

video highlights

Look at the map below and locate Gamla. Note its proximity to the Sea of Galilee and the towns of Bethsaida, Capernaum, and Korazin, where Jesus conducted much of His ministry.

1. What about Gamla surprised you?

2. Who were the Zealots, and what happened to them?

Galilee

120 Faith Lessons on the Life and Ministry of the Messiah

Synagogue of Gamla

3. What new information did you learn about the Jewish synagogue?

4. In what ways was Jesus' role as a rabbi important to God's plan of redemption?

Small Group Bible Discovery (15 minutes)

> *Participant's Guide pages 121–35.*
>
> During this time, a group with fewer than seven participants will stay together. A group with seven or more participants will break into small groups and reassemble as a large group during the final five minutes. Assign each group one of the following topics. If you have more than five small groups, assign some topics to more than one group.

Let's break into groups of three to five—people sitting near you—and study some of the Bible passages and truths mentioned in the video.

Turn to pages 121–35 in your Participant's Guide. There you'll find a list of five topics. You'll have ten minutes to read and discuss the topic I'll assign to you. Choose one person in your group to be a spokesperson for your group when we discuss these topics later.

> Assign each group a topic.

I'll signal you when one minute is left.

Topic A: The Lifestyle of a First-Century Rabbi

Jesus' role as a first-century Jewish rabbi provided the perfect setting in which to proclaim His message. Let's look at the lifestyle and teaching practices of typical rabbis who lived during Jesus' time.

✏ 1. What did many of the people who encountered Jesus consider Him to be? (See Luke 7:40; 12:13; 19:39.)

Suggested Response: a teacher (meaning rabbi). [Note: Popular rabbis during Jesus' time selected students called *talmidim,* who followed their rabbis in order to learn their interpretations of the Torah and to model their obedience to God's law.]

✏ 2. What do the following verses reveal about rabbis who lived during Jesus' day?

Scripture Source	The Rabbi's Life
Luke 8:1–3	Depended on the hospitality and financial support of other people
Matthew 26:55; Mark 6:6; Luke 4:14–16; 7:36, 40–47	Taught in synagogues, outdoors, in homes, and even the temple courts; sometimes traveled from village to village
Matthew 13:1–3	Sometimes taught through parables
Matthew 11:29–30	Encouraged their followers to take on the "yoke of Torah," which was obedience to the Torah as their rabbis interpreted it
Matthew 10:1–4; 17:24; 20:29; Luke 5:27–28	Chose disciples who would accompany them and learn to be like them
Luke 19:37; 23:49	Often had many disciples who followed them; Jesus also had women followers, which was unusual

small Group Bible Discovery

Topic A: The Lifestyle of a First-Century Rabbi

Jesus' role as a first-century Jewish rabbi provided the perfect setting in which to proclaim His message. Let's look at the lifestyle and teaching practices of typical rabbis who lived during Jesus' time.

1. What did many of the people who encountered Jesus consider Him to be? (See Luke 7:40; 12:13; 19:39.)

2. What do the following verses reveal about rabbis who lived during Jesus' day?

Scripture Source	The Rabbi's Life
Luke 8:1–3	
Matthew 26:55; Mark 6:6; Luke 4:14–16; 7:36, 40–47	
Matthew 13:1–3	
Matthew 11:29–30	
Matthew 10:1–4; 17:24; 20:29; Luke 5:27–28	
Luke 19:37; 23:49	

✏ 3. Each rabbi or teacher taught his disciples how the Torah should be obeyed. The system of obedience to the Torah was called the "yoke of Torah." Read Matthew 11:28–30 and answer the following questions:

a. What was unique about Jesus' "yoke"—His way of obedience to God?

Suggested Responses: Jesus' yoke was easy and simple to understand, and it provided genuine rest for people's souls. In contrast, some rabbis and Pharisees taught a yoke that was very complicated.

b. Why was it meaningful for Jesus to describe His message in this way?

Suggested Response: It was a concept that people of His day clearly understood.

c. How do you think Jesus' audience—common people, religious leaders, rabbis—reacted to this teaching?

Suggested Responses: The common people probably responded enthusiastically, while the religious leaders (who were often proud of their spirituality) may have ridiculed or become angry at the idea of an easy yoke presented by a gentle and humble rabbi.

THE TRUTH OF THE MATTER

To Be Called a "Rabbi"
In first-century Israel, the title *rabbi* meant "master" or "teacher." It was a term of respect or a description of activity. The position of "rabbi" didn't become an official office until after Jesus' time. Many diverse people believed Jesus to be a rabbi:
- A rich young ruler (Matthew 19:16–22).
- Pharisees who were experts in the law (Matthew 22:34–36).
- An unnamed man in the crowd (Luke 12:13).
- Sadducees (Luke 20:27–33).

Topic B: The Message of Jesus, the Rabbi

✏ 1. What was the basic theme of Jesus' message? (See Matthew 4:17.)

Suggested Response: to repent, because the kingdom of heaven was near.

✏ 2. Capernaum, a small village in which Jesus conducted some of His ministry, was located on the northern shore of the Sea of Galilee by the Via Maris, the crossroads of ancient civilization (see map on page 119 of your Participant's Guide). Why do you think Jesus chose Capernaum to be the hub of His ministry—His "hometown"? (See Isaiah 9:1–2; Matthew 4:12–17.)

Suggested Responses: God wanted His people to live in such a way that all the world would see them and know that He was God. Jesus not only fulfilled Isaiah's prophecy by choosing Capernaum as the hub for His ministry, He also placed Himself next to the most heavily traveled road of the ancient world—the Via Maris—the "Way of the Sea." By choosing Capernaum, He demonstrated God's kingdom to all the world.

3. Each rabbi or teacher taught his disciples how the Torah should be obeyed. The system of obedience to the Torah was called the "yoke of Torah." Read Matthew 11:28–30 and answer the following questions:

   a. What was unique about Jesus' "yoke"—His way of obedience to God?

   b. Why was it meaningful for Jesus to describe His message in this way?

   c. How do you think Jesus' audience—common people, religious leaders, rabbis—reacted to this teaching?

THE TRUTH OF THE MATTER

To Be Called a "Rabbi"

In first-century Israel, the title *rabbi* meant "master" or "teacher." It was a term of respect or a description of activity. The position of "rabbi" didn't become an official office until after Jesus' time. Many diverse people believed Jesus to be a rabbi:

- A rich young ruler (Matthew 19:16–22).
- Pharisees who were experts in the law (Matthew 22:34–36).
- An unnamed man in the crowd (Luke 12:13).
- Sadducees (Luke 20:27–33).

Topic B: The Message of Jesus, the Rabbi

1. What was the basic theme of Jesus' message? (See Matthew 4:17.)

2. Capernaum, a small village in which Jesus conducted some of His ministry, was located on the northern shore of the Sea of Galilee by the Via Maris, the crossroads of ancient civilization (see map on page 119). Why do you think Jesus chose Capernaum to be the hub of His ministry—His "hometown"? (See Isaiah 9:1–2; Matthew 4:12–17.)

3. For what did Jesus strongly condemn teachers of the law and Pharisees? (See Matthew 23:1–7.)

4. In contrast to the way a true disciple of Jesus would respond to His teaching, how did the inhabitants of

✏ 3. For what did Jesus strongly condemn teachers of the law and Pharisees? (See Matthew 23:1–7.)

Suggested Responses: They did not practice what they preached. They burdened people with rules. They did everything to draw attention to themselves and to be honored for their piety.

✏ 4. In contrast to the way a true disciple of Jesus would respond to His teaching, how did the inhabitants of Korazin and Bethsaida respond? (See Matthew 11:20–22.) In what way is this message important for people today?

Suggested Responses: Even after seeing Jesus' miracles and hearing His teaching, which ought to have brought them to their knees before God, the people didn't repent of their sins. Many people are like this today. They have heard the gospel message, have the evidence of God's work in history, and have seen evidence of God's blessing, yet still choose spiritual darkness.

✏ 5. Describe the astounding event that occurred one Sabbath in Nazareth when it was time for Jesus, the next scheduled reader, to read His assigned portion from the prophets. (See Luke 4:14–21.)

Suggested Responses: Jesus stood up in the synagogue and read His assigned portion of Scripture, which was from Isaiah. The portion was, in fact, about Jesus and explained His purpose. So He told the people that the verses He had just read had been fulfilled in their hearing. God even arranged the timing of that reading to fit Jesus' arrival in Nazareth!

DATA FILE

What Is a Disciple?

The Hebrew word for *disciple* is *talmid* (plural, *talmidim*). This word stresses the relationship between rabbi (teacher or master) and disciple (student). A *talmid* of Jesus' day would give up his entire life in order to be with his teacher. The disciple didn't only seek to know what the teacher knew, as is usually the case in our educational practice today. It was not enough just to *know* what the rabbi said. Rather, the foremost goal of any *talmid* was to become *like* the rabbi and do what the rabbi did (Luke 6:40). The Pharisees, for example, knew and taught the truth (according to Matthew 23:1–4), but many of them were not Jesus' disciples because they did not obey God's teaching.

Jesus' disciples became like Him in various ways. For example, they performed miracles, loved their enemies, and were persecuted and killed for their faith. Today, Jesus calls us to be His disciples—to know His message, to share it with others, and to model our lives after His. (See Matthew 28:19–20; John 8:31; 13:34–35.)

Topic B: The Message of Jesus, the Rabbi

1. What was the basic theme of Jesus' message? (See Matthew 4:17.)

2. Capernaum, a small village in which Jesus conducted some of His ministry, was located on the northern shore of the Sea of Galilee by the Via Maris, the crossroads of ancient civilization (see map on page 119). Why do you think Jesus chose Capernaum to be the hub of His ministry— His "hometown"? (See Isaiah 9:1–2; Matthew 4:12–17.)

3. For what did Jesus strongly condemn teachers of the law and Pharisees? (See Matthew 23:1–7.)

4. In contrast to the way a true disciple of Jesus would respond to His teaching, how did the inhabitants of

Korazin and Bethsaida respond? (See Matthew 11:20–22.) In what way is this message important for people today?

5. Describe the astounding event that occurred one Sabbath in Nazareth when it was time for Jesus, the next scheduled reader, to read His assigned portion from the prophets. (See Luke 4:14–21.)

DATA FILE

What Is a Disciple?

The Hebrew word for *disciple* is *talmid* (plural: *talmidim*). This word stresses the relationship between rabbi (teacher or master) and disciple (student). A *talmid* of Jesus' day would give up his entire life in order to be with his teacher. The disciple didn't only seek to know what the teacher knew, as is usually the case in our educational practice today. It was not enough just to *know* what the rabbi said. Rather, the foremost goal of any *talmid* was to become *like* the rabbi and do what the rabbi did (Luke 6:40). The Pharisees, for example, knew and taught the truth (according to Matthew 23:1–4), but many of them were not Jesus' disciples because they did not obey God's teaching.

Jesus' disciples became like Him in various ways. For example, they performed miracles, loved their enemies, and were persecuted and killed for their faith. Today, Jesus calls us to be His disciples—to know His message, to share it with others, and to model our lives after His. (See Matthew 28:19–20; John 8:31; 13:34–35.)

✏ 6.   Why did rabbis of Jesus' day wear the Jewish prayer shawl with tassels on it? (See Numbers 15:37–41.)

Suggested Responses: as a reminder of their covenant with God revealed in the five books of Moses—Genesis, Exodus, Leviticus, Numbers, and Deuteronomy, and of God's sacred and holy name. Its purpose was to remind them to obey God's laws.

✏ 7.   According to Jewish tradition, what was unique about the prayer shawl of the Messiah? (See Zechariah 8:23; Malachi 4:2; Mark 5:24–34.)

Suggested Responses: The Jews believed that God would be with the Messiah and because of that the Messiah would have the power to forgive and to heal, a power that was represented by the tassels. Thus the woman who touched the hem (tassel) of Jesus' garment was taking a step of faith, making a declaration that Jesus was the Messiah, and she was healed. Jesus commended her because of her faith in who He was.

DID YOU KNOW?

Understanding a Great Miracle

During Jesus' time, Jewish men wore two garments: a light tunic and a heavy mantle worn over the tunic (*tallit* in Hebrew). Attached to the corners of the *tallit* were the tassels (*tsitsityot*) that God had commanded the Israelites to wear (Numbers 15:37–41; Deuteronomy 22:12). The tassels reminded people of their obligations to God to keep all of His commandments, were intended to direct other people to God when the Messiah came, and reminded people that God was with His people. (The hem also communicated the wearer's status or rank.) One of the threads on each tassel had to be blue, a reminder that the Israelites were royalty because they were a "kingdom of priests."

According to Jewish tradition, the Messiah would have "healing" in His "wings" as represented by the tassels (Malachi 4:2). This tradition helps us understand the story of the diseased woman who reached out to grasp the hem—the tassel—of Jesus' mantle (Matthew 9:20–22; Luke 8:40–48). Her action was a demonstration of genuine faith (Mark 5:34). By grasping the tassel of Jesus' garment, she was affirming the prophet Zechariah's message that God was with Him (Zechariah 8:23) and that He was truly the Messiah.

In this case, as in others recorded in Scripture, faith was essential to God's willingness to work His power (Matthew 9:29–30; Mark 10:52; Matthew 13:58). By grasping Jesus' hem, the ailing, "unclean" (Numbers 5:1–2), and nameless woman demonstrated faith in who Jesus was and what He could do for her. God in turn released His healing power and performed a miracle.

6. Why did rabbis of Jesus' day wear the Jewish prayer shawl with tassels on it? (See Numbers 15:37–41.)

DID YOU KNOW?

Understanding a Great Miracle

During Jesus' time, Jewish men wore two garments: a light tunic and a heavy mantle worn over the tunic (*tallit* in Hebrew). Attached to the corners of the *tallit* were the tassels (*tsitsityot*) that God had commanded the Israelites to wear (Numbers 15:37–41; Deuteronomy 22:12). The tassels reminded people of their obligations to God to keep all of His commandments, were intended to direct other people to God when the Messiah came, and reminded people that God was with His people. (The hem also communicated the wearer's status or rank.) One of the threads on each tassel had to be blue, a reminder that the Israelites were royalty because they were a "kingdom of priests."

According to Jewish tradition, the Messiah would have "healing" in His "wings" as represented by the tassels (Malachi 4:2). This tradition helps us understand the story of the diseased woman who reached out to grasp the hem—the tassel—of Jesus' mantle (Matthew 9:20–22; Luke 8:40–48). Her action was a demonstration of genuine faith (Mark 5:34). By grasping the tassel of Jesus' garment, she was affirming the prophet Zechariah's message that God was with Him (Zechariah 8:23) and that He was truly the Messiah.

In this case, as in others recorded in Scripture, faith was essential to God's willingness to work His power (Matthew 9:29–30; Mark 10:52; Matthew 13:58). By grasping Jesus' hem, the ailing, "unclean" (Numbers 5:1–2), and nameless woman demonstrated faith in who Jesus was and what He could do for her. God in turn released His healing power and performed a miracle.

---

7. According to Jewish tradition, what was unique about the prayer shawl of the Messiah? (See Zechariah 8:23; Malachi 4:2; Mark 5:24–34.)

Topic C: The Zealots: No One But God

Jesus knew Zealots, addressed issues in which they were passionately interested, and shared their total commitment to serving God. Yet, His message about God's kingdom stood in stark contrast to their message, which advocated a violent overthrow of Roman oppression.

1. What did the devil tempt Jesus to do regarding God's kingdom? What was Jesus' commitment? (See Matthew 4:8–10.)

2. Consider how a Zealot might have received the following teachings of Jesus:

   a. Matthew 5:5

   b. Matthew 5:7

   c. Matthew 5:9

Topic C: The Zealots: No One But God

Jesus knew Zealots, addressed issues in which they were passionately interested, and shared their total commitment to serving God. Yet, His message about God's kingdom stood in stark contrast to their message, which advocated a violent overthrow of Roman oppression.

1. What did the devil tempt Jesus to do regarding God's kingdom? What was Jesus' commitment? (See Matthew 4:8–10.)

   Suggested Responses: Satan wanted Jesus to reject God's kingdom and accept in its place the glory and splendor of earthly kingdoms. Jesus, however, was committed totally to serving only God and His kingdom.

2. Consider how a Zealot might have received the following teachings of Jesus:

   a. Matthew 5:5

   Suggested Responses: laughed, ridiculed, demanded to know when the meek had ever inherited anything, wondered how this saying could ever be, etc.

   b. Matthew 5:7

   Suggested Responses: mocked the thought of mercy being returned in kind, considered Jesus to be naive, wondered what Jesus was talking about, etc.

   c. Matthew 5:9

   Suggested Responses: criticized Jesus for being naive; pointed out that violence was more effective than peacemaking; cited examples of how the Romans had persecuted peacemakers in the past; because they thought of themselves as the sons of God, they may have wondered what peacemaking had to do with being a son of God; etc.

   d. Matthew 5:38–42

   Suggested Responses: Resisting the evil of Rome was what the Zealots were all about, and these teachings are in direct opposition to everything the Zealots stood for and did. The Zealots probably could not even comprehend this teaching and perhaps would have responded in anger or thought that Jesus was just plain crazy.

   e. Matthew 5:43–48

   Suggested Responses: would have scoffed at the thought of loving the cruel Romans and praying for them, probably squirmed at the thought of loving enemies as a requirement to be sons of God, become angry because Jesus said even the tax collectors and pagans (whom the Zealots looked down on) loved those who loved them, might have had to reconsider their standards of perfection in God's eyes because of what Jesus said, etc.

3. Why was paying taxes to Caesar an issue for the pro-Roman Herodians and the Jewish Zealots? How did Jesus answer the loaded question He was asked? How did it satisfy, or not satisfy, both groups? (See Matthew 22:15–22; Mark 12:13–17.)

7. According to Jewish tradition, what was unique about the prayer shawl of the Messiah? (See Zechariah 8:23; Malachi 4:2; Mark 5:24–34.)

Topic C: The Zealots: No One But God

Jesus knew Zealots, addressed issues in which they were passionately interested, and shared their total commitment to serving God. Yet, His message about God's kingdom stood in stark contrast to their message, which advocated a violent overthrow of Roman oppression.

1. What did the devil tempt Jesus to do regarding God's kingdom? What was Jesus' commitment? (See Matthew 4:8–10.)

2. Consider how a Zealot might have received the following teachings of Jesus:

   a. Matthew 5:5

   b. Matthew 5:7

   c. Matthew 5:9

   d. Matthew 5:38–42

   e. Matthew 5:43–48

3. Why was paying taxes to Caesar an issue for the pro-Roman Herodians and the Jewish Zealots? How did Jesus answer the loaded question He was asked? How did it satisfy, or not satisfy, both groups? (See Matthew 22:15–22; Mark 12:13–17.)

4. As Jesus demonstrated His miraculous power, what unusual instructions did He give? What was He trying to avoid? (See Matthew 8:3–4; 9:29–30; Mark 1:40–44; Luke 8:51–56; John 6:14–15.)

DID YOU KNOW?

One of the men Jesus chose to be one of His disciples was Simon the Zealot (Mark 3:13–19). We do not know whether Simon gave up his support for Zealot tactics after joining Jesus, but the disciples' tendency to see the kingdom of God as a political entity may indicate Zealot influence. Some scholars believe that the reference to Simon as a "Zealot" meant that he was zealous. That perspective, although possible, is unlikely.

PLANNING NOTES:

Suggested Response: The Jewish people as a whole resented Roman rule and the taxes they were forced to pay. The Herodians supported paying taxes because they wanted to maintain the status quo and keep the power Rome had given them. The Zealots refused to pay taxes to anyone but God. So the question the Pharisees asked Jesus got right to the heart of the conflict between these groups. Jesus' answer amazed the people. The Herodians wouldn't have found fault with it. Although the Zealots couldn't argue against it in principle, it challenged their custom of not paying taxes.

4. As Jesus demonstrated His miraculous power, what unusual instructions did He give? What was He trying to avoid? (See Matthew 8:3–4; 9:29–30; Mark 1:40–44; Luke 8:51–56; John 6:14–15.)

Suggested Responses: He told people not to tell others that they had been healed. Miraculous demonstrations of power would have been very attractive to the Zealots, who were awaiting a Messiah who would oust the Roman rulers and establish His political kingdom in Israel. Because of His miraculous feeding of the five thousand, they had already tried to make him king by force, but He eluded them.

5. The word used to describe Barabbas in Luke 23:13–25 is the same word used to mean *Zealot*. What was the irony in Pilate's decision regarding Jesus?

Suggested Responses: Pilate found Jesus to be innocent of inciting rebellion, but according to the people's demands, he exchanged Jesus' life for the life of Barabbas—a condemned murderer and known insurrectionist (Zealot). [Note: No doubt the Sadducees (key religious rulers) and the Herodians, who generally were pro-Roman, didn't want Barabbas released.] The irony was that Jesus, in opposition to the Zealots, had resisted all attempts to make Him an earthly king. Instead, He had taught a message of love and self-sacrifice.

DID YOU KNOW?

One of the men Jesus chose to be one of His disciples was Simon the Zealot (Mark 3:13–19). We do not know whether Simon gave up his support for Zealot tactics after joining Jesus, but the disciples' tendency to see the kingdom of God as a political entity may indicate Zealot influence. Some scholars believe that the reference to Simon as a "Zealot" meant that he was zealous. That perspective, although possible, is unlikely.

    d. Matthew 5:38–42

    e. Matthew 5:43–48

3. Why was paying taxes to Caesar an issue for the pro-Roman Herodians and the Jewish Zealots? How did Jesus answer the loaded question He was asked? How did it satisfy, or not satisfy, both groups? (See Matthew 22:15–22; Mark 12:13–17.)

4. As Jesus demonstrated His miraculous power, what unusual instructions did He give? What was He trying to avoid? (See Matthew 8:3–4; 9:29–30; Mark 1:40–44; Luke 8:51–56; John 6:14–15.)

DID YOU KNOW?

One of the men Jesus chose to be one of His disciples was Simon the Zealot (Mark 3:13–19). We do not know whether Simon gave up his support for Zealot tactics after joining Jesus, but the disciples' tendency to see the kingdom of God as a political entity may indicate Zealot influence. Some scholars believe that the reference to Simon as a "Zealot" meant that he was zealous. That perspective, although possible, is unlikely.

5. The word used to describe Barabbas in Luke 23:13–25 is the same word used to mean *Zealot*. What was the irony in Pilate's decision regarding Jesus?

DATA FILE

Who Were the Zealots?

In about 45 B.C., a Jewish patriot named Hezekiah led a band of freedom fighters against the Romans and their supporters. Herod the Great captured Hezekiah and executed him, as he did to thousands of like-minded Jews during his reign. Although devout Jews continued to bitterly oppose Roman rule and taxation, there was no widespread resistance movement until Judea was officially incorporated into the Roman Empire in A.D. 6. At that time, Judah of Gamla, the son of Hezekiah, urged violent resistance. Supported by a popular Pharisee named Zadok, also from Galilee, Judah led a revolt. Judah was killed, his followers were scattered, and the Zealot movement began.

The term *Zealot* technically applies to a person who belonged to the party or "philosophy" that began in Gamla, but it often is applied to all Jewish rebels who resisted Roman authority and Jewish collaborators. For generations, the Zealots violently resisted the emperor's authority. They longed for a messiah who would raise up a great army, destroy their Roman overlords, and reestablish Jewish rule in Israel.

The Zealots based their zeal for God on the action of Phinehas, Aaron's grandson, who used a spear to defend God's name and destroy unfaithfulness to Torah among the Jewish people (Numbers 25:7–13). The Zealots interpreted this action to be a divine command to use violent action to defend God's name, which led to a long history of violent acts against Rome and brutal conflict between the Zealots and the Jews whom they believed cooperated with the pagan empire.

PLANNING NOTES:

DATA FILE

Who Were the Zealots?

In about 45 B.C., a Jewish patriot named Hezekiah led a band of freedom fighters against the Romans and their supporters. Herod the Great captured Hezekiah and executed him, as he did to thousands of like-minded Jews during his reign. Although devout Jews continued to bitterly oppose Roman rule and taxation, there was no widespread resistance movement until Judea was officially incorporated into the Roman Empire in A.D. 6. At that time, Judah of Gamla, the son of Hezekiah, urged violent resistance. Supported by a popular Pharisee named Zadok, also from Galilee, Judah led a revolt. Judah was killed, his followers were scattered, and the Zealot movement began.

The term *Zealot* technically applies to a person who belonged to the party or "philosophy" that began in Gamla, but it often is applied to all Jewish rebels who resisted Roman authority and Jewish collaborators. For generations, the Zealots violently resisted the emperor's authority. They longed for a messiah who would raise up a great army, destroy their Roman overlords, and reestablish Jewish rule in Israel.

The Zealots based their zeal for God on the action of Phinehas, Aaron's grandson, who used a spear to defend God's name and destroy unfaithfulness to Torah among the Jewish people (Numbers 25:7–13). The Zealots interpreted this action to be a divine command to use violent action to defend God's name, which led to a long history of violent acts against Rome and brutal conflict between the Zealots and the Jews whom they believed cooperated with the pagan empire.

The Zealots' creed can be summarized as follows:

- *There is only one God.* Exodus 20:3 revealed that "you shall have no other gods," so no one else could be acknowledged as king.
- *Israel is to serve God alone.*
- *The Torah and other writings of the Hebrew Bible are the only guide to righteous living.* The Zealots lived in strict conformity to the Torah.
- *Neither Rome nor Herod is a legitimate authority.* People are to use every means possible, including violence, to resist earthly authority.
- *Serving the Roman emperor in any way—whether in worship, slavery, or paying taxes—is apostasy against God.* Taxes are to be paid only to God.
- *Serving Rome, whether by choice or as a slave, violates God's supreme authority.*
- *God is on our side, so we will triumph in the end.* This belief led to the Zealots' reputation for incredible bravery and tolerance for suffering.
- *The Scriptures promise that the coming Anointed One will be a great military leader and king, like King David was.*

THE ZEALOT MOVEMENT

HASIDIM

Called the "Pious Ones," they resisted Hellenism by being totally devoted to Torah. They fought with Judah and the Maccabees against the Syrian Greeks (Seleucids) in 167 B.C.

The Hasmonaeans, the Maccabees' descendants, became as Hellenistic as the Seleucid Greeks.

Hasidim became two movements.

PHARISEES

- Resist Hellenism and the pagan worldview
- Totally devoted to Torah

ZEALOTS

- Resist Hellenism and the pagan worldview
- Totally devoted to Torah
- Were terrorists

ZEALOTS

Hezekiah
- Resisted Rome and Herod (47 B.C.)
- Was executed by Herod

Judah of Gamla
- Attacked Sepphoris in 4 B.C. to gain control of its arsenal
- Founded Zealot party with Zadok the Pharisee in A.D. 6, at the time of the census
- Was probably killed by Herod Antipas (see Acts 5:37)
- Beliefs: 1. God alone may rule Israel
            2. Pay taxes to no one but God
            3. Slavery is worse than death

Sons of Judah

Jacob
- Crucified for terrorism in A.D. 48

Simeon
- Crucified for terrorism in A.D. 48

Yair

Grandsons of Judah

Eleazar Ben Yair
- Son of Yair
- Commander of Masada
- Committed suicide in A.D. 73

Menahem
- Leader of a revolt in Jerusalem
- Killed by opponents in A.D. 66

5. The word used to describe Barabbas in Luke 23:13–25 is the same word used to mean *Zealot*. What was the irony in Pilate's decision regarding Jesus?

DATA FILE

Who Were the Zealots?

In about 45 B.C., a Jewish patriot named Hezekiah led a band of freedom fighters against the Romans and their supporters. Herod the Great captured Hezekiah and executed him, as he did to thousands of like-minded Jews during his reign. Although devout Jews continued to bitterly oppose Roman rule and taxation, there was no widespread resistance movement until Judea was officially incorporated into the Roman Empire in A.D. 6. At that time, Judah of Gamla, the son of Hezekiah, urged violent resistance. Supported by a popular Pharisee named Zadok, also from Galilee, Judah led a revolt. Judah was killed, his followers were scattered, and the Zealot movement began.

The term *Zealot* technically applies to a person who belonged to the party or "philosophy" that began in Gamla, but it often is applied to all Jewish rebels who resisted Roman authority and Jewish collaborators. For generations, the Zealots violently resisted the emperor's authority. They longed for a messiah who would raise up a great army, destroy their Roman overlords, and reestablish Jewish rule in Israel.

The Zealots based their zeal for God on the action of Phinehas, Aaron's grandson, who used a spear to defend God's name and destroy unfaithfulness to Torah among the Jewish people (Numbers 25:7–13). The Zealots interpreted this action to be a divine command to use violent action to defend God's name, which led to a long history of violent acts against Rome and brutal conflict between the Zealots and the Jews whom they believed cooperated with the pagan empire.

The Zealots' creed can be summarized as follows:

* *There is only one God.* Exodus 20:3 revealed that "you shall have no other gods," so no one else could be acknowledged as king.
* *Israel is to serve God alone.*
* *The Torah and other writings of the Hebrew Bible are the only guide to righteous living.* The Zealots lived in strict conformity to the Torah.
* *Neither Rome nor Herod is a legitimate authority.* People are to use every means possible, including violence, to resist earthly authority.
* *Serving the Roman emperor in any way—whether in worship, slavery, or paying taxes—is apostasy against God.* Taxes are to be paid only to God.
* *Serving Rome, whether by choice or as a slave, violates God's supreme authority.*
* *God is on our side, so we will triumph in the end.* This belief led to the Zealots' reputation for incredible bravery and tolerance for suffering.
* *The Scriptures promise that the coming Anointed One will be a great military leader and king, like King David was.*

DATA FILE

The End of the Zealots

The Zealot minority, although certainly influential, did not have the means to defeat the Roman Empire. Having rejected the kingdom and peace that Jesus offered, they came to a tragic end:

* Judah of Gamla, the movement's founder, was executed. His sons, Jacob and Simeon, were both crucified in approximately A.D. 48.
* Menahem, another of Judah's grandsons whom some believed to be the Messiah, seized Masada in A.D. 66 during the first true military action of the Jewish Revolt. (The Roman weapons in Masada equipped the Zealots.) Another Zealot later murdered Menahem.
* John of Gischala, a Zealot, futilely defended Jerusalem and the Temple Mount until the Romans conquered the city.
* In A.D. 73, the Romans laid siege to Masada. Eleazar Ben Yair, a descendant of Judah of Gamla, held out until there was no more hope. Then the Zealots in Masada, the last remaining Zealots, committed mass suicide.

THE ZEALOT MOVEMENT
HASIDIM

Called the "Pious Ones," they resisted Hellenism by being totally devoted to Torah. They fought with Judah and the Maccabees against the Syrian Greeks (Seleucids) in 167 B.C.

The Hasmonaeans, the Maccabees' descendants, became as Hellenistic as the Seleucid Greeks.

Hasidim became two movements.

PHARISEES
* Resist Hellenism and the pagan worldview
* Totally devoted to Torah

ZEALOTS
* Resist Hellenism and the pagan worldview
* Totally devoted to Torah
* Were terrorists

ZEALOTS

Hezekiah
* Resisted Rome and Herod (47 B.C.)
* Was executed by Herod

Judah of Gamla
* Attacked Sepphoris in 4 B.C. to gain control of its arsenal
* Founded Zealot party with Zadok the Pharisee in A.D. 6, at the time of the census
* Was probably killed by Herod Antipas (see Acts 5:37)
* Beliefs: 1. God alone may rule Israel
  2. Pay taxes to no one but God
  3. Slavery is worse than death

Sons of Judah

Jacob	Simeon	Yair
• Crucified for terrorism in A.D. 48	• Crucified for terrorism in A.D. 48	

Grandsons of Judah

Eleazar Ben Yair	Menahem
• Son of Yair	• Leader of a revolt in Jerusalem
• Commander of Masada	• Killed by opponents in A.D. 66
• Committed suicide in A.D. 73	

DATA FILE

The End of the Zealots

The Zealot minority, although certainly influential, did not have the means to defeat the Roman Empire. Having rejected the kingdom and peace that Jesus offered, they came to a tragic end:

- Judah of Gamla, the movement's founder, was executed. His sons, Jacob and Simeon, were both crucified in approximately A.D. 48.
- Menahem, another of Judah's grandsons whom some believed to be the Messiah, seized Masada in A.D. 66 during the first true military action of the Jewish Revolt. (The Roman weapons in Masada equipped the Zealots.) Another Zealot later murdered Menahem.
- John of Gischala, a Zealot, futilely defended Jerusalem and the Temple Mount until the Romans conquered the city.
- In A.D. 73, the Romans laid siege to Masada. Eleazar Ben Yair, a descendant of Judah of Gamla, held out until there was no more hope. Then the Zealots in Masada, the last remaining Zealots, committed mass suicide.

Topic D: Misunderstandings Concerning Jesus' Kingdom

1. What do the following verses reveal about how people misunderstood Jesus and His kingdom?

   a. *The disciples* (See Matthew 26:47–51; Mark 10:35–45.)

   Suggested Responses: James and John wanted rewards of honor. Jesus, in turn, told them to be servants. Simon Peter resisted Jesus' capture by using his sword, which was the way a Zealot would have responded.

   b. *The Romans* (See John 18:33–37.)

   Suggested Response: Pilate had heard that Jesus was "the king of the Jews." Given the political climate, that concerned him.

   c. *The crowd in the Garden of Gethsemane* (See Matthew 26:55–56.)

   Suggested Response: They came with swords and clubs, as if Jesus were leading a rebellion.

2. The Romans apparently feared that Jesus was a Zealot. Look up the following references to find evidence that could have raised their suspicions.

Scripture Reference	Was He a Zealot?
Mark 3:13–18	He had a Zealot disciple
Matthew 2:1–9	The wise men had sought the "king of the Jews"
Mark 11:15–18	In defense of God's house, He had driven buyers and sellers out of the temple
John 12:12–15	He rode into Jerusalem like a king, greeted by the praises of the crowd, who waved palm branches—a symbol of Jewish nationalism

The Zealots' creed can be summarized as follows:

- *There is only one God.* Exodus 20:3 revealed that "you shall have no other gods," so no one else could be acknowledged as king.
- *Israel is to serve God alone.*
- *The Torah and other writings of the Hebrew Bible are the only guide to righteous living.* The Zealots lived in strict conformity to the Torah.
- *Neither Rome nor Herod is a legitimate authority.* People are to use every means possible, including violence, to resist earthly authority.
- *Serving the Roman emperor in any way—whether in worship, slavery, or paying taxes—is apostasy against God.* Taxes are to be paid only to God.
- *Serving Rome, whether by choice or as a slave, violates God's supreme authority.*
- *God is on our side, so we will triumph in the end.* This belief led to the Zealots' reputation for incredible bravery and tolerance for suffering.
- *The Scriptures promise that the coming Anointed One will be a great military leader and king, like King David was.*

DATA FILE

The End of the Zealots

The Zealot minority, although certainly influential, did not have the means to defeat the Roman Empire. Having rejected the kingdom and peace that Jesus offered, they came to a tragic end:

- Judah of Gamla, the movement's founder, was executed. His sons, Jacob and Simeon, were both crucified in approximately A.D. 48.
- Menahem, another of Judah's grandsons whom some believed to be the Messiah, seized Masada in A.D. 66 during the first true military action of the Jewish Revolt. (The Roman weapons in Masada equipped the Zealots.) Another Zealot later murdered Menahem.
- John of Gischala, a Zealot, futilely defended Jerusalem and the Temple Mount until the Romans conquered the city.
- In A.D. 73, the Romans laid siege to Masada. Eleazar Ben Yair, a descendant of Judah of Gamla, held out until there was no more hope. Then the Zealots in Masada, the last remaining Zealots, committed mass suicide.

Topic D: Misunderstandings Concerning Jesus' Kingdom

1. What do the following verses reveal about how people misunderstood Jesus and His kingdom?

   a. *The disciples* (See Matthew 26:47–51; Mark 10:35–45.)

   b. *The Romans* (See John 18:33–37.)

   c. *The crowd in the Garden of Gethsemane* (See Matthew 26:55–56.)

2. The Romans apparently feared that Jesus was a Zealot. Look up the following references to find evidence that could have raised their suspicions.

Scripture Reference	Was He a Zealot?
Mark 3:13–18	
Matthew 2:1–9	
Mark 11:15–18	
John 12:12–15	

3. To clarify what His kingdom was about, what did Jesus say to Pilate, who no doubt wondered if Jesus was the political-military king that the Zealots awaited? (See John 18:36.)

    Suggested Response: Jesus told Pilate that His kingdom was not an earthly kingdom.

4. When Jesus appeared to His disciples after His resurrection, what did they ask Him that reflected the ideology of the Zealots? (See Acts 1:6.)

    Suggested Response: They wanted to know if He would restore political freedom to Israel at that time.

Topic E: Jesus Taught in Synagogues

The New Testament records more than ten occasions when Jesus ministered in synagogues, which provided a ready platform for His teaching. Imagine Jesus sitting on a stone bench or on the floor of a synagogue and listening, or on the *bema* (speaker's platform) holding the Torah scrolls. As we understand the role of the synagogues in Jewish life, we can better appreciate the actions and words of Jesus that took place there.

1. In which specific towns or regions did Jesus visit synagogues? (See Matthew 4:23; Mark 1:21; Luke 4:14–22, 44.) How important was the synagogue to His ministry?

    Suggested Response: Jesus taught in synagogues throughout Galilee (including Capernaum), preaching about His kingdom and healing people. He read from the Isaiah scroll in Nazareth, where He had been reared, and preached in synagogues in Judea. Clearly synagogues played a key role in His ministry, providing a ready platform from which to speak.

A Galilean Synagogue

132   Faith Lessons on the Life and Ministry of the Messiah

3. To clarify what His kingdom was about, what did Jesus say to Pilate, who no doubt wondered if Jesus was the political-military king that the Zealots awaited? (See John 18:36.)

4. When Jesus appeared to His disciples after His resurrection, what did they ask Him that reflected the ideology of the Zealots? (See Acts 1:6.)

Topic E: Jesus Taught in Synagogues

The New Testament records more than ten occasions when Jesus ministered in synagogues, which provided a ready platform for His teaching. Imagine Jesus sitting on a stone bench or on the floor of a synagogue and listening, or on the *bema* (speaker's platform) holding the Torah scrolls. As we understand the role of the synagogues in Jewish life, we can better appreciate the actions and words of Jesus that took place there.

1. In which specific towns or regions did Jesus visit synagogues? (See Matthew 4:23; Mark 1:21; Luke 4:14–22, 44.) How important was the synagogue to His ministry?

Session Five: The Rabbi   133

A Galilean Synagogue

2. Read the following Scripture passages and describe what Jesus' ministry in the synagogues involved.

Scripture	How Jesus Ministered
Matthew 12:9–13	
Luke 4:31–37	
Luke 4:16–22	
John 6:28–59	

✏ 2.   Read the following Scripture passages and describe what Jesus' ministry in the synagogues involved.

Scripture	How Jesus Ministered
Matthew 12:9–13	Healed people
Luke 4:31–37	Vanquished Satan's evil forces
Luke 4:16–22	Stood up, as a scheduled reader, to read from the scroll of Isaiah
John 6:28–59	Debated the interpretation of the Torah

DATA FILE

Synagogues of Jesus' Time

Synagogues have been a part of Jewish life since well before Jesus' time. They began as small assemblies of people for the purpose of study and prayer (perhaps as early as the time of Solomon's temple), and became particularly important during the Babylonian exile following the destruction of the first temple in Jerusalem. In Babylon, the Jews met regularly to study the Torah and reflect on the need to be obedient to God. The synagogue developed out of these regular meetings, becoming the center of Jewish social life as well as a place of study and prayer. The synagogue provided a place for the Jewish people to assemble and maintain their identity in a pagan land.

Even in the first century, the synagogue remained the focal point of Jewish community life. The synagogue served as school, meeting place, courtroom, seat of government, place of prayer, center for community celebrations, and in some cases may have provided lodging for travelers. In typical Galilean towns, synagogues occupied prominent places on an elevated platform in the town center or on the highest point in town, symbolizing the importance of living in the presence of God.

Outside each synagogue was a *mikveh* (plural: *mikvoth*) or ritual bath where worshipers symbolically cleansed their hearts before entering the synagogue. The *mikveh* had to be hewn out of rock or placed into the ground, and the water had to be "living"—flowing freely into the *mikveh* without being drawn. This tradition was in keeping with laws of the Torah regarding contact with "unclean" things (Numbers 19), bodily fluid (Leviticus 15), or other defiling objects such as idols.

The synagogue, a kind of democracy, was governed by local elders. Males thirteen years old or older could belong to it. A local ruler, called the *hazzan*, maintained the building and organized the prayer services (Mark 5:22, 35–38; Luke 13:14). He often taught in the synagogue school (especially in smaller villages), announced the arrival of the Sabbath with blasts on the shofar (ram's horn) on Friday evenings, and cared for the Torah scrolls and other sacred writings and brought them out at appropriate times (Luke 4:16–21).

Inside the synagogue, the leader of the service sat on a small, elevated platform on which a reading table, a menorah (a seven-branched candlestick), and a seat (sometimes referred to as the Moses' seat—Matthew 23:2) may have been placed. The members of the synagogue either sat on the floor or on stone benches or steps against the walls (the chief seats were those on the stone benches—Matthew 23:6). Common people sat on mats on the floor, which was usually paved with flagstones (although it was sometimes dirt and in later synagogues could have been an elaborate mosaic floor). Torah scrolls were kept in a permanent (but portable) chest called the holy ark—after the original ark of the covenant in which Moses placed the tablets of the law.

A Galilean Synagogue

2. Read the following Scripture passages and describe what Jesus' ministry in the synagogues involved.

Scripture	How Jesus Ministered
Matthew 12:9–13	
Luke 4:31–37	
Luke 4:16–22	
John 6:28–59	

DATA FILE

Synagogues of Jesus' Time

Synagogues have been a part of Jewish life since well before Jesus' time. They began as small assemblies of people for the purpose of study and prayer (perhaps as early as the time of Solomon's temple), and became particularly important during the Babylonian exile following the destruction of the first temple in Jerusalem. In Babylon, the Jews met regularly to study the Torah and reflect on the need to be obedient to God. The synagogue developed out of these regular meetings, becoming the center of Jewish social life as well as a place of study and prayer. The synagogue provided a place for the Jewish people to assemble and maintain their identity in a pagan land.

Even in the first century, the synagogue remained the focal point of Jewish community life. The synagogue served as school, meeting place, courtroom, seat of government, place of prayer, center for community celebrations, and in some cases may have provided lodging for travelers. In typical Galilean towns, synagogues occupied prominent places on an elevated platform in the town center or on the highest point in town, symbolizing the importance of living in the presence of God.

Outside each synagogue was a *mikveh* (plural: *mikvoth*) or ritual bath where worshipers symbolically cleansed their hearts before entering the synagogue. The *mikveh* had to be hewn out of rock or placed into the ground, and the water had to be "living"—flowing freely into the *mikveh* without being drawn. This tradition was in keeping with laws of the Torah regarding contact with "unclean" things (Numbers 19), bodily fluid (Leviticus 15), or other defiling objects such as idols.

The synagogue, a kind of democracy, was governed by local elders. Males thirteen years old or older could belong to it. A local ruler, called the *hazzan*, maintained the building and organized the prayer services (Mark 5:22, 35–38; Luke 13:14). He often taught in the synagogue school (especially in smaller villages), announced the arrival of the Sabbath with blasts on the shofar (ram's horn) on Friday evenings, and cared for the Torah scrolls and other sacred writings and brought them out at appropriate times (Luke 4:16–21).

DID YOU KNOW?

A Synagogue Education

Only boys attended synagogue schools. According to the Mishnah (the written record of the oral traditions of Jesus' time and afterward), students followed a specific educational plan. Since the learning of the community was passed orally, memorization of tradition and God's Word were essential. A typical education for a boy went as follows:

- At age five or six began memorizing and studying the written Torah.
- At age twelve studied the more complicated oral interpretations of the Torah.
- Became a religious adult at age thirteen.
- At age fifteen, a gifted student might continue his studies with a local rabbi in *beth midrash* (meaning "house of study" or secondary school), where he learned to apply the Torah and oral tradition to specific situations.
- The most gifted students would travel with famous itinerant rabbis, learning to understand and apply Torah and oral tradition in daily situations and seeking to "become like their rabbis."
- Learned a trade at age twenty.
- Demonstrated his full ability at age thirty.

By the time a student reached adulthood, he knew most Scriptures by heart and could tell whether someone quoted them correctly. Thus Jesus, in keeping with His culture, could say, "It is written . . ." and know that His audience would recognize an accurate quotation.

3. After the Babylonians destroyed the Temple in Jerusalem, the Jews could no longer worship God as they had for centuries. So they focused on studying God's law and making a different kind of sacrifice. What was that "new" sacrifice? (See Psalm 51:16–17; Isaiah 1:11–17.)

Suggested Responses: A true sacrifice was not shed blood or a burnt offering. Rather, it was the sacrifice of an obedient and contrite heart. It involved doing right actions, learning to follow God's truths, seeking justice, encouraging oppressed people, defending the cause of the fatherless, and pleading the case of the widows.

4. What did the apostle Paul express concerning the way in which Christians sacrifice to God? (See Romans 12:1–2, 9–21.)

Suggested Responses: Paul wrote that we are to offer our bodies as living sacrifices. We are to be holy and not conform to the world's values. We are to show sincere love and to honor other people above ourselves, zealously serve God, be joyful in hope, share with needy people, practice hospitality, love our persecutors, live in unity with each other, be humble, avoid revenge, live at peace as much as we can, etc.

The Rabbi

211

Session Five: The Rabbi

135

Inside the synagogue, the leader of the service sat on a small, elevated platform on which a reading table, a menorah (a seven-branched candlestick), and a seat (sometimes referred to as the Moses' seat—Matthew 23:2) may have been placed. The members of the synagogue either sat on the floor or on stone benches or steps against the walls (the chief seats were those on the stone benches—Matthew 23:6). Common people sat on mats on the floor, which was usually paved with flagstones (although it was sometimes dirt and in later synagogues could have been an elaborate mosaic floor). Torah scrolls were kept in a permanent (but portable) chest called the holy ark—after the original ark of the covenant in which Moses placed the tablets of the law.

3. After the Babylonians destroyed the Temple in Jerusalem, the Jews could no longer worship God as they had for centuries. So they focused on studying God's law and making a different kind of sacrifice. What was that "new" sacrifice? (See Psalm 51:16–17; Isaiah 1:11–17.)

4. What did the apostle Paul express concerning the way in which Christians sacrifice to God? (See Romans 12:1–2, 9–21.)

136

Faith Lessons on the Life and Ministry of the Messiah

DID YOU KNOW?

A Synagogue Education

Only boys attended synagogue schools. According to the Mishnah (the written record of the oral traditions of Jesus' time and afterward), students followed a specific educational plan. Since the learning of the community was passed orally, memorization of tradition and God's Word were essential. A typical education for a boy went as follows:

· At age five or six began memorizing and studying the written Torah.
· At age twelve studied the more complicated oral interpretations of the Torah.
· Became a religious adult at age thirteen.
· At age fifteen, a gifted student might continue his studies with a local rabbi in *beth midrash* (meaning "house of study" or secondary school), where he learned to apply the Torah and oral tradition to specific situations.
· The most gifted students would travel with famous itinerant rabbis, learning to understand and apply Torah and oral tradition in daily situations and seeking to "become like their rabbis."
· Learned a trade at age twenty.
· Demonstrated his full ability at age thirty.

By the time a student reached adulthood, he knew most Scriptures by heart and could tell whether someone quoted them correctly. Thus Jesus, in keeping with His culture, could say, "It is written . . ." and know that His audience would recognize an accurate quotation.

PLANNING NOTES:

After nine minutes, let participants know that they have one minute remaining. Then reassemble the entire group. After everyone is back together, begin asking one person from each small group to briefly share a key idea with the larger group. In some cases, you may not have time for every group to share their discoveries.

As time allows, let's briefly share the key ideas that your group discussed.

HIGHLIGHTS OF SABBATH WORSHIP

- Took place on Saturday morning in the synagogue.
- Began with several blessings offered to God, followed by the Shema: "Hear, O Israel: The LORD our God, the LORD is one" (Deuteronomy 6:4).
- The person selected to read the Torah would sit on the stone "Moses' seat" until the *hazzan* (temple ruler) brought the Torah scrolls. Then, the reader would stand up to read the words of Moses (Luke 4:16–21).
- As many as seven portions of Torah were read by different members of the synagogue community.
- A selection from the prophets was then read.
- A short sermon was offered. Interestingly, any member of the synagogue community could deliver the sermon. Often someone recognized for his wisdom and insight, or a visitor, offered the sermon. Even boys over age thirteen could, with permission, read or speak during the service. In this way, the community encouraged its youngest members to actively participate in its religious life.
- The service ended with a benediction. If a priest was present, he would offer the blessing of Aaron from the Torah (Numbers 6:24–26) at the end of the service. Aside from offering this blessing, priests and Levites could participate, but had no special role in synagogue life.

HIGHLIGHTS OF SABBATH WORSHIP

- Took place on Saturday morning in the synagogue.
- Began with several blessings offered to God, followed by the Shema: "Hear, O Israel: The LORD our God, the LORD is one" (Deuteronomy 6:4).
- The person selected to read the Torah would sit on the stone "Moses' seat" until the *hazzan* (temple ruler) brought the Torah scrolls. Then, the reader would stand up to read the words of Moses (Luke 4:16–21).
- As many as seven portions of Torah were read by different members of the synagogue community.
- A selection from the prophets was then read.
- A short sermon was offered. Interestingly, any member of the synagogue community could deliver the sermon. Often someone recognized for his wisdom and insight, or a visitor, offered the sermon. Even boys over age thirteen could, with permission, read or speak during the service. In this way, the community encouraged its youngest members to actively participate in its religious life.
- The service ended with a benediction. If a priest was present, he would offer the blessing of Aaron from the Torah (Numbers 6:24–26) at the end of the service. Aside from offering this blessing, priests and Levites could participate, but had no special role in synagogue life.

PLANNING NOTES:

faith Lesson

Time for Reflection (5 minutes)

It's time for each of us to think quietly about how we can apply what we've learned today. You'll find passages of Scripture on page 138 of the Participant's Guide. Let's each read these passages silently and take the next few minutes to consider some of the questions that follow.

Please do not talk during this time. It's a time when each of us can reflect on what it means to be a disciple of Jesus.

> *The Scripture passages and questions are reproduced in their entirety in the Participant's Guide on pages 138–40.*

To the Jews who had believed him, Jesus said, "If you hold to my teaching, you are really my disciples. Then you will know the truth, and the truth will set you free."

They answered him, "We are Abraham's descendants and have never been slaves of anyone. How can you say that we shall be set free?"

Jesus replied, "I tell you the truth, everyone who sins is a slave to sin. . . . So if the Son sets you free, you will be free indeed."

JOHN 8:31–34, 36

"Come to me, all you who are weary and burdened, and I will give you rest. Take my yoke upon you and learn from me, for I am gentle and humble in heart, and you will find rest for your souls. For my yoke is easy and my burden is light."

MATTHEW 11:28–30

When he had finished washing their feet, he put on his clothes and returned to his place. "Do you understand what I have done for you?" he asked them. "You call me 'Teacher' and 'Lord,' and rightly so, for that is what I am. Now that I, your Lord and Teacher, have washed your feet, you also should wash one another's feet. I have set you an example that you should do as I have done for you. . . .

A new command I give you: Love one another. As I have loved you, so you must love one another. By this all men will know that you are my disciples, if you love one another."

JOHN 13:12–15, 34–35

1. What is the true freedom that Jesus offers to His disciples? How is this like or unlike the freedom desired by the people of Jesus' day?

2. How is the freedom Jesus offers like or unlike the freedom you desire? Do you accept His offer, or are you holding out for a different kind of freedom?

3. In your own words, summarize the "yoke" that a *talmid*, a disciple of Jesus, takes on.

ꜰᴀɪᴛʜ ʟᴇssᴏɴ

Time for Reflection

Read the following passages of Scripture and take the next few minutes to consider what it means to be a disciple of Jesus.

> To the Jews who had believed him, Jesus said, "If you hold to my teaching, you are really my disciples. Then you will know the truth, and the truth will set you free."
>
> They answered him, "We are Abraham's descendants and have never been slaves of anyone. How can you say that we shall be set free?"
>
> Jesus replied, "I tell you the truth, everyone who sins is a slave to sin. . . . So if the Son sets you free, you will be free indeed."
>
> JOHN 8:31–34, 36

> "Come to me, all you who are weary and burdened, and I will give you rest. Take my yoke upon you and learn from me, for I am gentle and humble in heart, and you will find rest for your souls. For my yoke is easy and my burden is light."
>
> MATTHEW 11:28–30

> When he had finished washing their feet, he put on his clothes and returned to his place. "Do you understand what I have done for you?" he asked them. "You call me 'Teacher' and 'Lord,' and rightly so, for that is what I am. Now that I, your Lord and Teacher, have washed your feet, you also should wash one another's feet. I have set you an example that you should do as I have done for you. . . .
>
> A new command I give you: Love one another. As I have loved you, so you must love one another. By this all men will know that you are my disciples, if you love one another."
>
> JOHN 13:12–15, 34–35

1. What is the true freedom that Jesus offers to His disciples? How is this like or unlike the freedom desired by the people of Jesus' day?

2. How is the freedom Jesus offers like or unlike the freedom you desire? Do you accept His offer, or are you holding out for a different kind of freedom?

3. In your own words, summarize the "yoke" that a *talmid*, a disciple of Jesus, takes on.

WORTH OBSERVING

The Roots of Christian Community

The earliest Christians attended synagogues, although they had a new interpretation of the Torah since Jesus had been revealed as Messiah (Acts 13:14). It appears that the early church patterned itself after the synagogue, continuing the same practice of living and worshiping together as a community (Acts 2:42–47). Jesus' followers today, who have been made one body because of Jesus (1 Corinthians 12:12–13), would do well to remember that the roots of the church are in community living and worship. In our fractured, broken world, the picture of the community of God—the model of the synagogue—is one we would do well to put into practice.

PLANNING NOTES:

✐ 4.   As people look at you and your lifestyle, is it obvious that you are a disciple of Jesus? Why or why not?

✐ 5.   What changes in thought, word, and action do you need to make so that other people will know you are a *talmid* of Jesus?

> As soon as participants have spent five minutes reflecting on the above questions, get the entire group's attention and move to the next section.

WORTH OBSERVING

The Roots of Christian Community

The earliest Christians attended synagogues, although they had a new interpretation of the Torah since Jesus had been revealed as Messiah (Acts 13:14). It appears that the early church patterned itself after the synagogue, continuing the same practice of living and worshiping together as a community (Acts 2:42–47). Jesus' followers today, who have been made one body because of Jesus (1 Corinthians 12:12–13), would do well to remember that the roots of the church are in community living and worship. In our fractured, broken world, the picture of the community of God—the model of the synagogue—is one we would do well to put into practice.

Action Points (3 minutes)

> The following points are reproduced on pages 140–42 of the Participant's Guide:

Now it's time to wrap up our session.

> Give participants a moment to transition from their thoughtfulness to giving you their full attention.

I'd like to take a moment to summarize the key points we explored. After I have reviewed these points, I will give you a moment to jot down an action step (or steps) that you will commit to do this week as a result of what you have learned today.

> Read the following points and pause afterward so that participants can consider and write out their commitment.

✐ 1.   *Jesus came to earth to minister amidst a cauldron of conflicting ideas and tumultuous politics. Surrounded by a diverse array of belief systems, He assumed the role of a Jewish rabbi and taught a simple message that directed people toward fellowship with God. He also modeled the lifestyle of the kingdom of God and linked people's acceptance of His claim to be the Messiah to their willingness to follow the lifestyle He demonstrated.*

1. What is the true freedom that Jesus offers to His disciples? How is this like or unlike the freedom desired by the people of Jesus' day?

2. How is the freedom Jesus offers like or unlike the freedom you desire? Do you accept His offer, or are you holding out for a different kind of freedom?

3. In your own words, summarize the "yoke" that a *talmid*, a disciple of Jesus, takes on.

WORTH OBSERVING

The Roots of Christian Community
The earliest Christians attended synagogues, although they had a new interpretation of the Torah since Jesus had been revealed as Messiah (Acts 13:14). It appears that the early church patterned itself after the synagogue, continuing the same practice of living and worshiping together as a community (Acts 2:42–47). Jesus' followers today, who have been made one body because of Jesus (1 Corinthians 12:12–13), would do well to remember that the roots of the church are in community living and worship. In our fractured, broken world, the picture of the community of God—the model of the synagogue—is one we would do well to put into practice.

4. As people look at you and your lifestyle, is it obvious that you are a disciple of Jesus? Why or why not?

5. What changes in thought, word, and action do you need to make so that other people will know you are a *talmid* of Jesus?

Action Points

Take a few minutes to review the key points you explored today, then write down an action step (or steps) that you will commit to do this week as a result of what you have learned.

1. *Jesus came to earth to minister amidst a cauldron of conflicting ideas and tumultuous politics. Surrounded by a diverse array of belief systems, He assumed the role of a Jewish rabbi and taught a simple message that directed people toward fellowship with God. He also modeled the lifestyle of the kingdom of God and linked people's acceptance of His claim to be the Messiah to their willingness to follow the lifestyle He demonstrated.*

   Consider your lifestyle. In what ways does your life—at home, among friends, in the workplace—clearly direct people toward God?

Consider your lifestyle. In what ways does your life—at home, among friends, in the workplace—clearly direct people toward God?

Choose one aspect of your lifestyle that falls short of revealing the kingdom of God. What will you commit to do this week to more closely follow the lifestyle Jesus demonstrated?

2. *The way Jesus chose to point people toward God was to love them—even those whose inner hurt and brokenness led them to do things that were considered to be unacceptable or immoral.*

As His followers, we, too, are to point people toward God. Although using the tools of our culture to teach people about God is certainly important, our ultimate focus has to be on the hurts, needs, and cares of people and to minister to them as Jesus did.

Have you ever fallen into the trap of teaching about the kingdom of God while neglecting to truly love the people to whom you are ministering? What must you do to avoid treating people like that in the future?

What are the hurts, needs, and cares of some of the people God has brought across your path? In what ways, using the example of Jesus' life, can you reach out to touch the hearts of these hurting, needy people?

closing prayer

I minute

In this lesson, we've gained a better understanding of the world in which Jesus ministered and how His message was received by different groups of people. Let's close in prayer now, asking God to give us the courage to be His disciples and to reach out to hurting people with His love.

Dear God, You have done, and are doing, so much in our lives. Please help us not only to be devoted to You, but also to seek to be Your talmidim, to be like You. Help us to hear Your message. Help us to live according to Your ways and not our own. Bring our actions, our thoughts, and our words in line with how You want us to live as we reach out to our hurting world. In Your name we pray, Jesus, amen.

Choose one aspect of your lifestyle that falls short of revealing the kingdom of God. What will you commit to do this week to more closely follow the lifestyle Jesus demonstrated?

2. *The way Jesus chose to point people toward God was to love them—even those whose inner hurt and brokenness led them to do things that were considered to be unacceptable or immoral.*

As His followers, we, too, are to point people toward God. Although using the tools of our culture to teach people about God is certainly important, our ultimate focus has to be on the hurts, needs, and cares of people and to minister to them as Jesus did.

Have you ever fallen into the trap of teaching about the kingdom of God while neglecting to truly love the people to whom you are ministering? What must you do to avoid treating people like that in the future?

PLANNING NOTES:

Language of culture

Before You Lead

Synopsis

Jesus grew up in Nazareth, a rural village of about two to three hundred inhabitants in lower Galilee. Although we may picture Nazareth as a sheltered, out-of-the-way retreat from the world, it was actually located near some of the most sophisticated culture of the day. A main branch of the Via Maris—the international trade route of the world—passed nearby. And a mere three miles to the north, Herod Antipas, a son of Herod the Great, built the capital of his kingdom—a booming metropolis named Sepphoris.

This session's video was filmed in the recently excavated ruins of Sepphoris. Designed as Herod Antipas's administrative capital, this huge city covered as many as five hundred acres and housed as many as twenty-five to thirty thousand people. It boasted all the trappings of a modern, wealthy city of the Roman Empire. It was located on a hill, so it was visible for miles around. Rich villas with mosaic floors lined its modern streets. Herod's palace was magnificent. A colonnaded street led to the forum. An elaborate water system with a cistern a thousand feet long supplied the city. Its cultural amenities included a gymnasium and a theater that could seat more than four thousand people.

Not far away, in Nazareth, Jesus participated in a very different lifestyle. After receiving His basic education and traveling to Jerusalem for His first Passover, Jesus began to learn a trade from His father, who was a *tekton* (Matthew 13:55). The Greek word *tekton* is translated as "carpenter," but it actually means "a craftsman who builds." Although we typically picture Jesus as a carpenter who worked with wood, the building materials of Israel were primarily rocks and cut stones. Therefore, Jesus probably worked more with rocks and stones than with wood. As a stonemason, Jesus may even have helped His father construct buildings in Sepphoris.

Throughout His ministry, Jesus ministered to the hurts and needs of poor peasants, but He also interacted with and ministered to wealthy (often Hellenistic) people. For example, He shared meals and had discussions with influential religious leaders. Joanna, the wife of Cuza (the minister of finance for Herod Antipas), used her own funds to support the ministry of Jesus and His disciples. And people accused Jesus of befriending tax collectors, who were administrative officials in the upper echelon of first-century society in Israel. Although He spoke out against the oppressive use of wealth, Jesus appreciated wealthy people who had become wealthy honestly and used their wealth as a tool to advance the kingdom of God.

Ray Vander Laan points out how well Jesus understood the culture of His day. Jesus knew the day-to-day experiences, concerns, and joys of peasants, influential leaders, lepers, devout Jews, blind men, and many others, which enabled Him to minister effectively to them. Instead of isolating Himself from people, He interacted with them. Consequently, He knew the images, tools, and concepts He could use to effectively communicate God's truth to His diverse audience.

Many of the word pictures Jesus used came from the agricultural world of His time, particularly Galilee. For example, He used images from farming, fishing, and shepherding activities in His teaching. He used images from the world of religion—both Jewish and pagan. But Jesus also used word pictures drawn from aristocratic society—the world of culture, wealth, tax collectors, politics, royalty, and the theater. He was familiar enough with the sophisticated Hellenistic culture to use slices from it as illustrations. Thus He could communicate clearly to those in His audience who knew that world. Because Jesus could speak the language of His culture, He was a master teacher. He taught clearly and powerfully, inspiring cultural change through interaction with culture rather than isolation from it.

Key Points of This Lesson

1. *We need to discover and understand what shapes our culture.* Jesus participated in the culture of His world and learned its politics, concerns, trends, and passions. He interacted with many different kinds of men, women, and children: powerful leaders and impoverished peasants, religious teachers and lepers, farmers and fishermen, laborers and prostitutes, children of the rich and poor.

2. *Isolation from culture is not the solution to cultural change.* Jesus understood the culture, language, and people of His day. He knew what would communicate to the people of His world, and He used that knowledge with power.

    Without modifying or changing God's message, Jesus found ways to communicate in a "language" of words and ideas that people of His culture spoke and understood. He used the gifts and abilities He had in order to effectively communicate His message of repentance and salvation to everyone He met. In so doing, He made a lasting impact for God. If we are to reach people with Jesus' transforming message, we also need to work within our culture and communicate through the "language" of ideas and experiences that people in our world understand.

Session Outline (53 minutes)

I. Introduction (4 minutes)
Welcome

What's to Come

Questions to Think About

II. Show Video "Language of Culture" (21 minutes)

    III. Group Discovery (20 minutes)

        Video Highlights

        Small Group Bible Discovery

    IV. Faith Lesson (7 minutes)

        Time for Reflection

        Action Points

    V. Closing Prayer (1 minute)

Materials

No additional materials are needed for this session. Simply view the video prior to leading the session so you are familiar with its main points.

Language of culture

introduction

4 minutes

Welcome

> Assemble the participants together. Welcome them to session six of *Faith Lessons on the Life and Ministry of the Messiah*.

What's to Come

Just three miles from the small town of Nazareth where Jesus grew up, archaeologists are unearthing the sophisticated city of Sepphoris, the city Herod Antipas constructed as his administrative capital. It is possible that Jesus and his father, who were builders by trade, helped construct this sprawling city where more than twenty thousand people lived. Sepphoris also no doubt provided opportunities for Jesus to study the culture of His world and interact with the highly sophisticated people of His day. In this session, Ray Vander Laan directs our attention to the ways in which Jesus, a masterful teacher, used His understanding of culture to impact His world.

Questions to Think About

> *Participant's Guide page 143.*

> Ask each question and solicit a few responses from group members.

1. Have you experienced a situation in which you tried to communicate with another person, but you kept "missing" each other and couldn't seem to understand the other person's perspective? Describe what that was like.

   Suggested Responses: Encourage participants to share their experiences and consider why miscommunication occurs—often it is because people don't share the same cultural experiences or "speak the same language."

2. Identify some groups of people within our culture that have diverse life experiences or differing beliefs and therefore don't "speak the same language" or have difficulty understanding one another.

   Suggested Responses: will vary but may include urban teens and ranchers, professors and factory workers, pastors and securities traders, actors and homemakers, politicians and dog groomers, snowboarders and chess players, etc. (This could be amusing!)

Language of culture

questions to think about

1. Have you experienced a situation in which you tried to communicate with another person, but you kept "missing" each other and couldn't seem to understand the other person's perspective? Describe what that was like.

2. Identify some groups of people within our culture that have diverse life experiences or differing beliefs and therefore don't "speak the same language" or have difficulty understanding one another.

3. Think about Jesus' life and list some of the different kinds of people to whom He ministered. What do you think enabled Him to communicate effectively to those people?

PLANNING NOTES:

✏ 3. Think about Jesus' life and list some of the different kinds of people to whom He ministered. What do you think enabled Him to communicate effectively to those people?

Suggested Responses: The list will vary but may include lepers, blind people, fishermen, tax collectors, demon-possessed people, religious leaders, children, rulers, women, Zealots, etc. Responses to the second question will vary but may include He lived what He taught, loved His audience, took time to care for people, met people where they were, etc.

Let's keep these ideas in mind as we view the video.

video presentation

21 minutes   *Participant's Guide page 144.*

On page 144 of your Participant's Guide, you will find a space in which to take notes on key points as we watch this video.

Leader's Video Observations

Sepphoris, a City of the Herod Dynasty

Jesus

A Tekton of Nazareth

Understanding His Culture

Impacting His World

SESSION SIX

Language of Culture

Questions to Think About

1. Have you experienced a situation in which you tried to communicate with another person, but you kept "missing" each other and couldn't seem to understand the other person's perspective? Describe what that was like.

2. Identify some groups of people within our culture that have diverse life experiences or differing beliefs and therefore don't "speak the same language" or have difficulty understanding one another.

3. Think about Jesus' life and list some of the different kinds of people to whom He ministered. What do you think enabled Him to communicate effectively to those people?

144   Faith Lessons on the Life and Ministry of the Messiah

Video Notes

Sepphoris, a City of the Herod Dynasty

Jesus

    A Tekton of Nazareth

    Understanding His Culture

    Impacting His World

Group Discovery

20 minutes

> If your group has seven or more members, use the **Video Highlights** with the entire group (5 minutes), then break into small groups of three to five to discuss the **Small Group Bible Discovery** (10 minutes). Then reassemble the group to discuss the key points discovered (5 minutes).
>
> If your group has fewer than seven members, begin with the **Video Highlights** (5 minutes), then do one or more of the topics found in the **Small Group Bible Discovery** as a group (10 minutes). Finally, spend five minutes at the end discussing points that had an impact on participants.

Video Highlights (5 minutes)

> Here you'll ask one or more of the following questions that directly relate to the video the participants have just seen.

Look at the map of Herod the Great's kingdom on page 145 of your Participant's Guide. Note the specific territories for which each of Herod's four immediate successors was responsible.

1. In what ways do you think growing up so close to Sepphoris benefited Jesus and His ministry?

   Suggested Responses: He had a close-up view of the sophisticated culture of His day, was familiar with the political climate surrounding Herod Antipas, mingled with many different types of people, etc.

Kingdom of the Herods

video Highlights

Look at the map of Herod the Great's kingdom below. Note the specific territories for which each of Herod's four immediate successors was responsible.

1. In what ways do you think growing up so close to Sepphoris benefited Jesus and His ministry?

2. What did you learn about Jesus' vocation?

Kingdom of the Herods

✏ 2.   What did you learn about Jesus' vocation?

Suggested Responses: will vary, but most people have viewed Jesus as a carpenter, not a *tekton*, a builder or stonemason. Also, many people may not have realized that His work may have extended beyond the town of Nazareth and that He could have helped to build some of the great ancient cities.

✏ 3.   What did the examples of Jesus' teaching that Ray Vander Laan cited tell you about Jesus?

Suggested Responses: will vary but may include that He was a master teacher who knew His culture well; could converse on a wide range of subjects; skillfully drew on common experiences, history, the arts, and His knowledge of human nature to communicate His message; etc.

✏ 4.   Why is understanding culture well, according to this video, so important in ministering to people and reaching them effectively with the message of Christ?

Suggested Responses: The more we understand of culture, the better we understand people—their beliefs, their priorities, their passions, their lifestyle. We don't have to do what they do, but by learning their culture we can build bridges of understanding and communicate the message of Jesus in a language they understand.

Small Group Bible Discovery (15 minutes)

Participant's Guide pages 146–62.

During this time, a group with fewer than seven participants will stay together. A group with seven or more participants will break into small groups and reassemble as a large group during the final five minutes. Assign each group one of the following topics. If you have more than five small groups, assign some topics to more than one group.

Let's break into groups of three to five—people sitting near you—and study some of the Bible passages and truths mentioned in the video.

Turn to pages 146–62 in your Participant's Guide. There you'll find a list of five topics. You'll have ten minutes to read and discuss the topic I'll assign to you. Choose one person in your group to be a spokesperson for your group when we discuss these topics later.

Assign each group a topic.

I'll signal you when one minute is left.

video Highlights

Look at the map of Herod the Great's kingdom below. Note the specific territories for which each of Herod's four immediate successors was responsible.

1. In what ways do you think growing up so close to Sepphoris benefited Jesus and His ministry?

2. What did you learn about Jesus' vocation?

Kingdom of the Herods

3. What did the examples of Jesus' teaching that Ray Vander Laan cited tell you about Jesus?

4. Why is understanding culture well, according to this video, so important in ministering to people and reaching them effectively with the message of Christ?

small Group Bible Discovery

Topic A: The Significance of Nazareth

1. The small village of Nazareth in Lower Galilee was where Joseph and Mary made their home. At the time of Jesus' birth, they were in Bethlehem for the census required by Caesar Augustus. They had been told by angels that Jesus was the Son of God who would save His people from their sins. When King Herod sought to kill the infant Jesus, an angel warned Joseph and the family fled to Egypt, where they remained until Herod died and an angel told Joseph to return to Israel. (See Matthew 1:18–2:20; Luke 1:26–38.)

   a. When Joseph brought Mary and Jesus back to Israel, where did they settle? (See Matthew 2:21–23.)

Topic A: The Significance of Nazareth

1. The small village of Nazareth in Lower Galilee was where Joseph and Mary made their home. At the time of Jesus' birth, they were in Bethlehem for the census required by Caesar Augustus. They had been told by angels that Jesus was the Son of God who would save His people from their sins. When King Herod sought to kill the infant Jesus, an angel warned Joseph and the family fled to Egypt, where they remained until Herod died and an angel told Joseph to return to Israel. (See Matthew 1:18–2:20; Luke 1:26–38.)

   a. When Joseph brought Mary and Jesus back to Israel, where did they settle? (See Matthew 2:21–23.)

      Suggested Responses: It appears that Joseph wanted to return to Bethlehem, but when he realized that cruel Herod Archelaus was reigning in Judea, he went to Nazareth, which was ruled by Herod Antipas.

   b. Why was it important for them to live in Nazareth? (See Matthew 2:23.)

      Suggested Response: God's prophets had specified that the Messiah would be called a Nazarene.

Galilee

2. Since there is no record of a prophet specifically saying, "He will be called a Nazarene," let's explore the way in which Jesus' identity as a Nazarene fulfilled prophecy.

   a. How was Jesus identified by the people of His day? (See Mark 14:67; 16:6; Luke 4:34.)

      Suggested Responses: Jesus the Nazarene, Jesus of Nazareth.

   b. The meaning of the word *Nazareth* is necessary to our understanding of how Jesus fulfilled the words of the prophets. The Greek word translated *Nazareth* (or *Nazarene*) is most likely derived from the Hebrew

146   Faith Lessons on the Life and Ministry of the Messiah

3. What did the examples of Jesus' teaching that Ray Vander Laan cited tell you about Jesus?

4. Why is understanding culture well, according to this video, so important in ministering to people and reaching them effectively with the message of Christ?

small Group Bible Discovery

Topic A: The Significance of Nazareth

1. The small village of Nazareth in Lower Galilee was where Joseph and Mary made their home. At the time of Jesus' birth, they were in Bethlehem for the census required by Caesar Augustus. They had been told by angels that Jesus was the Son of God who would save His people from their sins. When King Herod sought to kill the infant Jesus, an angel warned Joseph and the family fled to Egypt, where they remained until Herod died and an angel told Joseph to return to Israel. (See Matthew 1:18–2:20; Luke 1:26–38.)

   a. When Joseph brought Mary and Jesus back to Israel, where did they settle? (See Matthew 2:21–23.)

Session Six: Language of Culture   147

   b. Why was it important for them to live in Nazareth? (See Matthew 2:23.)

2. Since there is no record of a prophet specifically saying, "He will be called a Nazarene," let's explore the way in which Jesus' identity as a Nazarene fulfilled prophecy.

   a. How was Jesus identified by the people of His day? (See Mark 14:67; 16:6; Luke 4:34.)

Galilee

word *netzer*, which means "shoot" or "branch" and is frequently used to refer to the royal line of David. In the following Scripture references, note the expressions the prophets used to describe the Messiah:

Prophecy	Expression Related to the Messiah
Isaiah 11:1–2	A "shoot" will come from the stump of Jesse (the line of David)
Isaiah 53:2	He grew up like a tender "shoot"
Jeremiah 23:5	A righteous "Branch" would come from David
Jeremiah 33:15	God would make a righteous "Branch" sprout from David's line
Zechariah 3:8	God would bring His servant, the "Branch"
Zechariah 6:12	The man whose name is the "Branch"

    c. The description "Jesus the Nazarene," meaning "Jesus the Branch," clearly linked Jesus to the prophecies stating that the Messiah would be the "Branch" that would grow out of Jesse's stump. What did Jesus say about Himself to confirm this identity? (See Revelation 22:16.)

    Suggested Response: that He is the "Root and the Offspring of David."

3. Based on their name and their Davidic lineage, the Nazarenes believed that the Messiah would come from their village because they were the "shoot" village.

    a. What does Luke 4:16–21 tell us about the Nazarenes?

    Suggested Response: They had a synagogue and were religious.

    b. What did other people think of Nazareth? (See John 1:46.)

    Suggested Response: They disliked Nazareth. [Note: Perhaps that is one reason why some people despised Jesus. See Isaiah 53:3.]

b. The meaning of the word *Nazareth* is necessary to our understanding of how Jesus fulfilled the words of the prophets. The Greek word translated *Nazareth* (or *Nazarene*) is most likely derived from the Hebrew word *netzer*, which means "shoot" or "branch" and is frequently used to refer to the royal line of David. In the following Scripture references, note the expressions the prophets used to describe the Messiah:

Prophecy	Expression Related to the Messiah
Isaiah 11:1–2	
Isaiah 53:2	
Jeremiah 23:5	
Jeremiah 33:15	
Zechariah 3:8	
Zechariah 6:12	

c. The description "Jesus the Nazarene," meaning "Jesus the Branch," clearly linked Jesus to the prophecies stating that the Messiah would be the "Branch" that would grow out of Jesse's stump. What did Jesus say about Himself to confirm this identity? (See Revelation 22:16.)

3. Based on their name and their Davidic lineage, the Nazarenes believed that the Messiah would come from their village because they were the "shoot" village.

a. What does Luke 4:16–21 tell us about the Nazarenes?

b. What did other people think of Nazareth? (See John 1:46.)

Topic B: Understanding Our Relationship to Jesus, the Image of the Olive Tree

When olive trees grow old, their branches no longer produce fruit, so the farmer will cut off those branches, leaving a stump several feet

The Olive Tree

DATA FILE

Sepphoris—A Window into Jesus' World

Sepphoris, like many cities of its day, had a tumultuous history:

- When Rome first invaded Israel, the Roman commander Pompey designated Sepphoris as the district capital of Galilee.
- Dating from at least the Hasmonaean period, the city was perched on top of a high hill surrounded by fertile, farm-dotted valleys.
- The inhabitants of the city resisted Herod the Great, however, so he slaughtered them in 37 B.C. and destroyed their city.
- People rebuilt Sepphoris and, led by the Zealots, its inhabitants revolted against Rome following Herod the Great's death in 4 B.C.
- Roman troops conquered and destroyed the city again.
- When Herod Antipas became king of Galilee, he began rebuilding Sepphoris as his capital.

Crowned by Herod's elaborate palace, Sepphoris was home to one of the largest theaters of the first century. The city was laid out in the latest Roman pattern with a colonnaded street leading to the forum. It also featured a gymnasium, an elaborate water system, and probably a bathing complex. Just three miles away, in the humble village of Nazareth, lived a Jewish boy—a stonemason by trade—who became known as Jesus of Nazareth. The beautiful and exciting city of Sepphoris, with its Hellenistic ideas, wealth, and power certainly impacted Nazareth and exposed Jesus to secular culture at a relatively young age.

Sepphoris: Bird on a Hill

Language of Culture

DATA FILE

Sepphoris—A Window into Jesus' World

Sepphoris, like many cities of its day, had a tumultuous history:

- When Rome first invaded Israel, the Roman commander Pompey designated Sepphoris as the district capital of Galilee.
- Dating from at least the Hasmonaean period, the city was perched on top of a high hill surrounded by fertile, farm-dotted valleys.
- The inhabitants of the city resisted Herod the Great, however, so he slaughtered them in 37 B.C. and destroyed their city.
- People rebuilt Sepphoris and, led by the Zealots, its inhabitants revolted against Rome following Herod the Great's death in 4 B.C.
- Roman troops conquered and destroyed the city again.
- When Herod Antipas became king of Galilee, he began rebuilding Sepphoris as his capital.

Crowned by Herod's elaborate palace, Sepphoris was home to one of the largest theaters of the first century. The city was laid out in the latest Roman pattern with a colonnaded street leading to the forum. It also featured a gymnasium, an elaborate water system, and probably a bathing complex. Just three miles away, in the humble village of Nazareth, lived a Jewish boy—a stonemason by trade—who became known as Jesus of Nazareth. The beautiful and exciting city of Sepphoris, with its Hellenistic ideas, wealth, and power certainly impacted Nazareth and exposed Jesus to secular culture at a relatively young age.

Sepphoris: Bird on a Hill

Topic B: Understanding Our Relationship to Jesus, the Image of the Olive Tree

When olive trees grow old, their branches no longer produce fruit, so the farmer will cut off those branches, leaving a stump several feet wide and tall. Soon, new shoots begin to grow out of the old stump, and new branches are sometimes grafted onto the old stump. The prophets, Jesus, and the apostle Paul used this image, which was familiar to the people of Jesus' day, to help explain His relationship to His people.

1. In order to understand the metaphor of the olive tree, we must know what it represents. What is the identity of the "stump" and the "shoot"? (See Isaiah 11:1–3.)

   Suggested Response: Jesse (David's father, who represents the people of Israel) is the "stump," and the Messiah is the "shoot."

The Olive Tree

2. In John 15:1, Jesus identifies Himself with the tree.

   a. What does Jesus reveal about God's relationship to the tree?

   Suggested Response: His Father is the gardener who tends the tree.

   b. What must God, the gardener, do to the "tree" that will not produce good fruit? (See Matthew 3:10; 7:19.)

   Suggested Response: Cut it down and throw it into the fire.

   c. Has God ever had to do this? What was the result? (See Isaiah 6:11–13.)

   Suggested Responses: God cut down the tree (Israel) once because it didn't produce fruit, but the stump—the "holy seed"—remained.

3. Based on their name and their Davidic lineage, the Nazarenes believed that the Messiah would come from their village because they were the "shoot" village.

   a. What does Luke 4:16–21 tell us about the Nazarenes?

   b. What did other people think of Nazareth? (See John 1:46.)

Topic B: Understanding Our Relationship to Jesus, the Image of the Olive Tree

When olive trees grow old, their branches no longer produce fruit, so the farmer will cut off those branches, leaving a stump several feet

The Olive Tree

wide and tall. Soon, new shoots begin to grow out of the old stump, and new branches are sometimes grafted onto the old stump. The prophets, Jesus, and the apostle Paul used this image, which was familiar to the people of Jesus' day, to help explain His relationship to His people.

1. In order to understand the metaphor of the olive tree, we must know what it represents. What is the identity of the "stump" and the "shoot"? (See Isaiah 11:1–3.)

2. In John 15:1, Jesus identifies Himself with the tree.

   a. What does Jesus reveal about God's relationship to the tree?

   b. What must God, the gardener, do to the "tree" that will not produce good fruit? (See Matthew 3:10; 7:19.)

   c. Has God ever had to do this? What was the result? (See Isaiah 6:11–13.)

3. What were early Christians called, and what did that description mean? (See Acts 24:5; Jeremiah 33:15.)

✐ 3.   What were early Christians called, and what did that description mean? (See Acts 24:5; Jeremiah 33:15.)

Suggested Response: Nazarenes, meaning "people of the branch."

✐ 4.   Romans 11:13–24 describes the relationship between Jesus the Nazarene, the Jewish people, and Gentile Christians. Fill in the blanks in the following:

   a.   Gentile Christians are not "natural" branches of the stump. They are <u>*wild olive shoots*</u> that have been <u>*grafted in*</u> among the others. (See Romans 11:17.)

   b.   Gentile Christians share in the <u>*nourishing sap*</u> from the olive root and must remember that they do not <u>*support*</u> the root, but in fact receive <u>*support from*</u> the root. (See Romans 11:17–18.)

✐ 5.   Gentile Christians, like Israel, are expected to produce fruit.

   a.   What enables the branches to produce fruit? (See John 15:4–5.)

Suggested Responses: Branches can't produce on their own, they must be nourished by the vine.

   b.   What will happen to branches that do not produce fruit? (See John 15:6; Romans 11:21–22.)

Suggested Response: They will be cut off and burned up.

Topic C: Jesus the Master Builder

Although Jesus was a trained *tekton* who could build with any material, He probably spent much of His time working as a stonemason, shaping and laying stones. Let's look at some of the images from the construction world that Jesus used as He taught His varied audiences.

✐ 1.   On what did Jesus say He would build His church? (See Matthew 16:18.)

Suggested Responses: a rock. Although there are different interpretations as to precisely what Jesus intended the rock to mean, two major viewpoints are: Jesus' identity as the Messiah, and the faith of His disciples as represented by Peter.

✐ 2.   After seeing the spectacular construction of Herod's temple, what claim did Jesus make? What impact did it have on His audience? (See John 2:19–22.)

Suggested Responses: He said that if "this" temple were destroyed, He would raise it again in three days. The Jews challenged His seemingly outrageous claim because everyone knew it had taken forty-six years to build the temple. But Jesus was referring to an even more miraculous resurrection—that of His physical body. After His resurrection, His disciples remembered His bold statement and believed.

✐ 3.   When addressing His disciples about their commitment to follow Him, Jesus drew an analogy between building a tower and becoming His disciple. What was His point? (See Luke 14:28–30.)

Suggested Responses: Jesus told them to weigh the cost, just as a person who wanted to build a tower would have to plan beforehand to ensure that he'd have

4. Romans 11:13–24 describes the relationship between Jesus the Nazarene, the Jewish people, and Gentile Christians. Fill in the blanks in the following:

a. Gentile Christians are not "natural" branches of the stump. They are _____ that have been _____ among the others. (See Romans 11:17.)

b. Gentile Christians share in the _____ from the olive root and must remember that they do not _____ the root, but in fact receive _____ the root. (See Romans 11:17–18.)

5. Gentile Christians, like Israel, are expected to produce fruit.

a. What enables the branches to produce fruit? (See John 15:4–5.)

b. What will happen to branches that do not produce fruit? (See John 15:6; Romans 11:21–22.)

Topic C: Jesus the Master Builder

Although Jesus was a trained *tekton* who could build with any material, He probably spent much of His time working as a stonemason, shaping and laying stones. Let's look at some of the images from the construction world that Jesus used as He taught His varied audiences.

1. On what did Jesus say He would build His church? (See Matthew 16:18.)

2. After seeing the spectacular construction of Herod's temple, what claim did Jesus make? What impact did it have on His audience? (See John 2:19–22.)

3. When addressing His disciples about their commitment to follow Him, Jesus drew an analogy between building a tower and becoming His disciple. What was His point? (See Luke 14:28–30.)

4. Read Matthew 21:42; Acts 4:11–12.

a. With which part of a building did Jesus identify Himself?

b. What does this metaphor say about His role?

5. Following Jesus' example, Peter also used images from stone construction to explain what it means to participate in the kingdom of God. (See 1 Peter 2:4–8.)

a. Who (or what) is Jesus in Peter's analogy?

enough money to complete it. The consequence of not planning would be public ridicule.

✏ 4. Read Matthew 21:42; Acts 4:11–12.

    a. With which part of a building did Jesus identify Himself?

       Suggested Responses: In fulfillment of prophecy, Jesus called Himself the capstone (cornerstone). He is the finishing stone of the structure, the crowning element.

    b. What does this metaphor say about His role?

       Suggested Responses: Jesus is the Cornerstone, the piece that holds everything together. He is the Messiah of whom the prophets spoke, the only one through whom salvation can come. When this stone is rejected, no other stone can replace it.

✏ 5. Following Jesus' example, Peter also used images from stone construction to explain what it means to participate in the kingdom of God. (See 1 Peter 2:4–8.)

    a. Who (or what) is Jesus in Peter's analogy?

       Suggested Responses: the Living Stone, the precious Cornerstone.

    b. What is Jesus the *tekton* building today, and with whom?

       Suggested Response: His church; God's people, like living stones, are being built into a spiritual house, a holy priesthood.

    c. What is Jesus to those who reject Him?

       Suggested Responses: a stumbling block, a rock that causes them to fall.

Topic D: Jesus and the Herods

From His birth until His death, Jesus' life on earth was intertwined with that of the Herod dynasty—Herod the Great, Herod Archelaus, Herod Antipas. Let's consider how Jesus may have been familiar enough with them to refer to them in His teaching.

✏ 1. What was the response of Herod the Great to the birth of Jesus, the "king of the Jews"? (See Matthew 2:1–8, 12–18.)

    Suggested Responses: When he learned of the birth through the Magi, Herod asked them, under the pretense of worshiping Him also, to reveal where Jesus was. After discovering that the Magi had ignored his request, Herod ordered every boy in Bethlehem two years of age and under to be killed.

✏ 2. When Joseph moved his family back to Israel, what caused him to settle in Nazareth, thereby fulfilling prophecy? (See Matthew 2:19–23.)

    Suggested Responses: Joseph heard that Herod Archelaus, whose cruelty rivaled that of his father, was ruling in Judea, and also was warned in a dream. So he took Mary and Jesus to the relative safety of Nazareth, which was ruled by Herod Antipas.

2. After seeing the spectacular construction of Herod's temple, what claim did Jesus make? What impact did it have on His audience? (See John 2:19–22.)

3. When addressing His disciples about their commitment to follow Him, Jesus drew an analogy between building a tower and becoming His disciple. What was His point? (See Luke 14:28–30.)

4. Read Matthew 21:42; Acts 4:11–12.

   a. With which part of a building did Jesus identify Himself?

   b. What does this metaphor say about His role?

5. Following Jesus' example, Peter also used images from stone construction to explain what it means to participate in the kingdom of God. (See 1 Peter 2:4–8.)

   a. Who (or what) is Jesus in Peter's analogy?

   b. What is Jesus the *tekton* building today, and with whom?

   c. What is Jesus to those who reject Him?

Topic D: Jesus and the Herods

From His birth until His death, Jesus' life on earth was intertwined with that of the Herod dynasty—Herod the Great, Herod Archelaus, Herod Antipas. Let's consider how Jesus may have been familiar enough with them to refer to them in His teaching.

1. What was the response of Herod the Great to the birth of Jesus, the "king of the Jews"? (See Matthew 2:1–8, 12–18.)

2. When Joseph moved his family back to Israel, what caused him to settle in Nazareth, thereby fulfilling prophecy? (See Matthew 2:19–23.)

✏ 3.   The lives of Herod Antipas and Jesus were closely intertwined. Herod Antipas was the only Herod to meet Jesus face-to-face. Let's take a closer look at their relationship.

a.   After Herod Antipas had John the Baptist killed, what impact did Jesus' ministry have on him? (See Matthew 14:1–2; Mark 6:14–16.)

Suggested Responses: He feared Jesus because he heard reports about Jesus and His miraculous powers and believed that Jesus was really John the Baptist raised from the dead.

b.   What was Herod Antipas's attitude toward Jesus after John's death? (See Luke 9:7–9; 13:31.)

Suggested Responses: He was confused about Jesus' true identity and wanted to see Him, but his intent was to kill Jesus.

c.   When Pilate sent Jesus to Herod Antipas, how did they respond to each other? (See Luke 23:8–11.)

Suggested Responses: At first, Herod was pleased and hoped to see Jesus perform a miracle. He asked many questions of Jesus, but Jesus didn't answer him. In response, Herod mocked Him.

✏ 4.   What great irony concerning the relationship between Herod Antipas and Jesus is revealed in Luke 8:1–3?

Suggested Responses: God used Joanna—the wife of Cuza, who managed the household of Herod Antipas—to help meet the financial needs of Jesus and His disciples. Herod was, in effect, financing Jesus' ministry!

✏ 5.   When Pharisees warned Jesus that Herod wanted to kill Him, what did Jesus say about Herod and about being in control of doing what God had called Him to do? (See Luke 13:31–33.)

Suggested Responses: Jesus called Herod a "fox," then said, in effect, "I'm really the one in control because I will do exactly what I plan to do." Rather than considering Herod to be crafty, Jesus was implying that Herod was a wimpy imposter, a weak pretender.

✏ 6.   How did the Herodians, the aristocratic Jews who supported Herod, respond to Jesus? Why? (See Matthew 22:15–22; Mark 3:6; John 11:49–50.)

Suggested Responses: They wanted to get Jesus into trouble and, ultimately, to kill Him. They apparently feared that Jesus would cause an uprising, leading the Romans to replace Herod Antipas with someone more effective. If this occurred, they would lose their power.

3. The lives of Herod Antipas and Jesus were closely intertwined. Herod Antipas was the only Herod to meet Jesus face-to-face. Let's take a closer look at their relationship.

a. After Herod Antipas had John the Baptist killed, what impact did Jesus' ministry have on him? (See Matthew 14:1–2; Mark 6:14–16.)

b. What was Herod Antipas's attitude toward Jesus after John's death? (See Luke 9:7–9; 13:31.)

c. When Pilate sent Jesus to Herod Antipas, how did they respond to each other? (See Luke 23:8–11.)

4. What great irony concerning the relationship between Herod Antipas and Jesus is revealed in Luke 8:1–3?

DID YOU KNOW?

In Jewish culture, the fox was sometimes compared to a lion. The fox was small and weak, although he might act like a powerful lion. Whereas great people are like lions in that they make good on their talk, petty nobodies who put on airs and pretend to be greater than they are resemble foxes. A fox is someone who acts big and talks big but is really a "nobody." A lion can make good on his talk because he is truly strong.[1] Jesus may also have been referring to the fact that Herod was only a tetrarch, not a king.

[1] From an article entitled: " That Small Fry Herod Antipas, or When a Fox Is Not a Fox" by Randall Buth.

5. When Pharisees warned Jesus that Herod wanted to kill Him, what did Jesus say about Herod and about being in control of doing what God had called Him to do? (See Luke 13:31–33.)

6. How did the Herodians, the aristocratic Jews who supported Herod, respond to Jesus? Why? (See Matthew 22:15–22; Mark 3:6; John 11:49–50.)

THE HEROD FAMILY TREE

Antipater (Idumaean)

HEROD THE GREAT

- Died in 4 B.C.
- Effective administrator, cruel, supported by Rome
- Visited by wise men, killed Bethlehem babies
- Greatest builder the ancient Near East ever knew
- Had 10 wives, three of whom were:

Cleopatra	Miriam	Malthace	

PHILIP

- Effective, popular king
- Ruled north and east of Galilee
- Built Caesarea Philippi

(Luke 3:1)

ANTIPAS

- Effective king
- Ruled Galilee and Perea
- Killed John the Baptist
- Built Tiberias and Sepphoris
- Tried Jesus before crucifixion

*(Luke 3:19; Luke 23:7–12;
Luke 9:7–9; Matthew 14:1–12;
Luke 13:32)*

ARCHELAUS

- Poor ruler, deposed by Romans
- Ruled Judea
- Mary and Joseph settle in Nazareth to avoid him

(Matthew 2:22)

HEROD AGRIPPA I

(Grandson of Herod the Great)

- King of Judea
- Killed James, put Peter in prison
- Struck down by an angel

(Acts 12:1–24)

AGRIPPA II

- King of Judea
- Paul defends his faith before him

(Acts 25:13–26:32)

DRUSILLA

—— *(Sisters of Agrippa II)* ——

- Married Felix, the Roman governor

(Acts 24:24)

BERNICE

- With her brother at Paul's defense

(Acts 25:13)

DID YOU KNOW?

In Jewish culture, the fox was sometimes compared to a lion. The fox was small and weak, although he might act like a powerful lion. Whereas great people are like lions in that they make good on their talk, petty nobodies who put on airs and pretend to be greater than they are resemble foxes. A fox is someone who acts big and talks big but is really a "nobody." A lion can make good on his talk because he is truly strong.[1] Jesus may also have been referring to the fact that Herod was only a tetrarch, not a king.

[1]From an article entitled: "That Small Fry Herod Antipas, or When a Fox Is Not a Fox" by Randall Buth.

THE HEROD FAMILY TREE

Antipater (Idumaean)

HEROD THE GREAT

- Died in 4 B.C.
- Effective administrator, cruel, supported by Rome
- Visited by wise men, killed Bethlehem babies
- Greatest builder the ancient Near East ever knew
- Had 10 wives, three of whom were:

Cleopatra   Miriam   Malthace

PHILIP   **ANTIPAS**   **ARCHELAUS**

- Effective, popular king
- Ruled north and east of Galilee
- Built Caesarea Philippi

(Luke 3:1)

- Effective king
- Ruled Galilee and Perea
- Killed John the Baptist
- Built Tiberias and Sepphoris
- Tried Jesus before crucifixion

(Luke 3:19; Luke 23:7–12; Luke 9:7–9; Matthew 14:1–12; Luke 13:32)

- Poor ruler, deposed by Romans
- Ruled Judea
- Mary and Joseph settle in Nazareth to avoid him

(Matthew 2:22)

HEROD AGRIPPA I

(Grandson of Herod the Great)

- King of Judea
- Killed James, put Peter in prison
- Struck down by an angel

(Acts 12:1–24)

AGRIPPA II   **DRUSILLA**   **BERNICE**

(Sisters of Agrippa II)

- King of Judea
- Paul defends his faith before him

(Acts 25:13–26:32)

- Married Felix, the Roman governor

(Acts 24:24)

- With her brother at Paul's defense

(Acts 25:13)

DID YOU KNOW?

In Jewish culture, the fox was sometimes compared to a lion. The fox was small and weak, although he might act like a powerful lion. Whereas great people are like lions in that they make good on their talk, petty nobodies who put on airs and pretend to be greater than they are resemble foxes. A fox is someone who acts big and talks big but is really a "nobody." A lion can make good on his talk because he is truly strong.[1] Jesus may also have been referring to the fact that Herod was only a tetrarch, not a king.

[1]From an article entitled: "That Small Fry Herod Antipas, or When a Fox Is Not a Fox" by Randall Buth.

5. When Pharisees warned Jesus that Herod wanted to kill Him, what did Jesus say about Herod and about being in control of doing what God had called Him to do? (See Luke 13:31–33.)

6. How did the Herodians, the aristocratic Jews who supported Herod, respond to Jesus? Why? (See Matthew 22:15–22; Mark 3:6; John 11:49–50.)

PROFILE OF A DYNASTY

The Legacy of Herod the Great

Few families in history have come as close to Jesus' message as the Herods. Many members of this ruling family knew of Jesus and His followers. Yet, one after the other, they killed or tried to kill anyone connected to Him. Maybe the Herod family, descended from Esau and Edom, simply fulfilled the prophecies (Genesis 25:23; Numbers 24:17; Obadiah 8–21).

Ruler	Notable Deeds	Last Days
Antipas: ruled Galilee and Perea 40+ years	Brought peace and prosperity; sensitive to Jewish religion yet married brother Philip's wife; built Sepphoris and Tiberias; had John the Baptist beheaded; met Jesus and plotted His death (Jesus opposed him)	Agrippa accused him of a plot; new emperor exiled him and claimed his property
Archelaus: ruled Judea, Samaria, Idumaea 10 years	Killed families of Jewish delegations who had gone to Rome to accuse him; known for his bloodthirstiness and evil qualities	Exiled to Gaul, then disappeared from history
Philip: ruled area north and east of the Sea of Galilee 37 years	A just ruler who mainly governed Gentiles; peace-loving	Died of natural causes at end of his reign
Agrippa I: ruled area north and east of Sea of Galilee, Judea 8 years	Ruled a large area; sought to stop Jesus' followers; killed James and imprisoned Peter and other disciples	An angel of God struck him down; eaten up by worms and died
Agrippa II: ruled small portion of his father's region, had limited rule in Jerusalem	Advanced Hellenistic culture; wounded during Jewish Revolt supporting Rome; heard Paul's stirring presentation of the gospel in Caesarea, but was not persuaded	Was wounded fighting for Rome against the Zealots at Gamla, but the specifics of his death are not known

PROFILE OF A DYNASTY

The Legacy of Herod the Great

Few families in history have come as close to Jesus' message as the Herods. Many members of this ruling family knew of Jesus and His followers. Yet, one after the other, they killed or tried to kill anyone connected to Him. Maybe the Herod family, descended from Esau and Edom, simply fulfilled the prophecies (Genesis 25:23; Numbers 24:17; Obadiah 8–21).

Ruler	Notable Deeds	Last Days
Antipas: ruled Galilee and Perea 40+ years	Brought peace and prosperity; sensitive to Jewish religion yet married brother Philip's wife; built Sepphoris and Tiberias; had John the Baptist beheaded; met Jesus and plotted His death (Jesus opposed him)	Agrippa accused him of a plot; new emperor exiled him and claimed his property
Archelaus: ruled Judea, Samaria, Idumaea 10 years	Killed families of Jewish delegations who had gone to Rome to accuse him; known for his bloodthirstiness and evil qualities	Exiled to Gaul, then disappeared from history
Philip: ruled area north and east of the Sea of Galilee 37 years	A just ruler who mainly governed Gentiles; peace-loving	Died of natural causes at end of his reign
Agrippa I: ruled area north and east of Sea of Galilee, Judea 8 years	Ruled a large area; sought to stop Jesus' followers; killed James and imprisoned Peter and other disciples	An angel of God struck him down; eaten up by worms and died
Agrippa II: ruled small portion of his father's region, had limited rule in Jerusalem	Advanced Hellenistic culture; wounded during Jewish Revolt supporting Rome; heard Paul's stirring presentation of the gospel in Caesarea, but was not persuaded	Was wounded fighting for Rome against the Zealots at Gamla, but the specifics of his death are not known

Topic E: Cultural Images in Jesus' Teaching

Jesus used word pictures and ideas designed to communicate effectively to His audiences. Let's now consider several elements of the world of wealth and power that were part of Jesus' teaching.

Royalty

1. Read Luke 19:11–27 and compare the parallels between Jesus' parable about the man of noble birth and widely known facts concerning Herod Archelaus:

Details in Jesus' Parable	True Herodian Facts
Luke 19:12: A man of noble birth went to distant country in order to become king.	Archelaus, a son of Herod the Great, went to Rome to request more land to govern than his father had bequeathed in his will.
Luke 19:14: His subjects hated him and sent a delegation to protest.	Jews from Judea and Jerusalem sent a delegation to Rome to request that someone other than Archelaus govern them.
Luke 19:27: Nobleman returned and killed those who didn't want him to become king.	When Archelaus returned from Rome, he executed the Jews who had gone to Rome to request that someone else govern them. He also killed their families and confiscated their property.

2. Compare Jesus' teaching in Luke 14:31–33 with a widely known fact concerning Herod Antipas:

Details in Jesus' Parable	True Herodian Facts
Luke 14:31–33: A king who is ready to battle another king should evaluate his ability to win, and if he cannot win, he should negotiate a peace.	After divorcing his wife, daughter of King Aretas of Nabatea, Herod had to defend himself against the army of Aretas, but he lost badly.

3. As recorded in Matthew 20:25–28, what did Jesus say to His disciples about the politicians of His day?

   Suggested Response: that they lorded over the Gentile population with a heavy hand rather than serving them.

WORTH OBSERVING

Although Jesus exposed and criticized some of the Pharisees, not all of the Pharisees were hypocrites. Some of them were not far from God's kingdom (Mark 12:34) or had entered it (Acts 15:5). Others supported Jesus and tried to protect Him (John 3:1–2; 7:50–51; Luke 13:31). Jesus never criticized them for being Pharisees, but He criticized their hypocrisy—the fact that they knew the truth but didn't live by it. Jesus commanded His followers to obey the Pharisees (Matthew 23:2–7) but not to imitate their hypocrisy. The apostle Paul remained a Pharisee after becoming a follower of Jesus. (See Acts 23:6; Philippians 3:4–5.)

Language of Culture

251

Session Six: Language of Culture   159

Topic E: Cultural Images in Jesus' Teaching

Jesus used word pictures and ideas designed to communicate effectively to His audiences. Let's now consider several elements of the world of wealth and power that were part of Jesus' teaching.

Royalty

1. Read Luke 19:11–27 and compare the parallels between Jesus' parable about the man of noble birth and widely known facts concerning Herod Archelaus:

Details in Jesus' Parable	True Herodian Facts
Luke 19:12:	Archelaus, a son of Herod the Great, went to Rome to request more land to govern than his father had bequeathed in his will.
Luke 19:14:	Jews from Judea and Jerusalem sent a delegation to Rome to request that someone other than Archelaus govern them.
Luke 19:27:	When Archelaus returned from Rome, he executed the Jews who had gone to Rome to request that someone else govern them. He also killed their families and confiscated their property.

160   Faith Lessons on the Life and Ministry of the Messiah

2. Compare Jesus' teaching in Luke 14:31–33 with a widely known fact concerning Herod Antipas:

Details in Jesus' Parable	True Herodian Facts
Luke 14:31–33:	After divorcing his wife, daughter of King Aretas of Nabatea, Herod had to defend himself against the army of Aretas, but he lost badly.

3. As recorded in Matthew 20:25–28, what did Jesus say to His disciples about the politicians of His day?

WORTH OBSERVING

Although Jesus exposed and criticized some of the Pharisees, not all of the Pharisees were hypocrites. Some of them were not far from God's kingdom (Mark 12:34) or had entered it (Acts 15:5). Others supported Jesus and tried to protect Him (John 3:1–2; 7:50–51; Luke 13:31). Jesus never criticized them for being Pharisees, but He criticized their hypocrisy—the fact that they knew the truth but didn't live by it. Jesus commanded His followers to obey the Pharisees (Matthew 23:2–7) but not to imitate their hypocrisy. The apostle Paul remained a Pharisee after becoming a follower of Jesus. (See Acts 23:6; Philippians 3:4–5.)

PLANNING NOTES:

The Theater

Herod the Great popularized the theater in Israel. The plays often focused on gods and goddesses, mocked honorable and sacred things, and were bawdy and obscene. Featured actors "painted" their faces to portray different characters or emotions, and leading actors were announced with trumpets. The Greek word for "stage actor" was *hypocrite.*

The Jewish community considered theaters to be immoral, and the Talmud taught that no one should attend them. There is no evidence that Jesus participated in or attended the theater, but He clearly was familiar with this aspect of His culture. By speaking its "language," he could communicate to those who knew the theater, including the pagans of the Decapolis.

4. How is each of the following examples related to stage actors, and what is the point of each teaching?

   a. Matthew 6:2–4

   Suggested Response: Jesus used the image of stage actors being announced with trumpets in order to encourage people to give to needy people quietly and humbly, without making a show so that other people would applaud.

   b. Matthew 6:16–18

   Suggested Response: Jesus used the image of stage actors who would paint their faces to express emotion in order to encourage people who were fasting to maintain their normal appearance so that other people would not know they were fasting.

   c. Matthew 23:23–28

   Suggested Response: Here Jesus used the imagery of stage actors who pretended, who did things for show, to strongly condemn some of the teachers of the law and some of the Pharisees. They did not practice what they taught. They were changeable, appearing to be one kind of person when they were really another.

Theater at Sepphoris

The Theater

Herod the Great popularized the theater in Israel. The plays often focused on gods and goddesses, mocked honorable and sacred things, and were bawdy and obscene. Featured actors "painted" their faces to portray different characters or emotions, and leading actors were announced with trumpets. The Greek word for "stage actor" was *hypocrite*.

The Jewish community considered theaters to be immoral, and the Talmud taught that no one should attend them. There is no evidence that Jesus participated in or attended the theater, but He clearly was familiar with this aspect of His culture. By speaking its "language," he could communicate to those who knew the theater, including the pagans of the Decapolis.

4. How is each of the following examples related to stage actors, and what is the point of each teaching?

   a. Matthew 6:2–4

Theater at Sepphoris

   b. Matthew 6:16–18

   c. Matthew 23:23–28

FOR FURTHER STUDY

The book *Roaring Lambs: A Gentle Plan to Radically Change Your World* by Robert Briner (Grand Rapids: Zondervan, 1993) makes a powerful case for learning to speak to a desperate culture in ways it understands. It includes many examples and recommendations.

After nine minutes, let participants know that they have one minute remaining. Then reassemble the entire group. After everyone is back together, begin asking one person from each small group to briefly share a key idea with the larger group. In some cases, you may not have time for every group to share their discoveries.

As time allows, let's briefly share the key ideas that your group discussed.

DATA FILE

The Theaters of Jesus' Day

More than any other person, Herod the Great was responsible for bringing the theater to Israel. His campaign to make humanistic Hellenism the world-view of his people included building theaters at Caesarea, Jericho, Jerusalem, Samaria, and Sidon. Many other places including Susita, Sepphoris, the Decapolis, and Beth Shan had theaters as well. Certainly the first-century theater, which often opposed the God-centered worldview of the Jews, was an important influence.

The splendor and size of Hellenistic theaters, such as the one in Sepphoris, were seductive and overwhelming to the Jewish people. Imagine the temptation of living in a small village such as Nazareth with a few hundred people and then having the opportunity to see sensual plays in a beautiful theater that could hold thousands of spectators. The religious community, realizing the pull of the theater, resisted it strongly. An ancient rabbi named Yitzak is quoted in the Megilla, a collection of Jewish sayings, as believing that Caesarea and Jerusalem could not prosper at the same time. Either one or the other would be in ruins. He clearly understood that the values represented by Caesarea and the theater were antithetical to those of Jerusalem and the temple.

Theater at Caesarea

FOR FURTHER STUDY

The book *Roaring Lambs: A Gentle Plan to Radically Change Your World* by Robert Briner (Grand Rapids: Zondervan, 1993) makes a powerful case for learning to speak to a desperate culture in ways it understands. It includes many examples and recommendations.

b. Matthew 6:16–18

c. Matthew 23:23–28

FOR FURTHER STUDY

The book *Roaring Lambs: A Gentle Plan to Radically Change Your World* by Robert Briner (Grand Rapids: Zondervan, 1993) makes a powerful case for learning to speak to a desperate culture in ways it understands. It includes many examples and recommendations.

DATA FILE

The Theaters of Jesus' Day

More than any other person, Herod the Great was responsible for bringing the theater to Israel. His campaign to make humanistic Hellenism the worldview of his people included building theaters at Caesarea, Jericho, Jerusalem, Samaria, and Sidon. Many other places including Susita, Sepphoris, the Decapolis, and Beth Shan had theaters as well. Certainly the first-century theater, which often opposed the God-centered worldview of the Jews, was an important influence.

The splendor and size of Hellenistic theaters, such as the one in Sepphoris, were seductive and overwhelming to the Jewish people. Imagine the temptation of living in a small village such as Nazareth with a few hundred people and then having the opportunity to see sensual plays in a beautiful theater that could hold thousands of spectators. The religious community, realizing the pull of the theater, resisted it strongly. An ancient rabbi named Yitzak is quoted in the Megilla, a collection of Jewish sayings, as believing that Caesarea and Jerusalem could not prosper at the same time. Either one or the other would be in ruins. He clearly understood that the values represented by Caesarea and the theater were antithetical to those of Jerusalem and the temple.

Theater at Caesarea

ғаітн ᴌᴇsson

Time for Reflection (4 minutes)

It's time for each of us to think quietly about how we can apply what we've learned today. On page 164 of the Participant's Guide, you'll find a passage of Scripture. Let's each read this passage silently and take the next few minutes to consider some of the questions that follow the Scripture passage.

Please do not talk during this time. It's a time when we can reflect on how Jesus communicated to the diverse people of His culture.

> *The Scripture passage and questions are reproduced in their entirety in the Participant's Guide on pages 164–65.*

"Be careful not to do your 'acts of righteousness' before men, to be seen by them. If you do, you will have no reward from your Father in heaven.

"So when you give to the needy, do not announce it with trumpets, as the hypocrites do in the synagogues and on the streets, to be honored by men. I tell you the truth, they have received their reward in full. But when you give to the needy, do not let your left hand know what your right hand is doing, so that your giving may be in secret. Then your Father, who sees what is done in secret, will reward you.

"And when you pray, do not be like the hypocrites, for they love to pray standing in the synagogues and on the street corners to be seen by men. I tell you the truth, they have received their reward in full. But when you pray, go into your room, close the door and pray to your Father, who is unseen. Then your Father, who sees what is done in secret, will reward you. And when you pray, do not keep on babbling like pagans, for they think they will be heard because of their many words. Do not be like them, for your Father knows what you need before you ask him."

MATTHEW 6:1–8

1. Note the various cultural images—the "language"—Jesus used in this short portion of Scripture to communicate with His audience.

2. In what ways have you spoken a "language" that is foreign to the secular culture around you when you have tried to communicate the gospel message to others?

3. In what ways are you effectively communicating God's truths to secular culture?

4. Jesus adjusted His teaching to the worldview of His audience without compromising His message. Can you think of a way in which you could tailor your sharing of God's truths to people at work? In your neighborhood? In your family? To children? To someone of a different race or ethnic group?

5. Is it appropriate to communicate the message of Jesus by means that are also used by secular culture? If so, in what way(s) might you be able to use popular music, theater, movies, television, or computer technology to communicate the gospel to people in your culture?

faith Lesson

Time for Reflection

Read the following passage of Scripture and take the next few minutes to consider the ways in which Jesus communicated to the diverse people of His culture.

"Be careful not to do your 'acts of righteousness' before men, to be seen by them. If you do, you will have no reward from your Father in heaven.

"So when you give to the needy, do not announce it with trumpets, as the hypocrites do in the synagogues and on the streets, to be honored by men. I tell you the truth, they have received their reward in full. But when you give to the needy, do not let your left hand know what your right hand is doing, so that your giving may be in secret. Then your Father, who sees what is done in secret, will reward you.

"And when you pray, do not be like the hypocrites, for they love to pray standing in the synagogues and on the street corners to be seen by men. I tell you the truth, they have received their reward in full. But when you pray, go into your room, close the door and pray to your Father, who is unseen. Then your Father, who sees what is done in secret, will reward you. And when you pray, do not keep on babbling like pagans, for they think they will be heard because of their many words. Do not be like them, for your Father knows what you need before you ask him."

MATTHEW 6:1–8

1. Note the various cultural images—the "language"—Jesus used in this short portion of Scripture to communicate with His audience.

2. In what ways have you spoken a "language" that is foreign to the secular culture around you when you have tried to communicate the gospel message to others?

3. In what ways are you effectively communicating God's truths to secular culture?

4. Jesus adjusted His teaching to the worldview of His audience without compromising His message. Can you think of a way in which you could tailor your sharing of God's truths to people at work? In your neighborhood? In your family? To children? To someone of a different race or ethnic group?

5. Is it appropriate to communicate the message of Jesus by means that are also used by secular culture? If so, in what way(s) might you be able to use popular music, theater, movies, television, or computer technology to communicate the gospel to people in your culture?

PLANNING NOTES:

Action Points (3 minutes)

The following points are reproduced on pages 166–67 of the Participant's Guide:

Now it's time to wrap up our session.

Give participants a moment to transition from their thoughtfulness to giving you their full attention.

I'd like to take a moment to summarize the key points we explored. After I have reviewed these points, I will give you a moment to jot down an action step (or steps) that you will commit to this week as a result of what you have learned today.

Read the following points and pause afterward so that participants can consider and write out their commitment.

1. *We need to discover and understand what shapes our culture.* Jesus participated in the culture of His world and learned its politics, concerns, trends, and passions. He interacted with many different kinds of men, women, and children: powerful leaders and impoverished peasants, religious teachers and lepers, farmers and fishermen, laborers and prostitutes, children of the rich and poor.

    Do you understand what's going on in the worlds of the people you meet— the issues that concern them, the trends that influence them, the passions that drive them, the fears that haunt them?

    What do you need to learn about your world in order to reach people effectively with Jesus' transforming message?

2. *Isolation from culture is not the solution to cultural change.* Jesus understood the culture, language, and people of His day. He knew what would communicate to the people of His world, and He used that knowledge with power. Without modifying or changing God's message, Jesus found ways to communicate in a "language" of words and ideas that people of His culture spoke and understood. He used the gifts and abilities He had in order to effectively communicate His message of repentance and salvation to everyone He met. In so doing, He made a lasting impact for God.

    If we are to reach people with Jesus' transforming message, we also need to work within our culture and communicate through the "language" of ideas and experiences that people in our world understand.

    God has given you a unique opportunity to reach people in your world—family members, classmates, neighbors, coworkers, community leaders—with His message. In what ways are you using words and ideas that your culture understands in order to faithfully communicate Jesus' message to people?

    What specific things will you do to broaden your understanding of your culture so that you can better communicate Jesus' message to the people of your world?

Action Points

Take a moment to review the key points you explored today, then write down an action step (or steps) that you will commit to this week as a result of what you have learned.

1. *We need to discover and understand what shapes our culture.* Jesus participated in the culture of His world and learned its politics, concerns, trends, and passions. He interacted with many different kinds of men, women, and children: powerful leaders and impoverished peasants, religious teachers and lepers, farmers and fishermen, laborers and prostitutes, children of the rich and poor.

   Do you understand what's going on in the worlds of the people you meet—the issues that concern them, the trends that influence them, the passions that drive them, the fears that haunt them?

   What do you need to learn about your world in order to reach people effectively with Jesus' transforming message?

2. *Isolation from culture is not the solution to cultural change.* Jesus understood the culture, language, and people of His day. He knew what would communicate to the people of His world, and He used that knowledge with power. Without modifying or changing God's message, Jesus found ways

to communicate in a "language" of words and ideas that people of His culture spoke and understood. He used the gifts and abilities He had in order to effectively communicate His message of repentance and salvation to everyone He met. In so doing, He made a lasting impact for God.

If we are to reach people with Jesus' transforming message, we also need to work within our culture and communicate through the "language" of ideas and experiences that people in our world understand.

God has given you a unique opportunity to reach people in your world—family members, classmates, neighbors, coworkers, community leaders—with His message. In what ways are you using words and ideas that your culture understands in order to faithfully communicate Jesus' message to people?

What specific things will you do to broaden your understanding of your culture so that you can better communicate Jesus' message to the people of your world?

PLANNING NOTES:

closing prayer

I minute

Jesus met people where they were. Without compromising His message or His way of living, Jesus reached out to people in all levels of society and made His message relevant to them. Let's close in prayer now, and ask God to work in our lives so that we can better communicate His message to the people around us.

Dear Lord, thank You that You came to earth in order to share God's truth and die on the cross for our sins. You communicated truth to Your culture using words and images that people understood. Please give us a love that makes us willing and ready to communicate Your love and truth in ways that people who do not yet know You can understand. Help us learn how to speak the language of our culture without compromising Your message. In Your name we pray, Jesus, amen.

DATA FILE

The Pharisees

Their History

When the Maccabees opposed the Greeks in 167 B.C., they were supported by a group of pious Jews called the Hasidim. These mighty warriors were devoted to God and sought to obey Him in everything they did. But eventually the Jewish leaders (descendants of the Maccabees) became as Hellenistic as the Greeks, and the devout Jews separated themselves from the Jewish leaders in Jerusalem.

Some of these separatists became Zealots who chose to battle the influence of paganism violently—among their fellow Jews as well as the Romans. Another group of separatists decided that violence would not work. These separatists believed (1) that God had allowed (even caused) the foreign oppression because His people had failed to obey the Torah and (2) that people should devote themselves to completely obeying every detail of law and separating themselves from all influences and people who might interfere with that devotion. These separatists took the name translated "separate" or "separatists" (*perushim*), which means "Pharisee" in English. Committed totally to God, they assumed the responsibility of leading Israel back to Him. By the time of Jesus, there were more than six thousand Pharisees.

The Pharisees' Beliefs

The Torah was the focus of the Pharisees' lives. They believed that Moses had given a two-part law: the written law of Torah and additional oral commandments that had been passed from generation to generation to help the faithful understand and apply the written law. The Pharisees continued to interpret and expand the Torah to cover every possible occurrence of unfaithfulness to the written law. As you might expect, this oral law became a complex guide to everyday life—far more complicated than most people could understand. In fact, the Pharisees' "yoke" of Torah—the method of obedience—was so difficult to understand that it sometimes obscured the very law they sought to obey.

DATA FILE

The Pharisees

Their History

When the Maccabees opposed the Greeks in 167 B.C., they were supported by a group of pious Jews called the Hasidim. These mighty warriors were devoted to God and sought to obey Him in everything they did. But eventually the Jewish leaders (descendants of the Maccabees) became as Hellenistic as the Greeks, and the devout Jews separated themselves from the Jewish leaders in Jerusalem.

Some of these separatists became Zealots who chose to battle the influence of paganism violently—among their fellow Jews as well as the Romans. Another group of separatists decided that violence would not work. These separatists believed (1) that God had allowed (even caused) the foreign oppression because His people had failed to obey the Torah and (2) that people should devote themselves to completely obeying every detail of law and separating themselves from all influences and people who might interfere with that devotion. These separatists took the name translated "separate" or "separatists" (perushim), which means "Pharisee" in English. Committed totally to God, they assumed the responsibility of leading Israel back to Him. By the time of Jesus, there were more than six thousand Pharisees.

The Pharisees' Beliefs

The Torah was the focus of the Pharisees' lives. They believed that Moses had given a two-part law: the written law of Torah and additional oral commandments that had been passed from generation to generation to help the faithful understand and apply the written law. The Pharisees continued to interpret and expand the Torah to cover every possible occurrence of unfaithfulness to the written law. As you might expect, this oral law became a complex guide to everyday life—far more complicated than most people could understand. In fact, the Pharisees' "yoke" of Torah—the method of obedience—was so difficult to understand that it sometimes obscured the very law they sought to obey.

PLANNING NOTES:

THE TRUTH OF THE MATTER

Jesus and the Pharisees

Many Pharisees were a powerful force for good among Jesus' people and had a theology similar to the one developed by the early Christians. Many Pharisees supported Jesus' ministry, frequently inviting Him to their homes (Luke 7:36; 14:1) and warning him of Herod's plot (Luke 13:31). Some Pharisees, in fact, accepted Christ (see Acts 15:5) and kept teaching other people (Acts 23:6; Philippians 3:4–6). Note the following beliefs that the Pharisees had in common with Jesus:

- Belief in the physical resurrection of the dead.
- Belief in a coming Judgment Day followed by reward or punishment.
- Expectation of the Messiah's return.
- Belief in angels.
- Recognition of a combination of free choice and divine control in human life.
- Belief that God was all wise, all knowing, just, merciful, and loving.
- Belief in the importance of completely obeying God's law.
- Belief in people's power to choose good or evil, using the Torah as their guide.

Despite these similarities, Jesus did have some conflicts with the Pharisees. Although many Pharisees set high moral standards and tried to remain devoted to God in a hostile world without resorting to the Zealots' violence, some Pharisees were not godly and righteous. Some were so zealous concerning interpretations of oral law that they violated the very letter of the Torah. Other Pharisees focused so much on obedience that they didn't notice or care about people's needs. Unfortunately, history perceives Pharisees as hypocrites and stubborn, uncaring, religious fanatics who rejected and hated Jesus and worked to obtain His arrest and conviction. Jesus, however, understood their thinking and often tailored His message to make sure the Pharisees would understand it.

It is important to realize that Jesus never criticized anyone for *being* a Pharisee. He criticized only hypocritical Pharisees (Matthew 23) and those who spoiled the entire group (Matthew 16:6, 11). Jesus instructed His disciples to obey what the Pharisees taught (Matthew 23:2–3) but not to practice their hypocrisy.

(continued on page 264)

Language of Culture

THE TRUTH OF THE MATTER

Jesus and the Pharisees

Many Pharisees were a powerful force for good among Jesus' people and had a theology similar to the one developed by the early Christians. Many Pharisees supported Jesus' ministry, frequently inviting Him to their homes (Luke 7:36; 14:1) and warning him of Herod's plot (Luke 13:31). Some Pharisees, in fact, accepted Christ (see Acts 15:5) and kept teaching other people (Acts 23:6; Philippians 3:4–6). Note the following beliefs that the Pharisees had in common with Jesus:

- Belief in the physical resurrection of the dead.
- Belief in a coming Judgment Day followed by reward or punishment.
- Expectation of the Messiah's return.
- Belief in angels.
- Recognition of a combination of free choice and divine control in human life.
- Belief that God was all wise, all knowing, just, merciful, and loving.
- Belief in the importance of completely obeying God's law.
- Belief in people's power to choose good or evil, using the Torah as their guide.

Despite these similarities, Jesus did have some conflicts with the Pharisees. Although many Pharisees set high moral standards and tried to remain devoted to God in a hostile world without resorting to the Zealots' violence, some Pharisees were not godly and righteous. Some were so zealous concerning interpretations of oral law that they violated the very letter of the Torah. Other Pharisees focused so much on obedience that they didn't notice or care about people's needs. Unfortunately, history perceives Pharisees as hypocrites and stubborn, uncaring, religious fanatics who rejected and hated Jesus and worked to obtain His arrest and conviction. Jesus, however, understood their thinking and often tailored His message to make sure the Pharisees would understand it.

It is important to realize that Jesus never criticized anyone for *being* a Pharisee. He criticized only hypocritical Pharisees (Matthew 23) and those who spoiled the entire group (Matthew 16:6, 11). Jesus instructed His

(continued on page 170)

(continued from page 262)

The Pharisees differed significantly from the Sadducees, another group of religious Jewish leaders with whom Jesus communicated. Notice the contrasts:

Pharisees	Sadducees
Committed to studying and obeying the Torah and oral law	Controlled the economy of the temple in Jerusalem; faithful to temple rituals but often Hellenistic in lifestyle
Had a minor role in the Sanhedrin—the ruling religious council used by the Herods and Romans as the instrument to govern the Jewish people	Had a majority in the Sanhedrin—the ruling religious council
Believed in the Torah and oral law	Believed in the written Torah and rejected oral law; opposed the Pharisees until the temple was destroyed in A.D. 70 (and they ceased to exist); believed study of Torah undermined temple ritual
Believed in bodily resurrection and angels	Didn't believe in bodily resurrection and most Pharisaical doctrine concerning angels and spirits
Gained authority based on piety and knowledge	Gained authority through position and birth
Worshiped in the synagogue	Believed synagogue worship undermined temple ritual and the economy of the temple (their income)
As a whole, were not intimidated by Jesus	Feared and hated Jesus, whose popularity might jeopardize their position in the Sanhedrin and Rome's support

(continued from page 169)

disciples to obey what the Pharisees taught (Matthew 23:2–3) but not to practice their hypocrisy.

The Pharisees differed significantly from the Sadducees, another group of religious Jewish leaders with whom Jesus communicated. Notice the contrasts:

Pharisees	Sadducees
Committed to studying and obeying the Torah and oral law	Controlled the economy of the temple in Jerusalem; faithful to temple rituals but often Hellenistic in lifestyle
Had a minor role in the Sanhedrin—the ruling religious council used by the Herods and Romans as the instrument to govern the Jewish people	Had a majority in the Sanhedrin—the ruling religious council
Believed in the Torah and oral law	Believed in the written Torah and rejected oral law; opposed the Pharisees until the temple was destroyed in A.D. 70 (and they ceased to exist); believed study of Torah undermined temple ritual
Believed in bodily resurrection and angels	Didn't believe in bodily resurrection and most Pharisaical doctrine concerning angels and spirits
Gained authority based on piety and knowledge	Gained authority through position and birth
Worshiped in the synagogue	Believed synagogue worship undermined temple ritual and the economy of the temple (their income)
As a whole, were not intimidated by Jesus	Feared and hated Jesus, whose popularity might jeopardize their position in the Sanhedrin and Rome's support

misguided faith

Before you Lead

Synopsis

The history of those who have sought to follow God is marked by situations in which God's people chose their own way of following Him and dealing with the problems of their day rather than choosing His way. Examples from the era that we have been studying in this series include the Pharisees, who believed that only single-minded dedication to the Torah would please God; the Zealots, who tried to bring about God's kingdom through violence; and the Essenes, who called for isolation and separation from the world. In this session, we will consider the great tragedy of Christianity—the terrible invasion of the Holy Land by the Christian Crusaders from Europe during the eleventh and twelfth centuries.

This session was filmed in Israel next to the ruins of a Crusader fort named Belvoir, which stands high above the Jordan Valley, isolated from the farmland and roadways below. Here, 50 knights, about 450 soldiers, and their families and supporting staff lived. In 1180, the fortress was placed under siege, which it withstood for about four years. In 1187, the siege began anew. After a total of about seven years under siege, the knights decided that the situation had gone on long enough. They surrendered, received free passage to the coast, and sailed back home to Europe.

The beautiful and seemingly peaceful location of this fort today gives little indication of the horror it represents. Instead of demonstrating the love, compassion, forgiveness, and self-sacrifice that Jesus used to communicate His message, the Crusaders decided that all people who did not belong to their tradition of Christianity should no longer live. So as they left Europe to liberate the Holy Land from the "infidels," the Crusaders brutally slaughtered innocent inhabitants of cities, towns, and villages. Entire Jewish communities were locked in their synagogues and burned to death. Entire towns were plundered because their inhabitants were Jewish or Muslim in ethnic or religious background. As they entered Turkey, the Crusaders slaughtered more "infidels," but the people they killed were orthodox Christians—brothers and sisters in the faith—who happened to look and dress like Muslims. All of this was done in the name of Jesus, with the full support of the popes and other religious leaders.

When the Crusaders chose to use violence and hatred as a means of presenting the gospel of peace, they defamed the name of Jesus. For nearly two hundred years, under the sign of the cross and in Jesus' name, the Crusaders' overall actions were not consistent with Jesus' commands. Although the Crusades did cause the gospel to be spread to new areas (primarily by the clergy who came after the Crusades), the Crusaders as a whole behaved in ways that greatly damaged the reputation of Christianity and turned many others—particularly Jews and Muslims—away from God. Even today, the Crusades influence people's perceptions of Christianity in the Middle East and stand as a wall between Christians and people of other faiths.

How do Christians today tell someone that Jesus Christ has a message of love when the focus of that message can still be viewed in the ruins of fortresses and battlements built by Christians who came to destroy and kill? The Crusades are indeed a sad chapter in Christian history. These "holy wars" illustrate how easy it is for Christians to justify methods and attitudes other than those that Jesus commanded and lived out. It is so important that we model our attitudes and behavior after His so that we can truly reflect Him to a spiritually dark and hurting world. We must demonstrate Jesus to people as He proclaimed Himself to be—Savior, not warrior.

Just as the Jews of the Old Testament were called to live on the crossroads of the world and demonstrate the living God to a watching, spiritually hungry world, Jesus calls His disciples to do the same. We are called to use Jesus' methods of love, kindness, and self-sacrifice in order to reflect to other people the character of the living God and the wonder of an ongoing, personal relationship with Him.

We must be as committed to the methods Jesus wants us to use as we are to the message of salvation He died to provide. If we are to be His disciples, we must become like Him in every way. Although we must always confront evil, we do this out of concern for those around us to whom we must be light and salt. We must be involved in our culture because Jesus' message is desperately needed in the world today. God gave it to us to give away, not to hoard in isolated hilltop fortresses.

Key Points of This Lesson

1. *When we present Jesus to other people using methods other than those that He used and taught, we send the wrong message and defame Jesus' reputation.* The era of the Crusades is a great tragedy of the Christian faith. The Crusaders slaughtered and plundered Jews, Muslims—even other Christians—in the name of Jesus. The damage done to Jesus' reputation and the walls erected between Christians and people of other faiths remain even to this day.

2. *Jesus wants us to confront the power of evil in our culture, but He wants us to do it as He did—not with the sword, but by offering His life.* So it's important for us, as we confront what is wrong, immoral, and unjust in our society, to do it in a way that models His attitudes and behavior. We must reject attitudes and methods that communicate that Christianity is anything like what the Crusaders demonstrated it to be. If we want others to know God through us, we must present Him as He has revealed Himself to be. If we are to be His disciples, we must become like Him in every way.

Session Outline (52 minutes)

I. Introduction (6 minutes)
Welcome
What's to Come
Questions to Think About

II. Show Video "Misguided Faith" (13 minutes)

III. Group Discovery (22 minutes)
Video Highlights
Small Group Bible Discovery

IV. Faith Lesson (10 minutes)
Time for Reflection
Action Points

V. Closing Prayer (1 minute)

Materials

No additional materials are needed for this session. Simply view the video prior to leading the session so you are familiar with its main points.

misguided faith

introduction

6 minutes

Welcome

Assemble the participants together. Welcome them to session seven of *Faith Lessons on the Life and Ministry of the Messiah.*

What's to Come

As a Jewish rabbi in first-century Israel, Jesus chose specific methods for delivering His message: demonstrating love and compassion, offering forgiveness, inviting people to accept salvation, and so on. He called upon those who would be His disciples to follow His example. Christians, however, have at times chosen methods other than those of Jesus—and with tragic results. The Crusades, which Ray Vander Laan focuses on in this session, are indeed a sad chapter of our Christian history. These "holy wars" illustrate how easy it is for Christians to justify methods, behaviors, and attitudes other than those that Jesus commanded and lived out. They are a reminder of how important it is to demonstrate Jesus to people as He truly proclaimed Himself to be—Savior, not warrior.

Questions to Think About

Participant's Guide page 171.

Ask each question and solicit a few responses from group members.

1. What do you think draws people to Jesus?

   Suggested Responses: will vary but may include His message of love and hope, His lifestyle, the fact that He rose from the dead and is alive today, the fact that He lived on this earth and knows our concerns, the fact that He sacrificed Himself for our sake, etc.

2. Think about the people who have guided you in your discovery of and walk with God. What about them drew you toward God?

   Suggested Responses: will vary but may include their obedience to God, their care for me, their devotion to studying God's Word, their concern for people in physical and spiritual need, etc.

SESSION SEVEN

misguided faith

questions to think about

1. What do you think draws people to Jesus?

2. Think about the people who have guided you in your discovery of and walk with God. What about them drew you toward God?

3. What things do Christians in our culture do that tend to turn people away from God rather than toward Him?

PLANNING NOTES:

✏ 3. What things do Christians in our culture do that tend to turn people away from God rather than toward Him?

Suggested Responses: will vary but may include abortion clinic bombings and the murders of abortionists (not all of which, of course, are done by Christians), insisting that non-Christians live or behave according to the same rules as Christians, proclaiming Jesus' message but not living by His rules (such as preachers who live immoral lives), appearing to judge people rather than love them, etc.

Let's keep these ideas in mind as we view the video.

video presentation
13 minutes

Participant's Guide page 172.

On page 172 of your Participant's Guide, you will find a space in which to take notes on key points as we watch this video.

Leader's Video Observations

The Crusaders' Fort

The Crusaders' Actions and Motivation

The Damaging Consequences of the Crusaders

Our Response: Choosing Jesus' Message and His Methods

misguided faith

questions to think about

1. What do you think draws people to Jesus?

2. Think about the people who have guided you in your discovery of and walk with God. What about them drew you toward God?

3. What things do Christians in our culture do that tend to turn people away from God rather than toward Him?

172   Faith Lessons on the Life and Ministry of the Messiah

video notes

The Crusaders' Fort

The Crusaders' Actions and Motivation

The Damaging Consequences of the Crusaders

Our Response: Choosing Jesus' Message and His Methods

PLANNING NOTES:

Group Discovery

If your group has seven or more members, use the **Video Highlights** with the entire group (5 minutes), then break into small groups of three to five to discuss the **Small Group Bible Discovery** (12 minutes). Then reassemble the group to discuss the key points discovered (5 minutes).

If your group has fewer than seven members, begin with the **Video Highlights** (5 minutes), then do one or more of the topics found in the **Small Group Bible Discovery** as a group (12 minutes). Finally, spend five minutes at the end discussing points that had an impact on participants.

Video Highlights (5 minutes)

Here you'll ask one or more of the following questions that directly relate to the video the participants have just seen.

Look at the map of the Roman Empire on page 173 of your Participant's Guide. Note how far the Crusaders had to travel to get to the Holy Land. Try to imagine the destruction and killing that took place all along their route. It's nearly impossible to comprehend what was done in the name of Jesus, isn't it?

1. What did you think when you saw the European-style Crusader fort high above the Jordan Valley?

   Suggested Responses: may include how out of place it seemed, how set in their ways the Crusaders were, how insensitive to the Jewish people and even the land of Palestine the Crusaders were, etc.

2. What stood out to you as you learned about the Crusades?

   Suggested Responses: Allow several participants to share their observations and perceptions.

The Roman World

video highlights

Look at the map of the Roman Empire below. Note how far the Crusaders had to travel to get to the Holy Land. Try to imagine the destruction and killing that took place all along their route. It's nearly impossible to comprehend what was done in the name of Jesus, isn't it?

1. What did you think when you saw the European-style Crusader fort high above the Jordan Valley?

2. What stood out to you as you learned about the Crusades?

The Roman World

PLANNING NOTES:

✍ 3. What happens to people's view of Christianity when those who are supposed to be imitating Jesus choose their own methods?

Suggested Responses: Unbelievers may see hypocrisy, hatred, cruelty, and criticism instead of seeing Jesus and His message. They may then reject or openly oppose anything that has to do with Christianity, which is a tragedy.

✍ 4. Do you agree with Ray Vander Laan that it's important not to use language that reminds people of the Crusades? Why or why not?

Suggested Responses: will vary. Encourage participants to seriously consider how other people, particularly unbelievers, perceive their words and actions.

DATA FILE

The Fortress of Belvoir

Built by the Knights of the Order of the Hospitalers in the twelfth century, this isolated fortress protected the eastern side of the Crusaders' kingdom. Perched on a hill of the Issachar Plateau 1,700 feet above the Jordan Valley, this fortress enabled the Crusaders to control the road below and "protected" its inhabitants from the local population. From their isolated position, the Crusaders were unable to exert any daily influence on the people in the valley below.

Muslims attacked the fortress from A.D. 1180–1184 and then besieged it again in 1187. After resisting sieges for a total of seven years, the 50 knights and 450 sol-

Belvoir

diers surrendered and left for Europe. The Muslims then destroyed the fortress so it could never be used again.

Today, the ruins of Belvoir stand as a grim monument to the tragedies that occur when people misunderstand Jesus' message and do not live by the truths He taught. Only by living *in* our culture and confronting evil as it presents itself in daily life are we able to influence it positively for Jesus. Jesus called His people to be community builders, not fortress builders. He called his people to confront evil with the weapons of love, forgiveness, and sacrifice.

Physical Details of the Fortress

- A moat encircled the fortress on three sides.
- The entrance was on the east side.
- Towers stood in each corner and in the center of the outer walls so archers could be closer to attackers. A huge tower defended the gate area.
- Small gates led from each tower into the moat, so knights could attack anyone trying to undermine the walls.
- Inside the outer walls (made of basalt) was a smaller fortress consisting of four vaulted, two-story walls and a courtyard. Upper-story rooms were frescoed plaster.
- Cisterns were dug beneath the vaulted rooms.
- A church made of limestone provided a place for worship on the second floor.

3. What happens to people's view of Christianity when those who are supposed to be imitating Jesus choose their own methods?

4. Do you agree with Ray Vander Laan that it's important not to use language that reminds people of the Crusades? Why or why not?

DATA FILE

The Fortress of Belvoir

Built by the Knights of the Order of the Hospitalers in the twelfth century, this isolated fortress protected the eastern side of the Crusaders' kingdom. Perched on a hill of the Issachar Plateau 1,700 feet above the Jordan Valley, this fortress enabled the Crusaders to control the road below and "protected" its inhabitants from the local population. From their isolated position, the Crusaders were unable to exert any daily influence on the people in the valley below.

Muslims attacked the fortress from A.D. 1180–1184 and then besieged it again in 1187. After resisting sieges for a total of seven years, the 50 knights and 450 soldiers surrendered and left for Europe. The Muslims then destroyed the fortress so it could never be used again.

Today, the ruins of Belvoir stand as a grim monument to the tragedies that occur when people misunderstand Jesus' message and do not live by the truths He taught. Only by living *in* our culture and confronting evil

as it presents itself in daily life are we able to influence it positively for Jesus. Jesus called His people to be community builders, not fortress builders. He called his people to confront evil with the weapons of love, forgiveness, and sacrifice.

Physical Details of the Fortress
- A moat encircled the fortress on three sides.
- The entrance was on the east side.
- Towers stood in each corner and in the center of the outer walls so archers could be closer to attackers. A huge tower defended the gate area.
- Small gates led from each tower into the moat, so knights could attack anyone trying to undermine the walls.
- Inside the outer walls (made of basalt) was a smaller fortress consisting of four vaulted, two-story walls and a courtyard. Upper-story rooms were frescoed plaster.
- Cisterns were dug beneath the vaulted rooms.
- A church made of limestone provided a place for worship on the second floor.

Belvoir

PROFILE OF A MOVEMENT

Soldiers of the Cross

On November 27, 1095, in Clermont, France, Pope Urban II called upon all true Christians to free the Holy Land from the Muslim infidels. Christian pilgrims were unable to visit holy sites, including the Church of the Holy Sepulchre—the most sacred of all shrines. That speech sparked a period of violent conflict between the Christian Europeans and the Muslims of the Middle East. Thousands of knights, serfs, peasants, and even a few kings sewed the sign of the cross on the front of their tunics and went to war for Jesus Christ. The Jews, without a country, were caught in between.

The First Crusade

This crusade began in Clermont, France, as knights, farmers, shopkeepers, and fortune seekers headed east through Germany and then south and east to the Holy Land. Determined to avenge Jesus' crucifixion in blood, the leaders of the Crusade massacred many Jews living in wealthy communities in Germany. Many other Jews committed suicide as the knights and unruly mob entered their towns. Tens of thousands of Muslims were also killed. The Crusaders continued to slaughter innocent people, even Orthodox Christians who had the misfortune to dress or look like Muslims.

Finally the Crusaders reached Jerusalem, which they captured on July 15, 1099. A terrible massacre ensued; streets were awash with the blood of innocent civilians. The Jews and Muslims who survived were sold into slavery, and Christianity had earned a reputation that would last for millennia.

The knights built great, European-style castles on high hills, far from roads and sometimes far from water. Soon the castles became places of refuge, escape, and even prisons. Having traveled thousands of miles to win the Holy Land and the infidels to God's truth, the European conquerors had no gospel to offer their subjects. They lived in isolation, not influencing the day-to-day lives of the common people. Jesus would not have recognized these soldiers who came to spread His kingdom because they knew so little of the methods He had taught and the way of sacrifice He had walked.

The Second Crusade

In 1144, an itinerant monk began urging soldiers to destroy the Jewish communities of Germany to avenge Jesus' crucifixion. As a result, many more innocent people were slaughtered in Jesus' name.

The Third Crusade

Spared the horrors of the first two Crusades, the Jewish communities in England were not as fortunate during this Crusade in 1170. Jews in York, Lynn, Norwich, Stamford, and other towns were massacred. Thus England, too, joined the roster of countries whose Christian armies distinguished themselves in their brutality against the "infidels."

(continued on page 280)

PROFILE OF A MOVEMENT

Soldiers of the Cross

On November 27, 1095, in Clermont, France, Pope Urban II called upon all true Christians to free the Holy Land from the Muslim infidels. Christian pilgrims were unable to visit holy sites, including the Church of the Holy Sepulchre—the most sacred of all shrines. That speech sparked a period of violent conflict between the Christian Europeans and the Muslims of the Middle East. Thousands of knights, serfs, peasants, and even a few kings sewed the sign of the cross on the front of their tunics and went to war for Jesus Christ. The Jews, without a country, were caught in between.

The First Crusade

This crusade began in Clermont, France, as knights, farmers, shopkeepers, and fortune seekers headed east through Germany and then south and east to the Holy Land. Determined to avenge Jesus' crucifixion in blood, the leaders of the Crusade massacred many Jews living in wealthy communities in Germany. Many other Jews committed suicide as the knights and unruly mob entered their towns. Tens of thousands of Muslims were also killed. The Crusaders continued to slaughter innocent people, even Orthodox Christians who had the misfortune to dress or look like Muslims.

Finally the Crusaders reached Jerusalem, which they captured on July 15, 1099. A terrible massacre ensued; streets were awash with the blood of innocent civilians. The Jews and Muslims who survived were sold into slavery, and Christianity had earned a reputation that would last for millennia.

The knights built great, European-style castles on high hills, far from roads and sometimes far from water. Soon the castles became places of refuge, escape, and even prisons. Having traveled thousands of miles to

win the Holy Land and the infidels to God's truth, the European conquerors had no gospel to offer their subjects. They lived in isolation, not influencing the day-to-day lives of the common people. Jesus would not have recognized these soldiers who came to spread His kingdom because they knew so little of the methods He had taught and the way of sacrifice He had walked.

The Second Crusade

In 1144, an itinerant monk began urging soldiers to destroy the Jewish communities of Germany to avenge Jesus' crucifixion. As a result, many more innocent people were slaughtered in Jesus' name.

The Third Crusade

Spared the horrors of the first two Crusades, the Jewish communities in England were not as fortunate during this Crusade in 1170. Jews in York, Lynn, Norwich, Stamford, and other towns were massacred. Thus England, too, joined the roster of countries whose Christian armies distinguished themselves in their brutality against the "infidels."

The Fourth Crusade

In 1198, Pope Innocent III began the Fourth Crusade. He ordered Jews to wear badges to identify themselves, then ordered them to be killed to atone for Jesus' death.

The Shepherds' Crusade

The Crusades formally ended in 1291 when the Holy Land was recaptured by the Muslims. But a few years later, European Jews were subjected to yet another Crusade. Nearly forty thousand, mostly teenage "Crusaders" pillaged, killed, and burned their way across Europe. Some sources indicate that 150 communities of Jews were exterminated by these "soldiers of the cross."

PLANNING NOTES:

(continued from page 278)

The Fourth Crusade

In 1198, Pope Innocent III began the Fourth Crusade. He ordered Jews to wear badges to identify themselves, then ordered them to be killed to atone for Jesus' death.

The Shepherds' Crusade

The Crusades formally ended in 1291 when the Holy Land was recaptured by the Muslims. But a few years later, European Jews were subjected to yet another Crusade. Nearly forty thousand, mostly teenage "Crusaders" pillaged, killed, and burned their way across Europe. Some sources indicate that 150 communities of Jews were exterminated by these "soldiers of the cross."

Small Group Bible Discovery (17 minutes)

Participant's Guide pages 178-87.

During this time, a group with fewer than seven participants will stay together. A group of seven or more participants will break into small groups and reassemble as a large group during the final five minutes. Assign each group one of the following topics. If you have more than four small groups, assign some topics to more than one group.

Let's break into groups of three to five—people sitting near you—and study some of the Bible passages and truths mentioned in the video.

Turn to pages 178-87 in your Participant's Guide. There you'll find a list of four topics. You'll have twelve minutes to read and discuss the topic I'll assign to you. Choose one person in your group to be a spokesperson for your group when we discuss these topics later.

Assign each group a topic.

I'll signal you when one minute is left.

Topic A: Jesus' Method of Confrontation

Jesus clearly advocated the confrontation of evil. Whereas our human response often is to confront using violence, Jesus confronted evil in different ways. Let's consider His methods of confrontation.

win the Holy Land and the infidels to God's truth, the European conquerors had no gospel to offer their subjects. They lived in isolation, not influencing the day-to-day lives of the common people. Jesus would not have recognized these soldiers who came to spread His kingdom because they knew so little of the methods He had taught and the way of sacrifice He had walked.

The Second Crusade

In 1144, an itinerant monk began urging soldiers to destroy the Jewish communities of Germany to avenge Jesus' crucifixion. As a result, many more innocent people were slaughtered in Jesus' name.

The Third Crusade

Spared the horrors of the first two Crusades, the Jewish communities in England were not as fortunate during this Crusade in 1170. Jews in York, Lynn, Norwich, Stamford, and other towns were massacred. Thus England, too, joined the roster of countries whose Christian armies distinguished themselves in their brutality against the "infidels."

The Fourth Crusade

In 1198, Pope Innocent III began the Fourth Crusade. He ordered Jews to wear badges to identify themselves, then ordered them to be killed to atone for Jesus' death.

The Shepherds' Crusade

The Crusades formally ended in 1291 when the Holy Land was recaptured by the Muslims. But a few years later, European Jews were subjected to yet another Crusade. Nearly forty thousand, mostly teenage "Crusaders" pillaged, killed, and burned their way across Europe. Some sources indicate that 150 communities of Jews were exterminated by these "soldiers of the cross."

small group bible discovery

Topic A: Jesus' Method of Confrontation

Jesus clearly advocated the confrontation of evil. Whereas our human response often is to confront using violence, Jesus confronted evil in different ways. Let's consider His methods of confrontation.

1. In each of the following Scripture passages, what did Jesus confront, and what can we learn from His attitudes and actions?

Scripture	What Did He Confront?	What Can We Learn from His Method?
Mark 5:1–20		
Matthew 15:21–28		
Matthew 16:21–25		

2. When Jesus healed the Canaanite woman's daughter (see Matthew 15:21–28 above), He was in the region of Tyre and Sidon.

✏ 1. In each of the following Scripture passages, what did Jesus confront, and what can we learn from His attitudes and actions?

Scripture	What Did He Confront?	What Can We Learn from His Method?
Mark 5:1–20	Evil, which presented itself in the form of a naked, violent man who was possessed by evil spirits	Jesus exercised His authority over the spirits and commanded them to leave the man. Afterward He sat down and spoke with the man. Then He told the man to tell his family what God had done for him.
Matthew 15:21–28	Evil, which presented itself in the form of a demon-possessed girl	This request for healing came from a Canaanite woman—a request Jesus easily could have ignored because she wasn't a Jew, but she had a persistent faith that Jesus honored by healing her daughter.
Matthew 16:21–25	Evil—Peter expressed Satan's temptation to abandon God's plan of salvation	Jesus clearly identified the evil source of Peter's words and rebuked them. Then He explained to His disciples the method and the cost of following Him.

✏ 2. When Jesus healed the Canaanite woman's daughter (see Matthew 15:21–28 above), He was in the region of Tyre and Sidon.

a. What was the reputation of that area? (See 1 Kings 16:31; Isaiah 23:17.)

Suggested Responses: It was an extremely pagan place, a center for immorality and Baal worship—and the home of Jezebel, King Ahab's wife.

b. Why did Jesus go there? (See Matthew 9:10–13.)

Suggested Response: He possibly wanted to demonstrate to His disciples that the gospel is for all people.

✏ 3. In His Sermon on the Mount, Jesus outlined His battle plan for confronting evil.

a. Which characteristics did Jesus call "blessed"? (See Matthew 5:5–10.)

Suggested Responses: meekness, hunger and thirst for righteousness, mercy, purity of heart, peacemaking, a willingness to be persecuted.

small Group Bible Discovery

Topic A: Jesus' Method of Confrontation

Jesus clearly advocated the confrontation of evil. Whereas our human response often is to confront using violence, Jesus confronted evil in different ways. Let's consider His methods of confrontation.

1. In each of the following Scripture passages, what did Jesus confront, and what can we learn from His attitudes and actions?

Scripture	What Did He Confront?	What Can We Learn from His Method?
Mark 5:1–20		
Matthew 15:21–28		
Matthew 16:21–25		

2. When Jesus healed the Canaanite woman's daughter (see Matthew 15:21–28 above), He was in the region of Tyre and Sidon.

   a. What was the reputation of that area? (See 1 Kings 16:31; Isaiah 23:17.)

   b. Why did Jesus go there? (See Matthew 9:10–13.)

3. In His Sermon on the Mount, Jesus outlined His battle plan for confronting evil.

   a. Which characteristics did Jesus call "blessed"? (See Matthew 5:5–10.)

   b. What is the purpose of following Jesus' battle plan? (See Matthew 5:13–16.)

   c. How are these characteristics and purposes like and unlike the Crusaders' ways of confronting evil? Our ways of confronting evil?

PLANNING NOTES:

b. What is the purpose of following Jesus' battle plan? (See Matthew 5:13–16.)

Suggested Responses: His followers are to be like salt—preserving and flavoring our culture; to be the light of the world—shining out the message of Jesus. We are to be like this so that everyone around us will see the good things we do and praise God.

c. How are these characteristics and purposes like and unlike the Crusaders' ways of confronting evil? Our ways of confronting evil?

Suggested Responses: Encourage participants to see the vast difference between Jesus' way of confronting evil and the violent, self-serving way in which the Crusaders conducted their campaign. Encourage them to do some soul-searching regarding their personal participation in Jesus' battle plan.

✏ 4. What did Jesus say His followers could expect to encounter as they lovingly carried out His commands and shared His message? What encouragement did He offer? (See Matthew 10:17–28.)

Suggested Responses: His followers would be beaten in synagogues, placed on trial before governors and kings, hated, and even persecuted unto death. He encouraged His followers to not back away from proclaiming His message, to seek to be like Him in every way, and to not be afraid of evil.

FACTS TO CONSIDER

As They Saw It

Many people during Jesus' time offered their own solutions to the problems of the day, as the following reveals:

Who Offered the Solution	What They Recommended	The Method of Jesus
Pharisees	National obedience to the Torah as a life commitment	Demonstrated His commitment to God by His obedience to the Torah
Essenes	Be separate from the world and wait for God to act	Had a similar theology, yet surrounded Himself with people He loved and to whom He ministered
Zealots	Violence is an appropriate means to bring about God's kingdom in Israel; it was a duty to throw off the chains of Roman rule by every means possible	Taught His disciples to love their enemies
Herodians, Sadducees	Preached cooperation with Rome; sought to maintain the status quo; were willing to compromise God's law	Was unwilling to compromise God's law in order to keep an earthly peace

a. What was the reputation of that area? (See 1 Kings 16:31; Isaiah 23:17.)

b. Why did Jesus go there? (See Matthew 9:10–13.)

3. In His Sermon on the Mount, Jesus outlined His battle plan for confronting evil.

a. Which characteristics did Jesus call "blessed"? (See Matthew 5:5–10.)

b. What is the purpose of following Jesus' battle plan? (See Matthew 5:13–16.)

c. How are these characteristics and purposes like and unlike the Crusaders' ways of confronting evil? Our ways of confronting evil?

4. What did Jesus say His followers could expect to encounter as they lovingly carried out His commands and shared His message? What encouragement did He offer? (See Matthew 10:17–28.)

FACTS TO CONSIDER

As They Saw It

Many people during Jesus' time offered their own solutions to the problems of the day, as the following reveals:

Who Offered the Solution	What They Recommended	The Method of Jesus
Pharisees	National obedience to the Torah as a life commitment	Demonstrated His commitment to God by His obedience to the Torah
Essenes	Be separate from the world and wait for God to act	Had a similar theology, yet surrounded Himself with people He loved and to whom He ministered
Zealots	Violence is an appropriate means to bring about God's kingdom in Israel; it was a duty to throw off the chains of Roman rule by every means possible	Taught His disciples to love their enemies
Herodians, Sadducees	Preached cooperation with Rome; sought to maintain the status quo; were willing to compromise God's law	Was unwilling to compromise God's law in order to keep an earthly peace

Topic B: God's People Are to Be Involved in Culture

The Crusaders abandoned Jesus' self-sacrificing methods and isolated themselves from culture. They dominated the political scene, yet had little influence on people's daily lives. God, however, calls His people to live on the crossroads of life so that the world may know that He is truly God.

1. What did God, through the prophet Isaiah, reveal about what His people are to do? (See Isaiah 43:12.)

   Suggested Response: God's people are to be His witnesses to the truth that He is God.

2. Jesus also instructed His disciples to be His witnesses.

   a. What did Jesus command all of His disciples (including us) to do? (See Matthew 28:19–20.)

      Suggested Response: To go into the world, share the message of Jesus, make disciples, baptize them, and teach them to obey Jesus' commands.

   b. In what ways are Jesus' disciples to accomplish this? (See Matthew 5:13–16.)

      Suggested Responses: We are to go out into the culture and be like salt and light so that the world will see the good things we do and praise God.

3. Read Matthew 15:29–38 and note the way in which Jesus demonstrated how to be involved in culture.

   Suggested Responses: When the crowds of people came to Him, Jesus loved them and healed them of their diseases. As a result, they praised the God of Israel. Then Jesus expressed great compassion for them because they hadn't eaten for three days, so He fed them.

4. In 1 Peter 2:11–12 what did the apostle Peter urge his readers to do? Contrast this with how the Crusaders lived.

   Suggested Responses: Christians are to remember that their real "citizenship" is in heaven. While on earth, they are to live such good lives among non-Christians that people will glorify God when He comes again. In contrast, the Crusaders demonstrated such evil in the name of Jesus that even today many Muslims and Jews regard the message of Jesus Christ with suspicion, and even contempt.

5. The apostle Paul took his involvement in culture very seriously.

   a. In 2 Corinthians 1:12, how did Paul describe his lifestyle?

      Suggested Response: He said he conducted himself in the world, in relationship with people, with godly sincerity and holiness.

Topic B: God's People Are to Be Involved in Culture

The Crusaders abandoned Jesus' self-sacrificing methods and isolated themselves from culture. They dominated the political scene, yet had little influence on people's daily lives. God, however, calls His people to live on the crossroads of life so that the world may know that He is truly God.

1. What did God, through the prophet Isaiah, reveal about what His people are to do? (See Isaiah 43:12.)

2. Jesus also instructed His disciples to be His witnesses.

   a. What did Jesus command all of His disciples (including us) to do? (See Matthew 28:19–20.)

   b. In what ways are Jesus' disciples to accomplish this? (See Matthew 5:13–16.)

3. Read Matthew 15:29–38 and note the way in which Jesus demonstrated how to be involved in culture.

4. In 1 Peter 2:11–12 what did the apostle Peter urge his readers to do? Contrast this with how the Crusaders lived.

5. The apostle Paul took his involvement in culture very seriously.

   a. In 2 Corinthians 1:12, how did Paul describe his lifestyle?

   b. Read 1 Corinthians 9:19–23 and note the specific ways in which the apostle Paul conducted himself in his culture. Contrast Paul's example with the conduct of the Crusaders, and with your own.

Paul's Conduct	The Crusader's Conduct	My Conduct
Although he was a free man, he was willing to make himself a slave in order to win others to Christ.		
Although he was free from the law, he was willing to come under the law.		

PLANNING NOTES:

b. Read 1 Corinthians 9:19–23 and note the specific ways in which the apostle Paul conducted himself in his culture. Contrast Paul's example with the conduct of the Crusaders, and with your own.

Paul's Conduct	The Crusader's Conduct	My Conduct
Although he was a free man, he was willing to make himself a slave in order to win others to Christ.	Came to rule and to enslave others	
Although he was free from the law, he was willing to come under the law.	Would come under no one's law; had their own	
Although he would not compromise obedience to Jesus, he was willing to adjust his lifestyle in order to relate to others.	Took their lifestyle with them—even building European forts in the Holy Land; had no interest in relating to others	
He was willing to become weak to win the weak.	Maintained their strength by isolation	
He did everything he could to win people to Jesus.	Did everything they could to destroy—not to win—people in the name of Jesus	

Topic C: Who Is Responsible for Jesus' Death?

As Jesus' trial progressed, some people in Jerusalem directed fierce anger and hatred toward Him. When Pilate believed Jesus to be innocent, the mob accepted responsibility for Jesus' death and willingly exclaimed, "Let his blood be on us and on our children!" (See Matthew 27:25.) Since then, many Christians, including the Crusaders, have blamed the Jews for killing Jesus. But did God place the blame for Jesus' death on that Jewish mob and their children? Did the mob speak for all Jews?

1. How did many Jewish people respond to Jesus and His teaching? (See Mark 11:18; Luke 20:39; 21:37–38.)

    Suggested Responses: Many people were amazed at Jesus' teaching, including some teachers of the law. People appreciated Him so much that they came to hear Him teach at the temple early in the morning. The chief priests and some teachers of the law wanted to kill Him, however.

2. What made it difficult for the chief priests and other religious leaders to arrest and kill Jesus? (See Matthew 26:3–5; Luke 19:47–48; 20:19; 22:1–6.)

    Suggested Responses: So many people supported Jesus and His teaching that the chief priests and other leaders were afraid to arrest Him—it could cause a riot.

4. In 1 Peter 2:11–12 what did the apostle Peter urge his readers to do? Contrast this with how the Crusaders lived.

5. The apostle Paul took his involvement in culture very seriously.

    a. In 2 Corinthians 1:12, how did Paul describe his lifestyle?

    b. Read 1 Corinthians 9:19–23 and note the specific ways in which the apostle Paul conducted himself in his culture. Contrast Paul's example with the conduct of the Crusaders, and with your own.

Paul's Conduct	The Crusader's Conduct	My Conduct
Although he was a free man, he was willing to make himself a slave in order to win others to Christ.		
Although he was free from the law, he was willing to come under the law.		

Paul's Conduct	The Crusader's Conduct	My Conduct
Although he would not compromise obedience to Jesus, he was willing to adjust his lifestyle in order to relate to others.		
He was willing to become weak to win the weak.		
He did everything he could to win people to Jesus.		

Topic C: Who Is Responsible for Jesus' Death?

As Jesus' trial progressed, some people in Jerusalem directed fierce anger and hatred toward Him. When Pilate believed Jesus to be innocent, the mob accepted responsibility for Jesus' death and willingly exclaimed, "Let his blood be on us and on our children!" (See Matthew 27:25.) Since then, many Christians, including the Crusaders, have blamed the Jews for killing Jesus. But did God place the blame for Jesus' death on that Jewish mob and their children? Did the mob speak for all Jews?

1. How did many Jewish people respond to Jesus and His teaching? (See Mark 11:18; Luke 20:39; 21:37–38.)

3. Which people plotted against Jesus and had Him arrested? (See Luke 19:47; John 11:45–53; 18:12–14.)

Suggested Responses: Some of the Sadducees (temple authorities), chief priests, teachers of the law, Pharisees, and Jewish elders plotted against Him. [Note: Not all of the Pharisees and other religious leaders plotted against Jesus.]

4. Who actually was responsible for Jesus' ill treatment and execution? (See Matthew 27:11–14, 26; Luke 18:31–33; 23:20–25; John 19:16.)

Suggested Response: Legally, the Romans were. They were responsible for wielding justice in Israel, especially in capital offenses. Many non-Jews were involved, including Roman soldiers, Herod, and Pilate—who made the final judgment.

5. As Jesus was being led away to be crucified, what did people do? (See Luke 23:26–27.)

Suggested Response: A large crowd followed, including Jewish women who mourned for Him.

6. What was Jesus' attitude toward those who crucified Him? (See Luke 23:34.)

Suggested Response: Jesus asked God to forgive them because they "did not know" what they were doing.

7. What did Ezekiel teach about each person's responsibility to God? (See Ezekiel 18:1–4, 19–20, 30.) How does this teaching apply to the Jews, including those who helped to kill Jesus?

Suggested Responses: Each person is responsible to God for his or her belief or unbelief. God will judge each person individually. The person who sins is responsible for those sins. So the Jews who wanted Jesus to be killed are responsible, not their children.

8. How did Paul, who knew that some of the Jews had supported Jesus' crucifixion, respond to the Jews? How did he say God responded to the Jews? (See Romans 10:1, 11–13; 11:1–5, 11.)

Suggested Responses: Paul prayed that the Jews would know the truth and put their trust in Jesus. God did not reject the Jews; some of them would choose salvation.

9. Read the following verses and answer each question:

a. For what purpose did Jesus die? (See John 1:29.)

Suggested Response: Jesus died as the Lamb of God—to take away the sins of the world. [Note: That includes the sins of everyone—Jews and Gentiles. All of us are responsible for Jesus' death because we are sinners.]

b. Who sent Jesus to die for the sins of the world? Ultimately, who decided that Jesus would give up His life as a sacrifice for us? (See John 3:16; 10:14–18.)

Suggested Responses: God sent Jesus to die, so that anyone who believes in Him can receive salvation and eternal life. Jesus Himself made the decision to die for our salvation.

Misguided Faith

2. What made it difficult for the chief priests and other religious leaders to arrest and kill Jesus? (See Matthew 26:3–5; Luke 19:47–48; 20:19; 22:1–6.)

3. Which people plotted against Jesus and had Him arrested? (See Luke 19:47; John 11:45–53; 18:12–14.)

4. Who actually was responsible for Jesus' ill treatment and execution? (See Matthew 27:11–14, 26; Luke 18:31–33; 23:20–25; John 19:16.)

5. As Jesus was being led away to be crucified, what did people do? (See Luke 23:26–27.)

6. What was Jesus' attitude toward those who crucified Him? (See Luke 23:34.)

7. What did Ezekiel teach about each person's responsibility to God? (See Ezekiel 18:1–4, 19–20, 30.) How does this teaching apply to the Jews, including those who helped to kill Jesus?

8. How did Paul, who knew that some of the Jews had supported Jesus' crucifixion, respond to the Jews? How did he say God responded to the Jews? (See Romans 10:1, 11–13; 11:1–5, 11.)

9. Read the following verses and answer each question:

   a. For what purpose did Jesus die? (See John 1:29.)

Topic D: Jesus Issues the Commands of God's Kingdom

In everything He did, Jesus displayed God's love. He loved us so much that He came to sacrifice Himself for the sins of the world. Instead of destroying all the opposition Jesus encountered, God chose to have His Son change the world with a confrontational love that reached out to meet people's needs.

Let's look at the instructions Jesus gave His disciples concerning how to live in their culture. As His disciples, we have the opportunity to conduct our lives in a way that will reflect Jesus and His gospel to spiritually blind, hurting people.

✏ 1. What command did Jesus give during the Last Supper to all who would be His disciples? Why is it important? (See John 13:34–35.)

Suggested Response: We are to love one another as Jesus loved us, so that people will know we are His disciples.

✏ 2. Instead of advocating violent, self-serving means such as those the Crusaders used, what did Jesus advocate as His way of changing the world? Write out how you would live out these commands.

Jesus' Commands	Living Them Out in the World
Matthew 5:5–7: Meekness, hungering and thirsting for righteousness, being merciful	
Matthew 5:8: Being pure in heart	
Matthew 5:9: Being a peacemaker	
Matthew 5:13–16: Being the "salt of the earth" and the "light of the world" so that people will see your good deeds and praise God	
Matthew 5:23–24: Before you bring your gifts to God, be reconciled to everyone	
Matthew 5:38–42: Do not fight back against an evil person; instead, go the "extra mile" voluntarily	
Matthew 5:43–48: Love your enemies and pray for those who persecute you	
Matthew 6:14–15: Willingly forgive people who sin against you	

b. Who sent Jesus to die for the sins of the world? Ultimately, who decided that Jesus would give up His life as a sacrifice for us? (See John 3:16; 10:14–18.)

Topic D: Jesus Issues the Commands of God's Kingdom

In everything He did, Jesus displayed God's love. He loved us so much that He came to sacrifice Himself for the sins of the world. Instead of destroying all the opposition Jesus encountered, God chose to have His Son change the world with a confrontational love that reached out to meet people's needs.

Let's look at the instructions Jesus gave His disciples concerning how to live in their culture. As His disciples, we have the opportunity to conduct our lives in a way that will reflect Jesus and His gospel to spiritually blind, hurting people.

1. What command did Jesus give during the Last Supper to all who would be His disciples? Why is it important? (See John 13:34–35.)

2. Instead of advocating violent, self-serving means such as those the Crusaders used, what did Jesus advocate as His way of changing the world? Write out how you would live out these commands.

Jesus' Commands	Living Them Out in the World
Matthew 5:5–7:	
Matthew 5:8:	
Matthew 5:9:	
Matthew 5:13–16:	
Matthew 5:23–24:	
Matthew 5:38–42:	
Matthew 5:43–48:	
Matthew 6:14–15:	

PLANNING NOTES:

> After eleven minutes, let participants know that they have one minute remaining. Then reassemble the entire group. After everyone is back together, begin asking one person from each small group to briefly share a key idea with the larger group. In some cases, you may not have time for every group to share their discoveries.

As time allows, let's briefly share the key ideas that your group discussed.

faith lesson

10 minutes

Time for Reflection (6 minutes)

It's time for each of us to think quietly about how we can apply what we've learned today. On pages 188–89 of your Participant's Guide, you'll find two passages of Scripture. Let's each read these passages silently and take the next few minutes to consider how we can follow the example of Jesus when confronting evil in our culture.

Please do not talk during this time. It's a time when we can reflect on today's lesson and how it applies to our lives.

> *The Scripture passages and questions are reproduced in their entirety in the Participant's Guide on pages 188–90.*

So Judas came to the grove, guiding a detachment of soldiers and some officials from the chief priests and Pharisees. They were carrying torches, lanterns and weapons.

Jesus, knowing all that was going to happen to him, went out and asked them, "Who is it you want?"

"Jesus of Nazareth," they replied.

"I am he," Jesus said. . . .

"If you are looking for me, then let these men go." . . .

Then Simon Peter, who had a sword, drew it and struck the high priest's servant, cutting off his right ear. (The servant's name was Malchus.)

Jesus commanded Peter, "Put your sword away! Shall I not drink the cup the Father has given me?"

JOHN 18:3–5, 8, 10–11

Finally, all of you, live in harmony with one another; be sympathetic, love as brothers, be compassionate and humble. Do not repay evil with evil or insult with insult, but with blessing, because to this you were called so that you may inherit a blessing. For,

> "Whoever would love life
> and see good days
> must keep his tongue from evil
> and his lips from deceitful speech.
> He must turn from evil and do good;
> he must seek peace and pursue it.
> For the eyes of the Lord are on the righteous

ꜰaith ʟesson

Time for Reflection

Read the following passages of Scripture and take the next few minutes to consider how we can follow the example of Jesus when confronting evil in our culture.

So Judas came to the grove, guiding a detachment of soldiers and some officials from the chief priests and Pharisees. They were carrying torches, lanterns and weapons. Jesus, knowing all that was going to happen to him, went out and asked them, "Who is it you want?"

"Jesus of Nazareth," they replied.

"I am he," Jesus said. . . .

"If you are looking for me, then let these men go. . . ."

Then Simon Peter, who had a sword, drew it and struck the high priest's servant, cutting off his right ear. (The servant's name was Malchus.)

Jesus commanded Peter, "Put your sword away! Shall I not drink the cup the Father has given me?"

JOHN 18:3–5, 8, 10–11

Finally, all of you, live in harmony with one another; be sympathetic, love as brothers, be compassionate and humble. Do not repay evil with evil or insult with insult, but with blessing, because to this you were called so that you may inherit a blessing. For,

"Whoever would love life
and see good days
must keep his tongue from evil
and his lips from deceitful speech.
He must turn from evil and do good;
he must seek peace and pursue it.
For the eyes of the Lord are on the righteous
and his ears are attentive to their prayer,
but the face of the Lord is against those who do evil."

and his ears are attentive to their prayer,
but the face of the Lord is against those who do evil."

Who is going to harm you if you are eager to do good? But even if you should suffer for what is right, you are blessed. "Do not fear what they fear; do not be frightened." But in your hearts set apart Christ as Lord. Always be prepared to give an answer to everyone who asks you to give the reason for the hope that you have. But do this with gentleness and respect, keeping a clear conscience, so that those who speak maliciously against your good behavior in Christ may be ashamed of their slander. It is better, if it is God's will, to suffer for doing good than for doing evil.

1 PETER 3:8–17

1. These Scripture passages reveal Peter the swordsman in the Garden of Gethsemane, then Peter the apostle and servant of Jesus. Does the Peter in the garden seem like the same person who said to live in harmony and be sympathetic, compassionate, humble, and loving?
   a. What fundamental change had taken place in Peter regarding his method of confronting evil? How is such a change possible?
   b. What became Peter's sole motivation?
   c. What do these passages say to you personally?

2. As other people observe your actions and attitudes, what do they see of Jesus?

3. When Peter cut off the servant's ear, Jesus said, "Put your sword away," indicating that His way was to follow a different path. To which of your actions would Jesus say, "Put your _____ away"?

Action Points (4 minutes)

The following points are reproduced on pages 191–92 of the Participant's Guide:

Now it's time to wrap up our session.

Give participants a moment to transition from their thoughtfulness to giving you their full attention.

I'd like to take a moment to summarize the key points we explored. After I have reviewed these points, I will give you a moment to jot down an action step (or steps) that you will commit to this week as a result of what you have learned today.

Read the following points and pause afterward so that participants can consider and write out their commitment.

1. *When we present Jesus to other people using methods other than those that He used and taught, we send the wrong message and defame Jesus' reputation.* The era of the Crusades is a great tragedy of the Christian faith. The Crusaders

Who is going to harm you if you are eager to do good? But even if you should suffer for what is right, you are blessed. "Do not fear what they fear; do not be frightened." But in your hearts set apart Christ as Lord. Always be prepared to give an answer to everyone who asks you to give the reason for the hope that you have. But do this with gentleness and respect, keeping a clear conscience, so that those who speak maliciously against your good behavior in Christ may be ashamed of their slander. It is better, if it is God's will, to suffer for doing good than for doing evil.

1 PETER 3:8–17

1. These Scripture passages reveal Peter the swordsman in the Garden of Gethsemane, then Peter the apostle and servant of Jesus. Does the Peter in the garden seem like the same person who said to live in harmony and be sympathetic, compassionate, humble, and loving?

a. What fundamental change had taken place in Peter regarding his method of confronting evil? How is such a change possible?

b. What became Peter's sole motivation?

c. What do these passages say to you personally?

2. As other people observe your actions and attitudes, what do they see of Jesus?

3. When Peter cut off the servant's ear, Jesus said, "Put your sword away," indicating that His way was to follow a different path. To which of your actions would Jesus say, "Put your _____ away"?

Action Points
Take a few moments to review the key points you explored today, then write down an action step (or steps) that you will commit to this week as a result of what you have learned.

1. *When we present Jesus to other people using methods other than those that He used and taught, we send the wrong message and defame Jesus' reputation. The era of the Crusades is a great tragedy of the Christian faith. The Crusaders slaughtered and plundered Jews, Muslims—even other Christians—in the name of Jesus. The damage done to Jesus' reputation and the walls erected between Christians and people of other faiths remain even to this day.*

Chances are, you will meet someone whose view of Christianity has been affected negatively by tragedies like the Crusades or who has been treated wrongfully by another Christian. What can you do to help such a person see who Jesus truly is?

If you know such a person, which steps will you take this week in an effort to undo the damage that has been done to Jesus' reputation?

2. *Jesus wants us to confront the power of evil in our culture, but He wants us to do it as He did—not with the sword, but by offering His life. So it's important for us, as we confront what*

slaughtered and plundered Jews, Muslims—even other Christians—in the name of Jesus. The damage done to Jesus' reputation and the walls erected between Christians and people of other faiths remain even to this day.

Chances are, you will meet someone whose view of Christianity has been affected negatively by tragedies like the Crusades or who has been treated wrongfully by another Christian. What can you do to help such a person see who Jesus truly is?

If you know such a person, which steps will you take this week in an effort to undo the damage that has been done to Jesus' reputation?

2. *Jesus wants us to confront the power of evil in our culture, but He wants us to do it as He did—not with the sword, but by offering His life.* So it's important for us, as we confront what is wrong, immoral, and unjust in our society, to do it in a way that models His attitudes and behavior. We must reject attitudes and methods that communicate that Christianity is anything like what the Crusaders demonstrated it to be. If we want others to know God through us, we must present Him as He has revealed Himself to be. If we are to be His disciples, we must become like Him in every way.

Think about the unique opportunities you have to bring Jesus' message to unbelievers through your actions and attitudes. What will you do this week to lovingly communicate His message—even if difficulties may follow?

What are you willing to do to help bridge the gap between yourself and non-Christians? In what way(s) can you be a "community" builder instead of a "fortress" builder in your culture?

What motivations, attitudes, or methods do you use as you confront evil in your culture that are your own rather than those of Jesus? What will you do to change those this week?

closing prayer
I minute

As we've seen, it's easy to substitute our own methods of living for the ways in which Jesus commanded us to live. As we close in prayer now, let us remember that we are His representatives. What we do communicates volumes about who He is. Obeying His commands makes a difference.

Dear God, it hurts to see how much the Crusades and other actions by Christians have defamed Your name and turned people against You. Please help us to follow Your ways. Continue to teach us, through Your Word and the Holy Spirit, how to live so that other people will see You in us. Fill us with Your Spirit so we can present Your claims faithfully and live as Jesus would have us live. Help us to be community builders, not fortress builders. Forgive us for the times when we have not followed Your way and have, through hatred or intolerance, communicated the wrong message about You. And give us opportunities to share with Jews and Muslims our sadness about the Crusades. In Your name we pray, Jesus, amen.

Action Points

Take a few moments to review the key points you explored today, then write down an action step (or steps) that you will commit to this week as a result of what you have learned.

1. *When we present Jesus to other people using methods other than those that He used and taught, we send the wrong message and defame Jesus' reputation.* The era of the Crusades is a great tragedy of the Christian faith. The Crusaders slaughtered and plundered Jews, Muslims—even other Christians—in the name of Jesus. The damage done to Jesus' reputation and the walls erected between Christians and people of other faiths remain even to this day.

   Chances are, you will meet someone whose view of Christianity has been affected negatively by tragedies like the Crusades or who has been treated wrongfully by another Christian. What can you do to help such a person see who Jesus truly is?

   If you know such a person, which steps will you take this week in an effort to undo the damage that has been done to Jesus' reputation?

2. *Jesus wants us to confront the power of evil in our culture, but He wants us to do it as He did—not with the sword, but by offering His life.* So it's important for us, as we confront what

   is wrong, immoral, and unjust in our society, to do it in a way that models His attitudes and behavior. We must reject attitudes and methods that communicate that Christianity is anything like what the Crusaders demonstrated it to be. If we want others to know God through us, we must present Him as He has revealed Himself to be. If we are to be His disciples, we must become like Him in every way.

   Think about the unique opportunities you have to bring Jesus' message to unbelievers through your actions and attitudes. What will you do this week to lovingly communicate His message—even if difficulties may follow?

   What are you willing to do to help bridge the gap between yourself and non-Christians? In what way(s) can you be a "community" builder instead of a "fortress" builder in your culture?

   What motivations, attitudes, or methods do you use as you confront evil in your culture that are your own rather than those of Jesus? What will you do to change those this week?

PLANNING NOTES:

A TRAGIC HISTORY

ca. A.D. 27–30	Jesus' ministry
66–73	First Jewish Revolt against Rome
70	Rome destroys Jerusalem
131–135	Second Jewish Revolt
315	Constantine forbids Jews from proselytizing
439	Jews denied right to hold public office and build new synagogues
600	Pope Gregory forbids Jews from eating with Christians
613	Forced baptisms in Spain; Jews who refuse are expelled and their children under age seven are given to Christians
632	Byzantine emperor Heraclius I forces Jews to either be baptized or be killed
1075	Pope Gregory VII prohibits Jews from holding office in Christian countries
1096	First Crusade (Jewish and Muslim communities are slaughtered across Europe, Turkey, and Israel)
1144	Second Crusade (mobs kill Jews throughout Europe)
1170	Third Crusade (Jews are killed throughout Europe)
1198	Pope Innocent III begins Fourth Crusade and orders Jews killed to atone for Jesus' death (Jews had to wear badges)
1291	Crusaders leave Palestine
1320	Shepherds' Crusade (120 communities of Jews are slaughtered in Europe)
1933–45	Nazi Holocaust

HISTORICAL PROFILE

The Jews: A History of Persecution

The New Testament records bitter disagreements over significant beliefs between some Jews (particularly the Sadducees and certain groups of Pharisees) and early Christians. Still, the disciples and apostles continued to try to persuade Jewish people to follow Jesus (Romans 12).

Long after New Testament times, Christians began to blame all Jews for rejecting and crucifying Jesus. Church fathers like Augustine and Justin

(continued on page 302)

A TRAGIC HISTORY

c.a. A.D. 27–30	Jesus' ministry
66–73	First Jewish Revolt against Rome
70	Rome destroys Jerusalem
131–135	Second Jewish Revolt
315	Constantine forbids Jews from proselytizing
439	Jews denied right to hold public office and build new synagogues
600	Pope Gregory forbids Jews from eating with Christians
613	Forced baptisms in Spain; Jews who refuse are expelled and their children under age seven are given to Christians
632	Byzantine emperor Heraclius I forces Jews to either be baptized or be killed
1075	Pope Gregory VII prohibits Jews from holding office in Christian countries
1096	First Crusade (Jewish and Muslim communities are slaughtered across Europe, Turkey, and Israel)
1144	Second Crusade (mobs kill Jews throughout Europe)
1170	Third Crusade (Jews are killed throughout Europe)
1198	Pope Innocent III begins Fourth Crusade and orders Jews killed to atone for Jesus' death (Jews had to wear badges)
1291	Crusaders leave Palestine
1320	Shepherds' Crusade (150 communities of Jews are slaughtered in Europe)
1933–45	Nazi Holocaust

HISTORICAL PROFILE

The Jews: A History of Persecution

The New Testament records bitter disagreements over significant beliefs between some Jews (particularly the Sadducees and certain groups of Pharisees) and early Christians. Still, the disciples and apostles continued to try to persuade Jewish people to follow Jesus (Romans 12).

Long after New Testament times, Christians began to blame all Jews for rejecting and crucifying Jesus. Church fathers like Augustine and Justin Martyr taught that the Jews were eternally cursed by God. Soon regular sermons were preached on the Christian holy days of Good Friday and Easter, blaming Jews for Jesus' death. (The fact that Jesus went willingly to His death because of the sins of all people was ignored. Little was said, too, about the Roman soldiers who actually crucified Jesus.)

Constantine, the first Christian emperor, passed many anti-Jewish laws. Popes like Gregory VII forbade interaction between Jews and Christians, and barred Jews from holding office. Jews, in the view of many Christians, were God's enemies. In spite of this oppression, Jewish communities survived and flourished. This increased Gentiles' resentment and led to more abuse of the Jews.

Forced conversions and baptisms of Jews became increasingly common, and local violence occasionally flared, wiping out entire communities. Absurd rumors, such as the accusation that Jews stole Christian children in order to use their blood to make unleavened bread for Passover, ran rampant. Consequently, although not a single example of this has ever been proved, thousands of innocent Jewish people died at the hands of their "Christian" neighbors.

Thus the Crusades simply expanded the violence against Jews to include Muslims as well. Yet, when the Crusades were over, the violence didn't end. Jewish property was routinely seized for hundreds of years. During the Inquisition (from the 1100s through the 1500s), entire communities of Jews were brutally tortured and destroyed, and thousands of others were forced to become Christians. Three hundred thousand Jews were expelled from Spain the year Columbus discovered America. In 1298, more than one hundred thousand Jews were killed in Germany;

PLANNING NOTES:

(continued from page 300)

Martyr taught that the Jews were eternally cursed by God. Soon regular sermons were preached on the Christian holy days of Good Friday and Easter, blaming Jews for Jesus' death. (The fact that Jesus went willingly to His death because of the sins of all people was ignored. Little was said, too, about the Roman soldiers who actually crucified Jesus.)

Constantine, the first Christian emperor, passed many anti-Jewish laws. Popes like Gregory VII forbade interaction between Jews and Christians, and barred Jews from holding office. Jews, in the view of many Christians, were God's enemies. In spite of this oppression, Jewish communities survived and flourished. This increased Gentiles' resentment and led to more abuse of the Jews.

Forced conversions and baptisms of Jews became increasingly common, and local violence occasionally flared, wiping out entire communities. Absurd rumors, such as the accusation that Jews stole Christian children in order to use their blood to make unleavened bread for Passover, ran rampant. Consequently, although not a single example of this has ever been proved, thousands of innocent Jewish people died at the hands of their "Christian" neighbors.

Thus the Crusades simply expanded the violence against Jews to include Muslims as well. Yet, when the Crusades were over, the violence didn't end. Jewish property was routinely seized for hundreds of years. During the Inquisition (from the 1100s through the 1500s), entire communities of Jews were brutally tortured and destroyed, and thousands of others were forced to become Christians. Three hundred thousand Jews were expelled from Spain the year Columbus discovered America. In 1298, more than one hundred thousand Jews were killed in Germany; two thousand were burned to death in Strasbourg. Martin Luther wrote "Against Jews and Their Lies," a strident treatise condemning Jews to the flames of hell forever. Jewish persecution continued in Russia, Poland, Hungary, and the Ukraine. Still the Jewish communities flourished. Then came the Holocaust . . . .

Only recently have formal steps been taken to renounce this part of Christian history. The Roman Catholic Church's Second Vatican Council affirmed the Jewish roots of Christianity and repudiated collective Jewish guilt for Jesus' death. The Lutheran Church in the United States recently voted to repudiate anti-Semitic teachings of Martin Luther. Many individual Christians have recognized the devastating effects that the Crusades had on non-Christians' views of Jesus and His teaching, and many are rediscovering the Jewish roots of Christianity.

HISTORICAL PROFILE

The Jews: A History of Persecution

The New Testament records bitter disagreements over significant beliefs between some Jews (particularly the Sadducees and certain groups of Pharisees) and early Christians. Still, the disciples and apostles continued to try to persuade Jewish people to follow Jesus (Romans 12).

Long after New Testament times, Christians began to blame all Jews for rejecting and crucifying Jesus. Church fathers like Augustine and Justin Martyr taught that the Jews were eternally cursed by God. Soon regular sermons were preached on the Christian holy days of Good Friday and Easter, blaming Jews for Jesus' death. (The fact that Jesus went willingly to His death because of the sins of all people was ignored. Little was said, too, about the Roman soldiers who actually crucified Jesus.)

Constantine, the first Christian emperor, passed many anti-Jewish laws. Popes like Gregory VII forbade interaction between Jews and Christians, and barred Jews from holding office. Jews, in the view of many Christians, were God's enemies. In spite of this oppression, Jewish communities survived and flourished. This increased Gentiles' resentment and led to more abuse of the Jews.

Forced conversions and baptisms of Jews became increasingly common, and local violence occasionally flared, wiping out entire communities. Absurd rumors, such as the accusation that Jews stole Christian children in order to use their blood to make unleavened bread for Passover, ran rampant. Consequently, although not a single example of this has ever been proved, thousands of innocent Jewish people died at the hands of their "Christian" neighbors.

Thus the Crusades simply expanded the violence against Jews to include Muslims as well. Yet, when the Crusades were over, the violence didn't end. Jewish property was routinely seized for hundreds of years. During the Inquisition (from the 1100s through the 1500s), entire communities of Jews were brutally tortured and destroyed, and thousands of others were forced to become Christians. Three hundred thousand Jews were expelled from Spain the year Columbus discovered America. In 1298, more than one hundred thousand Jews were killed in Germany;

two thousand were burned to death in Strasbourg. Martin Luther wrote "Against Jews and Their Lies," a strident treatise condemning Jews to the flames of hell forever. Jewish persecution continued in Russia, Poland, Hungary, and the Ukraine. Still the Jewish communities flourished. Then came the Holocaust . . . .

Only recently have formal steps been taken to renounce this part of Christian history. The Roman Catholic Church's Second Vatican Council affirmed the Jewish roots of Christianity and repudiated collective Jewish guilt for Jesus' death. The Lutheran Church in the United States recently voted to repudiate anti-Semitic teachings of Martin Luther. Many individual Christians have recognized the devastating effects that the Crusades had on non-Christians' views of Jesus and His teaching, and many are rediscovering the Jewish roots of Christianity.

PLANNING NOTES:

living water

before you lead

Synopsis

Israel's mountains, rocky plateaus, deep wadis, and windswept deserts help to create a wilderness panorama of breathtaking beauty and insidious danger. Wadis suddenly flood with water. The desert sun beats down on the hardy creatures and plants that have adapted to the dry, scorching heat. And in the midst of the most inhospitable places, one essential resource enables the wilderness to support life—water. As this video shows, that life-giving water changes everything.

This video takes you to En Gedi, an amazing oasis in the midst of the Judea Wilderness. Hardly more than one hundred feet or so from dry, desolate wilderness, water from a spring streams down a rock face and supports lush, jungle-like growth. Here, men and women through the centuries have collected water, soothed their parched throats, watered animals, and gathered the courage to enter the barren wilderness again. Here, David and his men no doubt grabbed refreshment while being chased from cave to cave and fortress to fortress by King Saul and his men.

Perhaps the precious, life-giving nature of pure water is one reason it is mentioned so many times in the Bible:

- We think of the psalmist describing how his soul thirsts for God "in a dry and weary land where there is no water" (Psalm 63:1). Or we recall this metaphor: "As the deer pants for streams of water, so my soul pants for you, O God" (Psalm 42:1).
- Biblical writers make a distinction between "living water," which flows constantly and is fresh, clean, pure, and life-giving, and stored "cistern" or "dead" water, which can be stagnant and dirty.
- Jesus, too, spoke of water. One day He sat by a well and asked a Samaritan woman for a drink (John 4). He then told her about the "living water" He could provide—water that could end her thirst. This water, He promised, would be like a spring of living water, welling up to eternal life.
- The prophet Jeremiah warned God's people against the incredible folly of forsaking God's living water and seeking out their own water—digging broken cisterns that couldn't even hold water (Jeremiah 2:13)!

These ancient images of the inhospitable wilderness and the living water that God freely gives to His people communicate an important message to Christians today. As Ray Vander Laan points out, living in our culture is in many ways like living in the Judea Wilderness. Life can be hot, dry, and barren, yet this is where we are called to live and to accomplish God's work. The wilderness is the home of thirsty, hungry people who need the message and love of Jesus. But living in the wilderness can sap our strength and make us weary of trying to serve the Lord and reach out to others.

God—the giver of living water—understands our weariness. He knows what it's like to give and give to people until it hurts. He knows the heat . . . the cold . . . the loneliness . . . the dry emptiness inside . . . the challenges of living for Jesus in the wilderness. That's why He encourages us to spend time every day refreshing ourselves in Him—our En Gedi oasis. We need to spend time reading His Word, praying to Him, listening for Him, sharing His truths with other Christians, and praising Him. When we do that, it's like drinking living water—being refreshed amidst the desert's heat, regaining strength when we are faint, and feeling spiritually alive again.

Yet each of us must make a choice. Will we look to God, our source of living water, for our refreshment? Or will we vainly dig our own cisterns—going out into the world to find what we think we need? Will we try to satisfy our spiritual thirst with things that cannot satisfy? Will we place our faith in our talents, hard work, friends, and success? Will we pursue things that look refreshing from a distance—like the Dead Sea—but have no life to give?

All such broken cisterns will fail us. Our ability to be effective Christians in a spiritually barren culture comes from God—our living water, our source of life. He is the Rock from which streams of water flow. He is our loving, eternal, all-sustaining God who freely gives living water to those who thirst. He is like an oasis in the wilderness that offers shade and flowing, "living" streams of pure water. We can always come to Him, be filled, and have something to share with other people. We don't have to dig our own cisterns.

Key Points of This Lesson

1. *Just as David and his men needed the life-giving, living water of En Gedi in order to survive their time in the wilderness, God's people today need God's pure, refreshing, living water in order to serve Him in the wilderness of life.* When we are nourished and filled with His living water, we will overflow with streams of living water that we can share with thirsty, needy people who live in a spiritually barren world (John 7:38). But in order to have anything to give, we need to have an En Gedi—times of devotion, Bible study, prayer, retreat, meditation—where we can meet with God to satisfy our own spiritual thirst.

2. *Accept no substitutes for living water! Although many things in our culture may look like living water, they all fail to give us life, to satisfy our thirst for God.* The Dead Sea, for example, looks refreshing from a distance, but its bitter saltwater cannot satisfy. It is equally foolish to turn our backs on God's pure, refreshing, life-giving water and try to dig our own cisterns, which if they hold water at all, can provide only dead, stagnant water.

Session Outline (54 minutes)

I. Introduction (3 minutes)
Welcome
What's to Come
Questions to Think About

II. Show Video "Living Water" (24 minutes)

III. Group Discovery (20 minutes)
Video Highlights
Small Group Bible Discovery

IV. Faith Lesson (6 minutes)
Time for Reflection
Action Points

V. Closing Prayer (1 minute)

Materials

No additional materials are needed for this session. Simply view the video prior to leading the session so you are familiar with its main points.

living water

introduction

3 minutes

Welcome

> Assemble the participants together. Welcome them to session eight of *Faith Lessons on the Life and Ministry of the Messiah.*

What's to Come

In this session, we'll see dramatic evidence of the difference life-giving water makes in the wilderness. We'll look at the Bible's imagery, how it compares the spiritual life that God offers to living water that continually refreshes and strengthens us. We will be reminded of our need to drink deeply of the living, pure, fresh streams of water that God offers us as we seek to live and accomplish His work in a culture that in many ways is like the dry, hot, barren wilderness.

Questions to Think About

> *Participant's Guide page 196.*

> Ask each question and solicit a few responses from group members.

✏ 1. When there is a drought and plants start to turn brown, wither, and die, what happens when water is provided?

Suggested Response: The plants respond to the water and start to green up and grow again.

✏ 2. Suppose you live in a dry region and someone offers you and everyone else in the area all the pure, running water you need if you but ask for it. So you ask every day and receive an abundance of water. But some people won't ask for the water, and some don't seem to know that they have access to an abundant supply. So they struggle to dig up the sunbaked ground in hopes of finding enough water to keep themselves alive. What would your response be to those people?

Suggested Responses: Encourage participants to consider the variety of options available to them—sharing, compassion, judgment, telling them about the water, inviting them to share in it, taking water to them, mocking their ignorance, condemning or grieving over their stubbornness, etc.

Let's keep these ideas in mind as we view the video.

SESSION EIGHT

living water

questions to think About

1. When there is a drought and plants start to turn brown, wither, and die, what happens when water is provided?

2. Suppose you live in a dry region and someone offers you and everyone else in the area all the pure, running water you need if you but ask for it. So you ask every day and receive an abundance of water. But some people won't ask for the water, and some don't seem to know that they have access to an abundant supply. So they struggle to dig up the sunbaked ground in hopes of finding enough water to keep themselves alive. What would your response be to those people?

video presentation
24 minutes

Participant's Guide page 197.

On page 197 of your Participant's Guide, you will find a space in which to take notes on key points as we watch this video.

Leader's Video Observations

Water in the Wilderness—A Spring of Life

The "Living Water" of God

The "Dead Water" of Our Own Cisterns

God as Our Oasis

video notes

Water in the Wilderness—A Spring of Life

The "Living Water" of God

The "Dead Water" of Our Own Cisterns

God as Our Oasis

PLANNING NOTES:

Group Discovery
20 minutes

If your group has seven or more members, use the **Video Highlights** with the entire group (5 minutes), then break into small groups of three to five to discuss the **Small Group Bible Discovery** (10 minutes). Then reassemble the group to discuss the key points discovered (5 minutes).

If your group has fewer than seven members, begin with the **Video Highlights** (5 minutes), then do one or more of the topics found in the **Small Group Bible Discovery** as a group (10 minutes). Finally, spend five minutes at the end discussing points that had an impact on participants.

Video Highlights (5 minutes)

Here you'll ask one or more of the following questions that directly relate to the video the participants have just seen.

1. Let's look at the map on page 198 of your Participant's Guide and find En Gedi. Notice how close it is to the Dead Sea (about a mile), how isolated it is from the civilization of the Judea Mountains, and how expansive the wilderness is from north to south. The abundant, rushing water of this spring would certainly be a relief in this part of the wilderness!

2. What did you notice about the oasis of En Gedi?

   Suggested Responses: will vary but may include its beauty, its close proximity to the wilderness, how all that life came from one spring, how green and full of life the oasis is in contrast to the barrenness that surrounds it, etc.

The Judea Wilderness

video highlights

1. Look at the map below and find En Gedi. Notice how close it is to the Dead Sea (about a mile), how isolated it is from the civilization of the Judea Mountains, and how expansive the wilderness is from north to south. The abundant, rushing water of this spring would certainly be a relief in this part of the wilderness!

2. What did you notice about the oasis of En Gedi?

The Judea Wilderness

✏ 3.   How do you think David and his men felt when they took refuge at this oasis?

   Suggested Responses: thankful for the coolness and the quantity of pure, running water; delighted to be in the shade; wishing they could stay in the oasis; etc.

✏ 4.   In what ways has your understanding of "living water" and "cistern water" changed as a result of this video?

   Suggested Responses: Allow participants to express what they have discovered.

✏ 5.   If life is indeed like the wilderness, why is spending time with God each day so important?

   Suggested Responses: Encourage participants to realize how desperately we need the refreshment of the oasis! In the wilderness we become tired, we give and give to people and need to be refreshed, we need to be replenished by God's living water so that we have something to share with others, etc.

DATA FILE

Oasis of En Gedi

The Oasis of En Gedi

Located along the eastern edge of the hot, barren Judea Wilderness where it seldom rains, this oasis is fed by springs. Miles away, in the Judea Mountains, rainfall seeps down into cracks in the rock until it emerges as water gushing from the rock. Just a few hundred yards west of the waterfall shown in the video, water literally streams from a rock.

Many Bible passages speak of water gushing from rock, such as Exodus 17:6; Deuteronomy 8:15; and Psalm 105:41. This adds to our understanding of God and His provision for us. The Bible describes God as the Rock from which water came (1 Corinthians 10:3–4; see also Deuteronomy 32:4, 31; Psalm 78:35).

Ibex

Since En Gedi belonged to the tribe of Judah, it was the place where David hid from King Saul. David and his men no doubt appreciated the cool shade, lush beauty, pools and streams of water, and abundant wildlife of En Gedi after hiding from Saul in the dry wilderness. In this context, David wrote Psalms 42 and 63. Today, desert goats known as ibex graze on the sparse grasses in the desert around En Gedi. They come to the oasis to drink even when people are nearby because they are so thirsty.

3. How do you think David and his men felt when they took refuge at this oasis?

4. In what ways has your understanding of "living water" and "cistern water" changed as a result of this video?

5. If life is indeed like the wilderness, why is spending time with God each day so important?

DATA FILE

The Oasis of En Gedi

Located along the eastern edge of the hot, barren Judea Wilderness where it seldom rains, this oasis is fed by springs. Miles away, in the Judea Mountains, rainfall seeps down into cracks in the rock until it emerges as water gushing from the rock. Just a few hundred yards west of the waterfall shown in the video, water literally streams from a rock.

Oasis of En Gedi

Many Bible passages speak of water gushing from rock, such as Exodus 17:6; Deuteronomy 8:15; and Psalm 105:41. This adds to our understanding of God and His provision for us. The Bible describes God as the Rock from which water came (1 Corinthians 10:3–4; see also Deuteronomy 32:4, 31; Psalm 78:35).

Ibex

Since En Gedi belonged to the tribe of Judah, it was the place where David hid from King Saul. David and his men no doubt appreciated the cool shade, lush beauty, pools and streams of water, and abundant wildlife of En Gedi after hiding from Saul in the dry wilderness. In this context, David wrote Psalms 42 and 63. Today, desert goats known as ibex graze on the sparse grasses in the desert around En Gedi. They come to the oasis to drink even when people are nearby because they are so thirsty.

Small Group Bible Discovery (15minutes)

> *Participant's Guide pages 201–11.*
>
> During this time, a group with fewer than seven participants will stay together. A group with seven or more participants will break into small groups and reassemble as a large group during the final five minutes. Assign each group one of the following topics. If you have more than four small groups, assign some topics to more than one group.

Let's break into groups of three to five—people sitting near you—and study some of the Bible passages and truths mentioned in the video.

Turn to pages 201–11 in your Participant's Guide. There you'll find a list of four topics. You'll have ten minutes to read and discuss the topic I'll assign to you. Choose one person in your group to be a spokesperson for your group when we discuss these topics later.

> Assign each group a topic.

I'll signal you when one minute is left.

> While participants are doing their Small Group Bible Discovery, rewind the video to the beginning of the song, "En Gedi." Replay the song during the Time for Reflection.

Topic A: God's Wonderful Gift of Living Water
The springs of En Gedi provide a vivid picture of God as living water.

1. To what did God liken Himself? (See Jeremiah 2:13; 17:13.)

   Suggested Response: the "spring of living water."

2. To what did David compare his thirst for God? (See Psalm 63:1.)

   Suggested Response: He thirsted and longed for God in the way a thirsty person in the barren wilderness thirsts for water.

3. To what did the prophet Jeremiah compare a person who trusts in himself or herself rather than in God? (See Jeremiah 17:5–6.)

   Suggested Response: A bush in the parched, salty wastelands.

4. Read Psalm 78:15–16; Isaiah 41:17–20; 58:11. List the images of living water and an oasis that illustrate what God provides for His people. Notice how similar these images are to the springs of En Gedi.

   Suggested Responses: God splits rocks in the desert to provide water as abundant as the seas; brings streams out of rocks and makes waters flow down like rivers; makes rivers flow on barren heights; makes springs flow in the valleys and parched ground; turns the desert into pools of water; puts fruitful, shade-giving trees in the wasteland so people would consider what He has done; guides His people in a sun-scorched land and makes them like a well-watered garden, watered by springs that never fail.

small Group bible Discovery

Topic A: God's Wonderful Gift of Living Water

The springs of En Gedi provide a vivid picture of God as living water.

1. To what did God liken Himself? (See Jeremiah 2:13; 17:13.)

2. To what did David compare his thirst for God? (See Psalm 63:1.)

3. To what did the prophet Jeremiah compare a person who trusts in himself or herself rather than in God? (See Jeremiah 17:5–6.)

4. Read Psalm 78:15–16; Isaiah 41:17–20; 58:11. List the images of living water and an oasis that illustrate what God provides for His people. Notice how similar these images are to the springs of En Gedi.

PLANNING NOTES:

✏ 5.   What did Jesus say about the "living water" He came to give? (See John 4:13–14.)

Suggested Responses: It takes away all thirst and becomes like a spring of water "welling up to eternal life" in the person who drinks it.

✏ 6.   At the end of the Sukkot, the Feast of Tabernacles, Jesus offered a bold invitation regarding living water. (See John 7:37–39.)

   a.   What did Jesus invite crowds of people to do?

        Suggested Responses: to recognize their spiritual thirst and drink the water He offered by believing in Him.

   b.   What did Jesus promise to those who did that?

        Suggested Response: that streams of living water would flow from within them.

   c.   Whom did John say the living water symbolizes?

        Suggested Responses: the Holy Spirit, a never-ending source of flowing, living water (like En Gedi).

DATA FILE

The Feast of Sukkot

During Old Testament times, God instituted a religious calendar for the Israelites to follow. The seventh day, the seventh year, and the end of seven "seven years" were significant to Him. Within each year, there were seven specified feasts (Leviticus 23), which included the Feast of Sukkot (or Tabernacles).

The weeklong celebration of Sukkot began after the fall harvest, a time to be especially thankful for God's blessings. Following God's command, the people came to Jerusalem and built booths of olive, palm, and myrtle branches (Nehemiah 8:15), which provided shade. The people were to leave enough space in the branches so that they could see the sky, reminding them of their wilderness years. These booths (*sukkot;* plural: *sukkah*) gave the feast its name.

For seven days, the people ate, lived, and slept in these booths. It was a time to praise God for His past gifts of freedom, land, and bountiful harvests. In fact, God commanded them to "rejoice" before Him (Leviticus 23:40).

A special element of the celebration of Sukkot involved living water. Sukkot took place at the end of the dry season, so the rains needed to begin immediately to ensure a bountiful harvest the following year. Thus the celebration of God's harvest was coupled with the people's fervent prayers for the next year's rains. The priests, too, added a ceremony that included a prayer for rain.

(continued on page 320)

202   Faith Lessons on the Life and Ministry of the Messiah

5. What did Jesus say about the "living water" He came to give? (See John 4:13–14.)

6. At the end of the Sukkot, the Feast of Tabernacles, Jesus offered a bold invitation regarding living water. (See John 7:37–39.)

    a. What did Jesus invite crowds of people to do?

    b. What did Jesus promise to those who did that?

    c. Whom did John say the living water symbolizes?

DATA FILE

The Feast of Sukkot

During Old Testament times, God instituted a religious calendar for the Israelites to follow. The seventh day, the seventh year, and the end of seven "seven years" were significant to Him. Within each year, there were seven specified feasts (Leviticus 23), which included the Feast of Sukkot (or Tabernacles).

The weeklong celebration of Sukkot began after the fall harvest, a time to be especially thankful for God's blessings. Following God's command, the people came to Jerusalem and built booths of olive, palm, and myrtle branches (Nehemiah 8:15), which provided shade. The people were to leave enough space in the branches so that they could see the sky, reminding them of their wilderness years. These booths (*sukkot*, plural: *sukkah*) gave the feast its name.

For seven days, the people ate, lived, and slept in these booths. It was a time to praise God for His past gifts of freedom, land, and bountiful harvests. In fact, God commanded them to "rejoice" before Him (Leviticus 23:40).

A special element of the celebration of Sukkot involved living water. Sukkot took place at the end of the dry season, so the rains needed to begin immediately to ensure a bountiful harvest the following year. Thus the celebration of God's harvest was coupled with the people's fervent prayers for the next year's rains. The priests, too, added a ceremony that included a prayer for rain.

During this ceremony, a procession of priests marched from the temple to the Pool of Siloam, which was fed by the Spring of Gihon. One priest filled a golden pitcher with water, and the procession returned to the temple. At that time, the priest carrying the pitcher stood near the top of the altar and solemnly poured the water into one of two silver funnels leading into the stone altar for the daily drink offerings. At this time, the people—accompanied by the Levitical choir—began a chant that meant, "O Lord, save us by sending rain as well." In this way, they asked God for life-giving rain.

Four great menorahs (more than seventy-five feet high) were also placed in the women's court of the temple. They commemorated the

(continued on page 204)

(continued from page 318)

During this ceremony, a procession of priests marched from the temple to the Pool of Siloam, which was fed by the Spring of Gihon. One priest filled a golden pitcher with water, and the procession returned to the temple. At that time, the priest carrying the pitcher stood near the top of the altar and solemnly poured the water into one of two silver funnels leading into the stone altar for the daily drink offerings. At this time, the people—accompanied by the Levitical choir—began a chant that meant, "O Lord, save us by sending rain as well." In this way, they asked God for life-giving rain.

Four great menorahs (more than seventy-five feet high) were also placed in the women's court of the temple. They commemorated the miraculous burning of a small amount of sacred oil for eight days in the menorah (eternal light) in the Holy of Holies after Judah Maccabee defeated the Greek army of Antiochus and reclaimed Jerusalem.

In the context of Sukkot, the water ceremony, and the menorahs blazing with light, Jesus presented the message of His new kingdom. He had traveled to Jerusalem for Sukkot (John 7:10) and had taught great crowds thronging the temple (John 7:14). On the "last and greatest day of the Feast" (John 7:37), during the water ceremony, the chanted prayers, and the plea made through the offering of living water, Jesus stood and said, "If anyone is thirsty, let him come to me and drink. Whoever believes in me, as the Scripture has said, streams of living water will flow from within him" (John 7:37–38). So, the setting in which Jesus chose to give this lesson, and the similarity of His meaning to Jewish tradition, meant that His shouted promise in the temple must have had stunning impact: "Let him come to *Me!*"

Sukkot is a feast that will be fully realized in heaven. There, God's people will experience living water (Revelation 7:17), His eternal presence (Revelation 21:22), and the light of God (Revelation 22:5). Whereas Sukkot taught the Jewish people to be joyful, in anticipation of heaven, imagine the most joyful celebration that ever existed lasting for eternity. That, indeed, is heaven!

(continued from page 203)

miraculous burning of a small amount of sacred oil for eight days in the menorah (eternal light) in the Holy of Holies after Judah Maccabee defeated the Greek army of Antiochus and reclaimed Jerusalem.

In the context of Sukkot, the water ceremony, and the menorahs blazing with light, Jesus presented the message of His new kingdom. He had traveled to Jerusalem for Sukkot (John 7:10) and had taught great crowds thronging the temple (John 7:14). On the "last and greatest day of the Feast" (John 7:37), during the water ceremony, the chanted prayers, and the plea made through the offering of living water, Jesus stood and said, "If anyone is thirsty, let him come to me and drink. Whoever believes in me, as the Scripture has said, streams of living water will flow from within him" (John 7:37–38). So, the setting in which Jesus chose to give this lesson, and the similarity of His meaning to Jewish tradition, meant that His shouted promise in the temple must have had stunning impact: "Let him come to *Me!*"

Sukkot is a feast that will be fully realized in heaven. There, God's people will experience living water (Revelation 7:17), His eternal presence (Revelation 21:22), and the light of God (Revelation 22:5). Whereas Sukkot taught the Jewish people to be joyful, in anticipation of heaven, imagine the most joyful celebration that ever existed lasting for eternity. That, indeed, is heaven!

Topic B: Living Water or Broken Cisterns — The Choice Is Ours

Cisterns represent, in one sense, our own efforts and strength. In the language of Scripture, trying to live without God is like turning away from the gushing, cool springs of En Gedi to seek dirty water from broken cisterns.

1. Psalm 107:4–9 describes the condition of the Jews during their desert wanderings and what God did for them.

   a. What was their condition before they turned to God?

      Suggested Responses: They were lost, hungry, thirsty, and their lives were "ebbed away."

   b. After they turned to God—their source of living water—what did He do for them?

      Suggested Responses: God delivered them from their awful circumstances and led them to a habitable place where they could live. He satisfied their thirst and met their hunger with "good things."

A Broken Cistern

2. Before the Israelites entered the Promised Land, what serious warning did God give to His people? (See Deuteronomy 8:10–18.)

   Suggested Responses: God told them to praise Him for what He had provided, to continue to remember and obey Him. Otherwise, they would become complacent and proud and forget what God had done for them. They would begin to think that they had made all the good things happen rather than God. He reminded them that He was the one who provided for them.

Water from Rock

Topic B: Living Water or Broken Cisterns—The Choice Is Ours

Cisterns represent, in one sense, our own efforts and strength. In the language of Scripture, trying to live without God is like turning away from the gushing, cool springs of En Gedi to seek dirty water from broken cisterns.

1. Psalm 107:4–9 describes the condition of the Jews during their desert wanderings and what God did for them.

   a. What was their condition before they turned to God?

   b. After they turned to God—their source of living water—what did He do for them?

A Broken Cistern

2. Before the Israelites entered the Promised Land, what serious warning did God give to His people? (See Deuteronomy 8:10–18.)

Water from Rock

3. In Jeremiah 2:13, we discover what God's people did once they were settled in the Promised Land.

   a. Which two sins did God's people commit?

   b. What does this verse reveal about our human tendencies?

✎ 3.   In Jeremiah 2:13, we discover what God's people did once they were settled in the Promised Land.

   a.   Which two sins did God's people commit?

   Suggested Responses: They forsook God (the spring of living water) and dug their own cisterns that could not hold water. [Note: This is another way of saying that they became unfaithful to God. They became proud of what they had done for themselves, forgot that He was their provider, and worshiped other gods.]

   b.   What does this verse reveal about our human tendencies?

   Suggested Responses: may include that we quickly become proud, forgetting what God provides; how foolish we are to turn away from the pure, flowing water that God provides in order to pursue the work of our own hands, which is nothing more than dirty, stagnant cistern water; etc.

✎ 4.   What is the tragedy of turning away from God and depending upon our own cisterns? (See Jeremiah 14:3–4.)

   Suggested Responses: Jeremiah reveals a terrible picture of people going to empty cisterns and walking away with dashed hopes, dismay, and spiritual desolation.

✎ 5.   In contrast, when a person spends time in God's "oasis"—praying, reading and meditating on the Bible, worshiping, obeying God—instead of trying to dig his or her own cistern, what is he or she compared to in Psalm 1:1–3?

   Suggested Response: The person who delights in God and studies and obeys His Word is like a tree planted by streams of water. He or she remains fruitful and prosperous.

DATA FILE

What Was "Cistern Water"?   **An Essene Cistern**

In Israel, the rainy season is only five months long, from November through March. Since fresh springs like those at En Gedi are rare, most ancient cities, towns, and even households used cisterns to catch and store runoff from rooftops, courtyards, or even streets. So cistern water wasn't like the clean, fresh, cool, flowing water of a spring. It was likely to be stale and dirty—perhaps even fouled by dead animals.

Furthermore, cisterns were dug by hand out of solid rock and were plastered so they would hold water. They needed constant care because the plaster tended to fall off, which allowed the precious water to leak out. When a cistern failed to hold water, it created a desperate situation for the people who depended on it.

2. Before the Israelites entered the Promised Land, what serious warning did God give to His people? (See Deuteronomy 8:10–18.)

Water from Rock

3. In Jeremiah 2:13, we discover what God's people did once they were settled in the Promised Land.

   a. Which two sins did God's people commit?

   b. What does this verse reveal about our human tendencies?

4. What is the tragedy of turning away from God and depending upon our own cisterns? (See Jeremiah 14:3–4.)

5. In contrast, when a person spends time in God's "oasis"—praying, reading and meditating on the Bible, worshiping, obeying God—instead of trying to dig his or her own cistern, what is he or she compared to in Psalm 1:1–3?

DATA FILE

What Was "Cistern Water"?

An Essene Cistern

In Israel, the rainy season is only five months long, from November through March. Since fresh springs like those at En Gedi are rare, most ancient cities, towns, and even households used cisterns to catch and store runoff from rooftops, courtyards, or even streets. So cistern water wasn't like the clean, fresh, cool, flowing water of a spring. It was likely to be stale and dirty—perhaps even fouled by dead animals.

Furthermore, cisterns were dug by hand out of solid rock and were plastered so they would hold water. They needed constant care because the plaster tended to fall off, which allowed the precious water to leak out. When a cistern failed to hold water, it created a desperate situation for the people who depended on it.

DID YOU KNOW?

Cisterns Were Used for More Than Water!

Served as prisons	(Joseph) Genesis 37:21–28; (Jeremiah) Jeremiah 38:6–13
Symbolized prosperity	2 Kings 18:28–32
Served as hiding places	1 Samuel 13:6
Used as tombs	Jeremiah 41:7–9
Built by kings as well as common people	2 Chronicles 26:9–10
Used in teaching metaphors	Proverbs 5:15–18

Topic C: Living in the Wilderness

As the Jews—God's chosen people—faced the scorching, dry wilderness, God responded to their needs. Using the desert metaphor to describe the struggles of life, and En Gedi with its freshwater springs to describe God's provision, we can say that God still meets the needs of His people in the wilderness of life.

1. How did God provide for the Israelites as they wandered in the wilderness? (See Psalm 105:37–41.)

   Suggested Responses: He strengthened them, cared for them, gave them light at night, and provided bread, meat, and fresh, "living" water.

2. What did God promise to do for the Israelites if they faithfully obeyed His commands, loved Him, and served Him devotedly? (See Deuteronomy 11:10–15.)

   Suggested Response: to provide water in the autumn and spring so their crops and animals would prosper and they would have plenty to eat.

3. What does Psalm 107:1, 8–9 reveal about God—and how we should respond to Him?

   Suggested Responses: God is good, and His love is eternal. We should thank Him for His love and the wonderful things He does—satisfying the thirsty and filling the hungry with good things.

4. What does God promise to do for the poor and needy? Why? (See Isaiah 41:17–20.)

   Suggested Responses: God will not forsake them. He will provide an abundance of "living" water and cause fruit and shade trees to grow in the wilderness. He will do this so that people will see and know that He has done it. He wants to receive the glory and praise.

208   Faith Lessons on the Life and Ministry of the Messiah

DID YOU KNOW?

Cisterns Were Used for More Than Water!

Served as prisons	(Joseph) Genesis 37:21–28; (Jeremiah) Jeremiah 38:6–13
Symbololized of prosperity	2 Kings 18:28–32
Served as hiding places	1 Samuel 13:6
Used as tombs	Jeremiah 41:7–9
Built by kings as well as common people	2 Chronicles 26:9–10
Used in teaching metaphors	Proverbs 5:15–18

Topic C: Living in the Wilderness

As the Jews—God's chosen people—faced the scorching, dry wilderness, God responded to their needs. Using the desert metaphor to describe the struggles of life, and En Gedi with its freshwater springs to describe God's provision, we can say that God still meets the needs of His people in the wilderness of life.

1. How did God provide for the Israelites as they wandered in the wilderness? (See Psalm 105:37–41.)

2. What did God promise to do for the Israelites if they faithfully obeyed His commands, loved Him, and served Him devotedly? (See Deuteronomy 11:10–15.)

Session Eight: Living Water   209

3. What does Psalm 107:1, 8–9 reveal about God—and how we should respond to Him?

4. What does God promise to do for the poor and needy? Why? (See Isaiah 41:17–20.)

5. What did Isaiah prophesy concerning the future of God's people and His eternal provision for them? (See Isaiah 35:6–10.)

6. What beautiful image did Jeremiah use to describe a person who trusts in God and His provision? (See Jeremiah 17:7–8.)

7. As God provides for us, what does He expect us to do? (See John 7:38; Mark 9:41.)

5. What did Isaiah prophesy concerning the future of God's people and His eternal provision for them? (See Isaiah 35:6–10.)

    Suggested Responses: He describes God's eternal kingdom where people will be filled with joy and even the wilderness will be transformed. "Living" water will gush forth in the wilderness, the burning sand will turn into a refreshing pool, the cracked ground will provide springs. Beautiful plants will grow in the former haunts of predators, and people traveling on the "Way of Holiness" will be safe.

6. What beautiful image did Jeremiah use to describe a person who trusts in God and His provision? (See Jeremiah 17:7–8.)

    Suggested Responses: Such a person is compared to a tree located by streams of water. Such a tree continues to flourish when difficult times come and remains fruitful even when everything around it withers and dies.

7. As God provides for us, what does He expect us to do? (See John 7:38; Mark 9:41.)

    Suggested Responses: We have been given His living water, which wells up from within us, and we are to share it with other people.

Topic D: Our God—An Oasis in the Wilderness

Trusting God for survival means taking the time to come to our "En Gedi" to be refreshed from the rigors of the wilderness of life. The biblical wilderness metaphors used for God communicated powerfully to those who experienced life as wanderers in a danger-filled wilderness. When we see God in this way, and ask Him for help, He will respond with encouragement and comfort.

1. Which imagery did Paul use to describe the Israelites' source of spiritual "living" water that quenched their spiritual thirst? (See 1 Corinthians 10:1–4.)

    Suggested Response: They drank from the "spiritual rock" that accompanied them—Jesus Christ.

2. Life in the wilderness is often like being in the brutal heat of the sun. It dries us out, weakens us, and overheats us. In the context of wilderness living, what do the following verses reveal about God as our oasis?

Scripture	God as Our Oasis
Psalm 18:2	He is our rock, fortress, deliverer, shield, stronghold in whom we take refuge
Psalm 61:1–4	He hears our cry when we grow faint, leads us to the "rock," provides a safe dwelling place, shelters us in the shade and protection of His wings
Psalm 91:1–2	We can find rest in His shadow and trust in Him as our refuge and fortress
Psalm 121:5–8	He watches over our lives and is our shade and protector; He protects us from harm during all of our comings and goings
Isaiah 25:4–5	He is a refuge for the poor, needy, distressed; provides shelter and shade from the storms, the heat, and ruthless enemies

Topic D: Our God—An Oasis in the Wilderness

Trusting God for survival means taking the time to come to our "En Gedi" to be refreshed from the rigors of the wilderness of life. The biblical wilderness metaphors used for God communicated powerfully to those who experienced life as wanderers in a danger-filled wilderness. When we see God in this way, and ask Him for help, He will respond with encouragement and comfort.

1. Which imagery did Paul use to describe the Israelites' source of spiritual "living" water that quenched their spiritual thirst? (See 1 Corinthians 10:1–4.)

2. Life in the wilderness is often like being in the brutal heat of the sun. It dries us out, weakens us, and overheats us. In the context of wilderness living, what do the following verses reveal about God as our oasis?

Scripture	God as Our Oasis
Psalm 18:2	
Psalm 61:1–4	
Psalm 91:1–2	
Psalm 121:5–8	
Isaiah 25:4–5	

✏ 3.   The Word of God helps provide the refreshment and nourishment we need to survive the wilderness. Which images did the psalmist use to describe the Word of God? (See Psalm 19:9b–11.)

Suggested Responses: He said God's Words were more precious than gold and sweeter than honey from the honeycomb. [Note: Honey was the only naturally sweet substance ancient people had. As such, it was highly valued. The Bible describes God's blessings as being like honey.]

✏ 4.   Living in the "wilderness" of culture is not without purpose. The wilderness is where we learn to depend on God, and it is where we are called to be witnesses for Him.

   a.   As we live in the "wilderness" of our culture, what does God do for us? (See Isaiah 58:11.)

   Suggested Responses: He will guide, satisfy, and strengthen us in the wilderness so that we will be like a well-watered garden, a spring that does not fail.

   b.   What enables us to keep being effective for God while we are in the wilderness? (See Jeremiah 17:5–8.)

   Suggested Responses: We must not depend on ourselves for strength. If we do, we will continue to live in the barren "desert." But if we trust in the Lord, we will be like trees planted by nourishing water that remain green and fruitful despite the heat and drought of life.

✏ 5.   When God finally establishes His heavenly kingdom, what does He promise to do for those who believe in Him? (See Isaiah 35:6–7.)

Suggested Responses: God will save His people and heal them. He will make the wilderness like an oasis, providing streams of water, placing pools of cool water where burning sand used to be, and making once-desolate land fertile, etc.

After nine minutes, let participants know that they have one minute remaining. Then reassemble the entire group. After everyone is back together, begin asking one person from each small group to briefly share a key idea with the larger group. In some cases, you may not have time for every group to share their discoveries.

As time allows, let's briefly share the key ideas that your group discussed.

3. The Word of God helps provide the refreshment and nourishment we need to survive the wilderness. Which images did the psalmist use to describe the Word of God? (See Psalm 19:9b–11.)

4. Living in the "wilderness" of culture is not without purpose. The wilderness is where we learn to depend on God, and it is where we are called to be witnesses for Him.

   a. As we live in the "wilderness" of our culture, what does God do for us? (See Isaiah 58:11.)

   b. What enables us to keep being effective for God while we are in the wilderness? (See Jeremiah 17:5–8.)

5. When God finally establishes His heavenly kingdom, what does He promise to do for those who believe in Him? (See Isaiah 35:6–7.)

faith lesson

6 minutes

Time for Reflection (3 minutes)

It's time for each of us to think quietly about how we can apply what we've learned today. On page 212 of the Participant's Guide, you'll find the words to the song, "En Gedi." Listen carefully as we play this song again. Then let's each take a few minutes to consider some of the questions that follow.

Please do not talk during this time. It's a time when we can reflect on today's lesson and how much we need the refreshment of God's living water.

> Replay the closing song, "En Gedi," which is at the end of the video.

Life is not so easy,
As a Christian standing stone.
It's a barren wilderness,
You can't make it on your own.
For work to be a good thing
You must face the dusty heat.
But you're called to find some rest,
Gaining strength to not be beat.
Do not dig a cistern,
Letting pleasures get ahead.
For the water you need clean,
Will be stale and dry instead.
But the waters of En Gedi,
Are fresh and flow with life.
So find the Lord in prayer,
Quench your thirst, and end your strife.
Oh, En Gedi, taking refuge in the Lord,
En Gedi, letting Jesus' words reward.
Drinking living water,
Resting in the shade.
Finding all the comfort,
To never be afraid.
En Gedi, a quiet peace with God.

—BEN LAPPENGA

1. How does living in your culture (the desert wilderness) affect your desire for God (the oasis of En Gedi)?

2. In what ways has God been like the oasis of En Gedi for you? How does that help you face the wilderness of today?

3. Where can you find an "En Gedi," a place where you can become restored with God's shade and living water, in the midst of your busy days?

4. Although it is tempting to stay at En Gedi—the refreshing oasis of God's presence—God calls you to live in a difficult world (the wilderness) so that you can be His witness. How effectively are you reaching out to spiritually thirsty people in the wilderness?

ꜰaith Lesson

Time for Reflection

Review the words to the song, "En Gedi," and spend a few minutes reflecting on how essential the refreshment of God's living water is in your life.

> Life is not so easy,
> As a Christian standing stone.
> It's a barren wilderness,
> You can't make it on your own.
> For work to be a good thing
> You must face the dusty heat.
> But you're called to find some rest,
> Gaining strength to not be beat.
> Do not dig a cistern,
> Letting pleasures get ahead.
> For the water you need clean,
> Will be stale and dry instead.
> But the waters of En Gedi,
> Are fresh and flow with life.
> So find the Lord in prayer,
> Quench your thirst, and end your strife.
> Oh, En Gedi, taking refuge in the Lord,
> En Gedi, letting Jesus' words reward.
> Drinking living water,
> Resting in the shade.
> Finding all the comfort,
> To never be afraid.
> En Gedi, a quiet peace with God.
>
> —Ben Lappenga

1. How does living in your culture (the desert wilderness) affect your desire for God (the oasis of En Gedi)?

2. In what ways has God been like the oasis of En Gedi for you? How does that help you face the wilderness of today?

3. Where can you find an "En Gedi," a place where you can become restored with God's shade and living water, in the midst of your busy days?

4. Although it is tempting to stay at En Gedi—the refreshing oasis of God's presence—God calls you to live in a difficult world (the wilderness) so that you can be His witness. How effectively are you reaching out to spiritually thirsty people in the wilderness?

Action Points (3 minutes)

> *The following points are reproduced on pages 214–15 of the Participant's Guide:*

Now it's time to wrap up our session.

> Give participants a moment to transition from their thoughtfulness to giving you their full attention.

I'd like to take a moment to summarize the key points we explored. After I have reviewed these points, I will give you a moment to jot down an action step (or steps) that you will commit to this week as a result of what you have learned today.

> Read the following points and pause afterward so that participants can consider and write out their commitment.

✏ 1. *Just as David and his men needed the life-giving, living water of En Gedi in order to survive their time in the wilderness, God's people today need God's life-giving, living water in order to serve Him in the wilderness of life.*

When we are nourished and filled with His living water, we will overflow with streams of living water that we can share with thirsty, needy people who live in a spiritually barren world (John 7:38). But in order to have anything to give, we need to have an En Gedi—times of devotion, Bible study, prayer, retreat, meditation—where we can meet with God to satisfy our own spiritual thirst.

What will you do this coming week to guarantee that you will have time with God—your "oasis" who will give you what you need in order to flourish?

✏ 2. *Accept no substitutes for living water! Although many things in our culture may look like living water, they all fail to give us life, to satisfy our thirst for God.* The Dead Sea, for example, looks refreshing from a distance, but its bitter saltwater cannot satisfy. It is equally foolish to turn our backs on God's pure, refreshing, life-giving water and try to dig our own cisterns, which if they hold water at all, can provide only dead, stagnant water.

Which "cisterns" have you built in the past? And which "cisterns" are you building, or are you tempted to build, today? Which "Dead Seas" seem inviting to you?

What will you do to seek out God's "living water" this week?

Action Points

Take a few minutes to review the key points you explored today, then write down an action step (or steps) that you will commit to this week as a result of what you have learned.

1. *Just as David and his men needed the life-giving, living water of En Gedi in order to survive their time in the wilderness, God's people today need God's life-giving, living water in order to serve Him in the wilderness of life.*

   When we are nourished and filled with His living water, we will overflow with streams of living water that we can share with thirsty, needy people who live in a spiritually barren world (John 7:38). But in order to have anything to give, we need to have an En Gedi—times of devotion, Bible study, prayer, retreat, meditation—where we can meet with God to satisfy our own spiritual thirst.

   What will you do this coming week to guarantee that you will have time with God—your "oasis" who will give you what you need in order to flourish?

2. *Accept no substitutes for living water! Although many things in our culture may look like living water, they all fail to give us life, to satisfy our thirst for God. The Dead Sea, for example, looks refreshing from a distance, but its bitter saltwater cannot satisfy.* It is equally foolish to turn our backs on God's pure, refreshing, life-giving water and try to dig our own cisterns, which if they hold water at all, can provide only dead, stagnant water.

Which "cisterns" have you built in the past? And which "cisterns" are you building, or are tempted to build, today? Which "Dead Seas" seem inviting to you?

What will you do to seek out God's "living water" this week?

closing prayer

As we close this session today, let's focus on our need for God—the provider of living water—as we face each day in the wilderness of life.

Dear God, thank You for loving us so much. You know what it's like to face wilderness experiences, and You are with us, ready to provide living water that will satisfy our deepest needs. How easy it is for us to forget what You have done for us in the past and to start digging our own cisterns. Forgive us for our lack of faith. We want to be like trees rooted by streams of water that produce much fruit, and we can't be like that on our own. We need You. Draw us close to You every day. Make us realize that we need Your oasis every day as we face difficult challenges and heavy responsibilities. And when we travel through desert times, remind us that You are still with us, guiding our steps and providing for our needs. In Jesus' name, amen.

Additional Resources

History

Connolly, Peter. *Living in the Time of Jesus of Nazareth.* Tel Aviv: Steimatzky, 1983.

Ward, Kaari. *Jesus and His Times.* New York: Reader's Digest, 1987.

Whiston, William, trans. *The Works of Josephus: Complete and Unabridged.* Peabody, Mass.: Hendrikson Publishers, 1987.

Wood, Leon. Revised by David O'Brien. *A Survey of Israel's History.* Grand Rapids: Zondervan, 1986.

Jewish Roots of Christianity

Stern, David H. *Jewish New Testament Commentary.* Clarksville, Md.: Jewish New Testament Publications, 1992.

Wilson, Marvin R. *Our Father Abraham: Jewish Roots of the Christian Faith.* Grand Rapids: Eerdmans, 1986.

Young, Brad H. *Jesus the Jewish Theologian.* Peabody, Mass.: Hendrickson Publishers, 1995.

Geography

Beitzel, Barry J. *The Moody Atlas of Bible Lands.* Chicago: Moody Press, 1993.

Gardner, Joseph L. *Reader's Digest Atlas of the Bible.* New York: Reader's Digest, 1993.

General Background

Alexander, David, and Pat Alexander, eds. *Eerdmans' Handbook to the Bible.* Grand Rapids: Eerdmans, 1983.

Butler, Trent C., ed. *Holman Bible Dictionary.* Nashville: Holman Bible Publishers, 1991.

Edersheim, Alfred. *The Life and Times of Jesus the Messiah.* Peabody, Mass.: Hendrickson Publishers, 1994.

Archaeological Background

Charlesworth, James H. *Jesus Within Judaism: New Light from Exciting Archaeological Discoveries.* New York: Doubleday, 1988.

Finegan, Jack. *The Archaeology of the New Testament: The Life of Jesus and the Beginning of the Early Church.* Princeton: Princeton University Press, 1978.

Mazar, Amihai. *Archaeology of the Land of the Bible: 10,000–586 B.C.E.* New York: Doubleday, 1990.

To learn more about the specific backgrounds of this set of videos, consult the following resources:

Avigad, Nahman. "Jerusalem in Flames—The Burnt House Captures a Moment in Time." *Biblical Archaeology Review* (November–December 1983).

Barkey, Gabriel. "The Garden Tomb—Was Jesus Buried Here?" *Biblical Archaeology Review* (March–April 1986).

Ben Dov, Meir. "Herod's Mighty Temple Mount." *Biblical Archaeology Review* (November–December 1986).

Bivin, David. "The Miraculous Catch." *Jerusalem Perspective* (March–April 1992).

Burrell, Barbara, Kathryn Gleason, and Ehud Netzer. "Uncovering Herod's Seaside Palace." *Biblical Archaeology Review* (May–June 1993).

Edersheim, Alfred. *The Temple*. London: James Clarke & Co., 1959.

Edwards, William D., Wesley J. Gabel, and Floyd E. Hosmer. "On the Physical Death of Jesus Christ." *Journal of American Medical Association (JAMA)* (March 21, 1986).

Flusser, David. "To Bury Caiaphas, Not to Praise Him." *Jerusalem Perspective* (July–October 1991).

Greenhut, Zvi. "Burial Cave of the Caiaphas Family." *Biblical Archaeology Review* (September–October 1992).

Hareuveni, Nogah. *Nature in Our Biblical Heritage*. Kiryat Ono, Israel: Neot Kedumim, Ltd., 1980.

Hepper, F. Nigel. *Baker Encyclopedia of Bible Plants: Flowers and Trees, Fruits and Vegetables, Ecology*. Ed. by J. Gordon Melton. Grand Rapids: Baker, 1993.

"The 'High Priest' of the Jewish Quarter." *Biblical Archaeology Review* (May–June 1992).

Hirschfeld, Yizhar, and Giora Solar. "Sumptuous Roman Baths Uncovered Near Sea of Galilee." *Biblical Archaeology Review* (November–December 1984).

Hohlfelder, Robert L. "Caesarea Maritima: Herod the Great's City on the Sea." *National Geographic* (February 1987).

Holum, Kenneth G. *King Herod's Dream: Caesarea on the Sea*. New York: W. W. Norton, 1988.

Mazar, Benjamin. "Excavations Near Temple Mount Reveal Splendors of Herodian Jerusalem." *Biblical Archaeology Review* (July–August 1980).

Nun, Mendel. *Ancient Stone Anchors and Net Sinkers from the Sea of Galilee*. Israel: Kibbutz Ein Gev, 1993. (Also available from *Jerusalem Perspective*.)

_____. "Fish, Storms, and a Boat." *Jerusalem Perspective* (March–April 1990).

_____. "The Kingdom of Heaven Is Like a Seine." *Jerusalem Perspective* (November–December 1989).

_____. "Net Upon the Waters: Fish and Fishermen in Jesus' Time." *Biblical Archaeology Review* (November–December 1993).

_____. *The Sea of Galilee and Its Fishermen in the New Testament*. Israel: Kibbutz Ein Gev, 1993. (Also available from *Jerusalem Perspective*.)

Pileggi, David. "A Life on the Kinneret." *Jerusalem Perspective* (November–December 1989).

Pixner, Bargil. *With Jesus Through Galilee According to the Fifth Gospel*. Rosh Pina, Israel: Corazin Publishing, 1992.

Pope, Marvin, H. "Hosanna: What It Really Means." *Bible Review* (April 1988).

Riech, Ronny. "Ossuary Inscriptions from the Caiaphas Tomb." *Jerusalem Perspective* (July–October 1991).

_____. "Six Stone Water Jars." *Jerusalem Perspective* (July–September 1995).

Ritmeyer, Kathleen. "A Pilgrim's Journey." *Biblical Archaeology Review* (November–December 1989).

Ritmeyer, Kathleen, and Leen Ritmeyer. "Reconstructing Herod's Temple Mount in Jerusalem." *Biblical Archaeology Review* (November–December 1989).

_____. "Reconstructing the Triple Gate." *Biblical Archaeology Review* (November–December 1989).

Ritmeyer, Leen. "The Ark of the Covenant: Where It Stood in Solomon's Temple." *Biblical Archaeology Review* (January–February 1996).

_____. "Quarrying and Transporting Stones for Herod's Temple Mount." *Biblical Archaeology Review* (November–December 1989).

Sarna, Nahum M. *The JPS Torah Commentary: Exodus.* New York: Jewish Publication Society, 1991.

"Sea of Galilee Museum Opens Its Doors." *Jerusalem Perspective* (July–September 1995).

Shanks, Hershel. "Excavating in the Shadow of the Temple Mount." *Biblical Archaeology Review* (November–December 1986).

"Shavuot." *Encyclopedia Judaica,* Volume 14. Jerusalem: Keter Publishing House, 1980.

Stern, David. *Jewish New Testament Commentary.* Clarksville, Md.: Jewish New Testament Publications, 1992.

Taylor, Joan E. "The Garden of Gethsemane." *Biblical Archaeology Review* (July–August 1995).

Tzaferis, Vassilios. "Crucifixion—The Archaeological Evidence." *Biblical Archaeology Review* (January–February 1985).

_____. "A Pilgrimage to the Site of the Swine Miracle." *Biblical Archaeology Review* (March–April 1989).

_____. "Susita." *Biblical Archaeology Review* (September–October 1990).

Vann, Lindley. "Herod's Harbor Construction Recovered Underwater." *Biblical Archaeology Review* (May–June 1983).

transform your life through a journey of discovery into the world of the bible

Faith Lessons Video Series
Ray Vander Laan

Filmed on location in Israel, **Faith Lessons** is a unique video series that brings God's Word to life with astounding relevance. By weaving together the Bible's fascinating historical, cultural, religious, and geographical contexts, teacher and historian Ray Vander Laan reveals keen insights into Scripture's significance for modern believers. These illuminating "faith lessons" afford a new understanding of the Bible that will ground your convictions and transform your life.

The **Faith Lessons** video series is ideal for use at home, especially in personal and family Bible studies. Individual believers and families will gain vital insights from long-ago times and cultures through this innovative approach to Bible study.

"Nothing has opened and illuminated the Scriptures for me quite like the Faith Lessons series."

—Dr. James Dobson

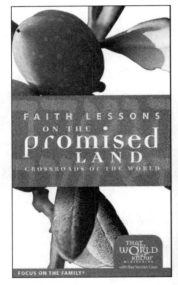

Faith Lessons on the Promised Land
Crossroads of the World
Volume One
0-310-67864-1

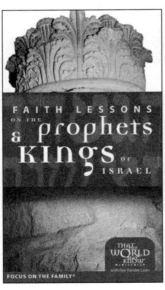

Faith Lessons on the Prophets & Kings of Israel
Volume Two
0-310-67865-X

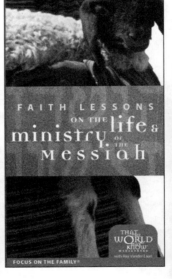

Faith Lessons on the Life & Ministry of the Messiah
Volume Three
0-310-67866-8

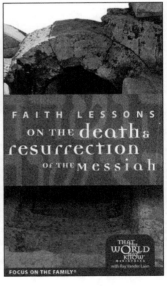

Faith Lessons on the Death & Resurrection of the Messiah
Volume Four
0-310-67867-6

Travel back in time to see the sights, hear the sounds, and experience the wonder of Jesus—all through the power of interactive CD-ROM.

Jesus
An Interactive Journey

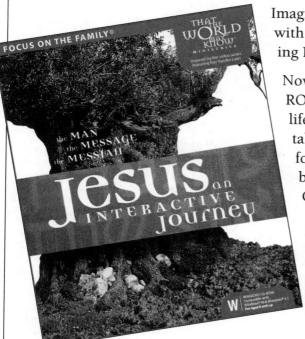

Imagine traveling back in time for a life-changing encounter with Christ . . . meeting the people who knew Him . . . retracing His footsteps . . . seeing firsthand what His life was like.

Now, through the cutting-edge technology of interactive CD-ROM, you can make that incredible voyage—back to the life and times of Jesus! This exciting multimedia adventure takes you there, giving you an entirely new appreciation for the fascinating historical, geographical, and cultural backdrop that will enhance your understanding of the Gospel.

An innovative "Visitor's Center" is your gateway to more than 180 different avenues of study, from Christ's birth to His resurrection. With a click of the mouse, you'll be guided to dozens of colorful locales, where you'll experience through the eyes and ears of ancient Jews and Romans what Christ's world was really like.

Or take a self-guided tour and stroll at your own pace through the lively marketplace to learn about trade and commerce, pause to listen in on the people, or go to the synagogue to gain a better understanding of the religious practices of the day.

The high technology and vast amount of material in this unique presentation will captivate you for hours, while providing a solid understanding of the Gospel and its relevance to today's believer. It's great for personal and family Bible study, Christian schools, and a wide variety of church uses.

Compatible with Windows® 95 and Windows® 3.1

We want to hear from you. Please send your comments about this book
to us in care of the address below. Thank you.

ZondervanPublishingHouse
Grand Rapids, Michigan 49530
http://www.zondervan.com